Permanent Markers

Permanent Markers

Race, Ancestry, and the Body
after the Genome

· ·

SARAH ABEL

The University of North Carolina Press Chapel Hill

This book was published with the assistance of the Lilian R. Furst Fund of the University of North Carolina Press.

Set in Charis by Westchester Publishing Services
Manufactured in the United States of America

The University of North Carolina Press has been a member of the Green Press Initiative since 2003.

Library of Congress Cataloging-in-Publication Data
Names: Abel, Sarah (Cultural anthropologist), author.
Title: Permanent markers : race, ancestry, and the body after the genome / Sarah Abel.
Description: Chapel Hill : University of North Carolina Press, [2021] | Includes bibliographical references and index.
Identifiers: LCCN 2021046312| ISBN 9781469665146 (cloth ; alk. paper) | ISBN 9781469665153 (paperback ; alk. paper) | ISBN 9781469665160 (ebook)
Subjects: LCSH: Genetic genealogy—United States. | Genetic genealogy—Brazil. | DNA—Analysis—Social aspects. | Genomics—Social aspects. | Human genetics—Social aspects. | Identity (Psychology) | Biotechnology industries—Social aspects. | United States—Race relations—History. | Brazil—Race relations—History.
Classification: LCC CS21.3 .A24 2021 | DDC 929.1072 23/eng/20211—dc14
LC record available at https://lccn.loc.gov/2021046312

Contents

Figures

Note on Language

Throughout this book, I employ various familiar anthropological terms and concepts that, in the context of the burgeoning world of DNA ancestry testing, are fast acquiring additional meanings and usages. In the interests of clarity, I have tried to reserve the use of inverted commas for new or potentially ambiguous uses of concepts. As I explore throughout the text, the terms "race" and "ethnicity" are contested categories that can take on very distinct meanings in different scientific disciplines and cultural contexts. Where they appear without inverted commas, they should usually be interpreted (unless signaled otherwise) as shorthand for "the concept of race/ethnicity." Conversely, I use quotation marks to signal when they are used to convey an idea of concrete biological essences (human "races," genetic "ethnicities," "racial" mixture). The word "color" appears in quotation marks when it refers to the Brazilian concept *cor* (meaning an ensemble of racialized physical traits typically used as a basis for subjective evaluations about a person's ancestry, social standing, attractiveness, etc.). Throughout the book, citations of Brazilian interviewees and authors appear in my own English translation; in some cases, however, Portuguese words and phrases appear in italics, either to signal that no direct equivalent exists in English or to retain a particular nuance found in the original language. With regard to the various categories (racial, ethnic, genetic) that appear throughout my work, I have generally retained the original labels and nomenclatures used by DNA testing companies, scientists, and other social actors. One exception is my decision to capitalize the racial labels "Black" and "White" in the body of the text (original typographies are maintained in citations), to underline that these terms are not merely adjectives denoting skin color but sociopolitical categories with specific histories and local meanings.

Permanent Markers

Introduction

The World in Our DNA

. . . .

The camera focuses in on a young woman with a mass of curly hair. She is facing forward, her eyes downcast, gazing fixedly on something in her lap. Behind her, slightly out of focus, rows of people sit facing the camera, some leaning forward expectantly. The woman blinks, her forehead creases, her lips purse and tremble; she is holding back tears.

The image cuts to a young man already wiping a tear from his eye. He stares transfixed at a piece of paper, his mouth hanging open in awe.

Cut again, and now we see a woman whose face is suddenly transformed from a nonchalant grin to a mask of shock. An envelope lies open on the table in front of her. The scene cuts to a black screen, with the words: "Would you dare to question who you really are?"

These scenes began to appear on various social networking websites in June 2016. They were the product of a short film made by Danish travel company Momondo and the U.S. genetic testing company AncestryDNA. Titled "The DNA Journey," it featured a group of sixty-seven people from around the world and all walks of life receiving the results of their personalized DNA ancestry tests. After discussing their own national or ethnic identity and laying bare their personal prejudices toward other nationalities, the participants were invariably shown laughing and shedding tears as their preconceptions were blown away by the diverse array of origins displayed in their DNA results. An Englishman who expressed a dislike for Germans grinned wryly as he discovered he had 5 percent German ancestry, while a Frenchwoman who was attributed zero percent French ancestry exclaimed that genetic tests should be made compulsory, because "if people knew their heritage like that, who would be stupid enough to think of such a thing as a pure race?" At its climax, the video showed two of the participants embracing joyfully, to the applause of the others, as they learned they were "cousins." Imparting these genetic results, over and over again, were two White, bespectacled scientists whose air of benevolent authority seemed to sum up the power of genetics to reveal deep and awesome truths about human identity.

The film closed with a final uplifting message: "You have more in common with the world than you think. An open world begins with an open mind."[1] To drive the point home, viewers were also invited to enter an online competition for the chance to win a DNA test and a free trip to any of the countries listed in their results. Released just three weeks before the United Kingdom's vote to leave the European Union, the video went viral, accumulating some 28 million views on the travel company's Facebook page and 5 million on YouTube in its first week and gaining more than 320 million video views globally in the space of a year.[2] For many viewers, the film represented a ray of hope amid a rising tide of political nationalism and a growing refugee crisis—topics that dominated global headlines that summer. It also epitomized a belief that the spread of genetic knowledge has the potential to eliminate prejudice and transform human relations for the better. But is combating xenophobia and racial oppression really as simple as taking a DNA test?

Self-Discovery through the Genome

This is a book about the relationships between bodies and identities, and the collision between a century of anthropological thought about race with the arrival of consumer genomics. It follows in the wake of a long-standing body of scholarship that has sought to separate out the influence of biology and culture on human identities. According to the orthodoxy established by the UNESCO Statements on Race in the 1950s, religion, nationality, language, and ethnic affiliation are all cultural constructs: fluid, mutable, and overlapping, and by no means determined by, or even fundamentally linked to, a person's physical features or genetic inheritance.[3] While patterns of genetic variation have been found to reflect underlying biological structures— the relics of the migrations of early modern humans into different world regions—fundamentally, all living humans are understood to be members of one extended family.

The catalyst for this scientific consensus was among the darkest chapters in European history: the imprisonment, forced sterilization, and mass murder of groups designated "racially impure" or "asocial" by the Nazi and other racial-supremacist regimes during the Second World War. These extreme and lethal attempts to eugenically "purify" national bodies of their "dysgenic" components rested on a noxious brand of biological determinism that the UNESCO scientists sought to short-circuit, once and for all. Their objective was ambitious. By separating the biological facts from the social fictions about human difference, they aimed to foster a world free of the scourge of racism. The influence of this international effort has been far-reaching, and today the adage that "there is only one race: the human race" passes for common sense in many parts of the world.

Yet in the decades since the 1950s, scientists have significantly expanded their technical capacities to study life on a molecular scale. As the ability to monitor and map human genetic material has flourished, the symbolic power attributed to genetics as a source of profound knowledge about human origins has grown and grown. The sequencing of the human genome in the early 2000s marked a watershed. At that time, scientists from the Human Genome Project (HGP) made the pronouncement that "in genetic terms, all human beings, regardless of race, are more than 99.9 percent the same"[4]—once more emphasizing the fundamental disjunction between biological and social conceptions of difference. But the two decades that followed the decoding of the human genome have seen a proliferation of research into the proportion of the genome that encodes humankind's genetic diversity.[5] In academic circles, this has injected new life into debates over the capacity of genomics to revolutionize our understanding of human diversity versus its potential to "geneticize" existing concepts of race, ethnicity, and kinship. Among the general public, this potential has taken concrete form in the personal genomics industry.

For many people, taking a DNA ancestry test offers the first inroad to a new kind of self-discovery. Since their emergence in the early 2000s, direct-to-consumer (DTC) genetic ancestry-testing companies have encouraged clients to treat their genome as a source of profound and intimate self-knowledge, presenting DNA as an "umbilical cord," linking the individual to the deep history of our species.[6] Originally dismissed by critics as faddish and pseudo-scientific, the DNA ancestry-testing market has since grown into a global multimillion-dollar industry that caters to customers' desires to discover their unique "ethnic mix" and genetic health predispositions and reconnect with lost relatives through the most basic aspect of their biology: their DNA. At the time of writing, it is estimated that more than 30 million commercial DNA ancestry-testing kits have been processed by companies worldwide.[7]

In public discourse, DNA ancestry tests are ascribed a dual function: the ability to challenge chauvinistic conceptions of identity and ethnic or racial prejudices while making visible the biological connections between us to demonstrate, truly, that "we are all related." The online reactions of viewers of the Momondo video, written in several languages on the company's

Facebook page in June 2016, reflected some of these ideas. While the video made no mention of "race" or "racism," instead revolving around national identities and prejudices, the concept of race dominated in the comments. For instance, a British man wrote: "Race is an idea, a social construct based on appearance, tradition and prejudice—it has almost no scientific meaning at all. . . . Our differences are utterly superficial," while a Brazilian woman stated, "If everyone knew their genetic inheritance, the number of Aryan idiots would fall right down."

Yet other interpretations abound. A man from the United States commented on the video, seeing it as offering proof of the biological bases of human "races": "Race was not a social construct or created by men, but it was created. . . . Pursuit of resources, geography, and climate naturally selected the five groups or races from which all of us descend. . . . But I did chuckle a bit when the English fellow was surprised that he was [5] percent German. The modern English are of course descended from the Germanic tribe called the Angles." Some viewers with a background in genetics applauded the film's message but disagreed with its portrayal of the relationship between genetic inheritance and identity: "A DNA test can't tell us that we're 'X% Portuguese or Chinese.' What it can tell is that 'X% of the Portuguese (or Chinese or whatever) have this or that haplotype in common with you.'" Some scoffed at the emotions presented in the video, pointing out that the participants "had to be actors." Commentators from France, where commercial DNA ancestry testing is prohibited, were largely skeptical of the whole affair. One wrote, "Without any explanation this is meaningless. . . . How are they giving nationalities as percentages? What genes are they looking at?" while another exclaimed, "Someone reassure me, tell me I'm not the only one who is profoundly shocked by the idea of giving your DNA to an American company who will determine the percentage of Jewish race in your genes and keep the sample indefinitely to do whatever they like with?"[8]

As these comments show, the tantalizing thought that our DNA holds the key to our identity inevitably gives way to a series of more troubling questions. Is it racist for companies to provide estimates of their customers' "Jewish"—or for that matter, "sub-Saharan African" or "Native American"—genomic ancestry? Can a DNA test really tell us we are "5 percent German," and if so what does that mean? Are DNA ancestry tests the final proof of the inexistence of biological "races," or precisely the opposite? Such questions are habitually raised in connection with genomic ancestry testing, and in turn they echo broader debates about the impact of genomics on scientific and lay understandings of the relationships between bodies and identities. At the heart of this dilemma lies the long shadow cast by the worst excesses of scientific racism, weighed against the strategic reinvigoration of racial and ethnic categories in recent decades as a means of combating the structural inequalities caused by racism.

To find a way through these debates, this book presents the first comparative study of how DNA ancestry data and technologies have been mobilized in connection with the histories and legacies of transatlantic slavery in the United States and Brazil and the local responses and international reverberations these initiatives have provoked. One advantage of this comparative approach is that it allows me to show that genomic data are necessarily read in the light of various cultural and political discourses about race, ancestry, and identity, meaning that they can never be regarded as universal or unambiguous in their scope and meaning. In both countries, we encounter strong desires to incorporate DNA ancestry data into personal identities as a way to abolish, blur, or reimagine the contours of ethnoracial categories. These efforts, however, are always in tension with local embodied experiences of race and racism—hinting that these are resilient, structural phenomena that cannot simply be undone by a strong dose of genetic logic. My analysis of how DNA ancestry data are constructed in academic and commercial labs, meanwhile, calls into question whether these enterprises are really engaged in producing alternatives to conventional forms of race- and ethnicity-based thinking as much as finding ways to reproduce conventional conceptions of ancestry *through* genetics. A more fundamental question I pose is whether transforming our identities is necessary or desirable for combating racism and deconstructing modes of race-thinking. In this respect, the final chapters of this book examine the potential of DNA ancestry tests as a tool for recuperating ancestral identities obscured by historical trauma. Overall, rather than offering emancipation from "outdated" racial myths, I propose that DNA ancestry tests act as a constant reminder of the ways that we continue to be marked, as individuals and societies, by the oppositional identities produced by slavery and colonialism.

Science and the (Re)making of Race

Since its genesis in the early 2000s, the DNA ancestry-testing market has been criticized by geneticists and social scientists alike, in large part because of how companies encourage clients to use their genetic data to inform and shape their personal identities, a tendency that is seen by many as violating the consensus of the nature/culture divide. Yet, while some geneticists attempt to draw a distinction between their own *scientific* work and the commercial activities of DNA ancestry-testing companies, the scrutiny of social scientists has also brought up uncomfortable questions about how race is dealt with in mainstream contemporary genomic research.

The theories and data produced by modern population genetics were significant for the reconfiguration of race as a biological concept in the wake of the Second World War.[9] The field's pioneers proposed a new definition of "races" as "genetically open systems" that overlapped and changed over time, rather than being fixed and discrete types. In particular, the use of *invisible* factors such as blood type alleles to map out human diversity— rather than morphological features (skull shape, skin color, and so on) that could easily feed back into old stereotypes of racial difference—was seen as an important source of the field's credibility and objectivity.[10] Yet, like other anthropological disciplines, population geneticists disagreed about the utility of race as a term for describing patterns of human genetic variation. The problem often arose when attempting to apply the *ideal* genetic definition of race to the study of actual, heterogeneous populations that have at different times been referred to as "races."[11] For instance, Theodosius Dobzhansky, one of the field's founders and an advocate for maintaining race as a classificatory device, noted that in practice the genetic differentiation among human "races" was generally "so poorly delimited that their very number is estimated from two to about one hundred."[12] In a well-known 1972 study, U.S. bioinformatician Richard Lewontin claimed to have settled the debate by calculating that around 85 percent of all human genetic variation could be accounted for by differences between individuals, irrespective of racial or ethnic classification. Lewontin concluded, "Human racial classification is of no social value and is positively destructive of social and human relations. Since such racial classification is now seen to be of virtually no genetic or taxonomic significance, either, no justification can be offered for its continuance."[13]

The transition to the (relative) dominance of a "no-race" stance on human diversity within genetics by the late twentieth century was not simply the result of emerging empirical findings; it began as a broad ideological shift spearheaded by academics who, concerned by the racist political agendas their research was being used to support, began to question the assumption that human groups were biologically destined to be unequal and sought other ways of studying and conceptualizing human biological diversity.[14]

Nonetheless, ever since the postwar period, voices from within the discipline have cautioned against this stance becoming a dogma in its own right, which they feel could detract from the study of substantive genetic differences between populations.[15]

Evidence presented by recent social studies of science, not to mention a proliferation of articles authored by geneticists, demonstrate that there is currently no single consensus within the discipline about the suitability of applying the concept of race in genomic research.[16] The issue is complex. Some have argued that the ability of model-based clustering algorithms to habitually sort DNA samples, taken from populations around the world, into roughly continental groups offers support for the validity of race as a taxonomic category in genetics.[17] Critics point out that the form and distribution of these clusters depends both on the programming of the statistical software (e.g., how many clusters the program is asked to produce from the data) and the sampling method used. For instance, sampling a small number of geographically isolated populations is likely to yield racelike clusters, whereas sampling populations on a geographic gradient is more likely to produce overlapping clines.[18] Some interpret this as a question of terminology. For instance, certain scientists (particularly those of an older generation) may retain some version of the classic population genetics definition of "races" as "biological sub-groups within the single species, *Homo sapiens*, in which the similar heredity which the whole species has in common far outweighs the relative and minor ways in which the sub-groups differ."[19] Others may agree that such broad genetic classifications *can* be made, but disagree with calling them "races," preferring instead to use less evocative terms like "population," which could refer to a genetic cluster of any magnitude, with or without a particular regional origin, and allows for the fact that significant levels of genetic mixture and variation exist both within and between conventional "racial" groups.[20] Finally, some geneticists have argued the continued importance of paying attention to race when selecting which populations to sample and study. The most nuanced arguments have come from members of historically marginalized groups, who point to a troubling Eurocentric bias in genetic and genomic research globally.[21] For instance, an important criticism of the HGP was that its findings (including the statement about the overwhelming genetic similarity of humankind) were based on a sampling of mainly Euro-descendant individuals from Utah, France, and Venezuela, whose genomes were presented as an "average" blueprint for all humans.[22] Without claiming that geneticists *should* attempt to validate the biological existence of "races," these critics argued that conducting genetic research in a "population-blind" manner could end up perpetuating the exclusion of ethnic and racial minorities from important fields like biomedical studies, preventing these populations from benefiting fully from the outcomes of genomic research.[23]

Although geneticists today have differing perspectives on the use of race within their own studies (variously, as a taxonomic category, a lens of analysis, or an object of study), most are at pains to defend the antiracist credentials of their field and to establish that human genetic variation can be studied without legitimizing racist agendas or reinvigorating biological-essentialist conceptions of race. The habitual warnings of social scientists have put geneticists on the defensive, and interdisciplinary discussions on the subject can feel more like a turf war over who is "qualified" or "responsible enough" to talk about race.

This was a theme that cropped up repeatedly during my fieldwork. During an interview with a biological anthropologist in the United States, I asked whether he and his team dealt with the concept of race in their research. He shot back at me, "I don't use the term race. Do you?" To some geneticists, social scientists appear obsessed with race, or else in denial that there exist substantive biological differences among humans that are worthy of study. As the prominent Harvard geneticist David Reich wrote in a much-circulated op-ed for the *New York Times* in 2018: "I am worried that well-meaning people who deny the possibility of substantial biological differences among human populations are digging themselves into an indefensible position, one that will not survive the onslaught of science. I am also worried that whatever discoveries are made—and we truly have no idea yet what they will be—will be cited as 'scientific proof' that racist prejudices and agendas have been correct all along, and that those well-meaning people will not understand the science well enough to push back against these claims."[24]

My entry to these debates was through my PhD research, which I developed as part of an international research project, EUROTAST, funded by the European Union, which examined the histories and legacies of the transatlantic trade in enslaved Africans from various disciplinary perspectives, drawing in particular on new techniques in modern and ancient genomics.[25] As a social scientist, my contribution within this network was to reflect on current debates surrounding the uses of DNA ancestry testing to reconstruct African ethnic identities effaced by slavery and the broader impacts this phenomenon was having on the definition of racial and ethnic identities in Brazil and the United States. As I go on to describe further below, the extent to which African identities and kinship ties were destroyed or maintained through slavery in different parts of the Americas has been a topic of long-standing anthropological and sociological debate. Far from being a purely intellectual matter, studies in this area have been used to both challenge and uphold racist political discourses about the cultural "particularities" and social exceptionalism of African-descendant populations.[26] More recently, on the other hand, debates have revolved around the relevance of genetic ancestry for initiatives aimed at restorative justice and negotiating reparations for slavery—or, conversely, their propensity to geneticize conceptions of race and ethnicity and reinvigorate forms of biological racism.[27]

Before embarking on this research, I was trained in a social-constructionist tradition that treated the ample evidence for the social origins of race as proof of its biological irrelevance—the social and the biological being regarded as mutually exclusive ontological spheres. Yet, like others who have engaged critically with genetic population research into American societies, I found this stance difficult to square with the conventional use of racelike genetic categories to describe the biogeographical ancestry of the region and the ability of genetic studies to reflect the racial and gendered dynamics of colonialism, slavery, and their aftermaths (e.g., the implementation of eugenic policies such as segregation, selective immigration, and racial Whitening), whose traces are still imprinted collectively in the genomes of contemporary American and Caribbean populations.[28] This notion that biological and social forms of knowledge are intrinsically separate was likewise hard to reconcile with the increasingly mundane way that members of the public are using genomic ancestry data to feed back into their understandings of their family origins or ethnic makeup without leading scholars to the untenable conclusion that these people (numbering in the tens of millions around the world) are simply "getting identity wrong" by mixing up *genetic* data with *social* relations.

Nonetheless, social constructionism offers numerous useful tools and insights for studying the relationships between genomic science and systems of racial thought. In particular, by approaching race not as something that exists a priori in the world (i.e., human "races") but as a set of beliefs about human difference that have developed, adapted, and diversified over time and in different places in response to specific sociopolitical circumstances, social-constructionist approaches allow us to trace the various forms and impacts of racial thinking without making prescriptive assumptions about what race *is* or *is not*, what it *should* or *should not* do. By insisting on the subjective, contextual, and relational ways in which we produce knowledge about the world, these approaches equip us to understand how a set of DNA ancestry results, for instance, could be used to deconstruct racial ideologies in one context and reinforce them in another.

In this book I approach race as the product of a set of interrelated worldviews that have *multiple* meanings and effects, spanning the sociocultural to the biologic. Modern concepts of race emerged from Europe's colonial experiences in the Americas and other parts of the world. In their desire for cheap labor to exploit the natural resources of the "New World," European powers proclaimed their "natural" dominance over Indigenous Americans and Africans, whom they regarded as lesser forms of humanity, with varying potential for civilization.[29] In colonial societies, autochthonous European notions about lineage and heredity (expressed through the biocultural metaphor of "blood") combined with new ideas about ancestry and geographical origin to define the legal status and socioeconomic possibilities of colonial subjects.[30] This emergent racial logic governed who could be enslaved and who was automatically free; who labored to produce wealth and who profited from this labor; who could marry whom and what legal and social status their children could inherit. In time, these racial schemas came to shape entire societies, to the point that Eurocentric philosophers and scientists began to claim, from the eighteenth century onward, that the unequal relations of domination and oppression among "races"—observable the world over—were part of the *natural* order of things. During the nineteenth and early twentieth century, a great amount of work went into fashioning race as a global and standardized scientific concept. Far from proving the coherency of race as a biological concept, these efforts attest to the constant work needed to fix and stabilize a fundamentally fluid and flawed idea.[31]

Race was constructed historically, but it is not simply a figment of the imagination. It is, as Amade M'charek suggests, a fiction: not in the sense of something to be opposed against *fact*, but rather in the sense of "something both *made* and *made up*."[32] Racism (which is both the source and the product of these fictions) structures worlds, conditioning the way that individuals inhabit and move through societies, their education and work possibilities, their health outcomes, kinship and social networks, their conditions of life and death.[33] Moreover, the effects of racism are not only—or always—perceived psychologically; they may also register biologically. For instance, social epidemiologists have linked the manifestation of certain diseases and the incidence of premature mortality, among other indicators, to structural, institutional, and interpersonal forms of racism, describing these health outcomes as the *embodied* effects of racisms.[34] These structured, material distinctions have the circular effect of reinforcing the tangibility of racial differences, both for individuals and the clinicians who treat them, something that has led in recent decades to renewed claims that race constitutes a valid biological as well as social category.[35] A counter proposal, first put forward by anthropologists Carol C. Mukhopadhyay and Yolanda T. Moses in the late 1990s, argues that race should not be separated out into its social and biological effects, but rather understood through a biocultural lens that "situate[s] human biodiversity *within* a sociocultural framework, in effect reuniting culture and biology by embedding biology in society and culture."[36] An advantage of biocultural approaches is that they take seriously the materiality and embodied experiences of race by treating them not as innate but as the biological imprint of sociopolitical ideologies and structures of domination. In other words, they regard the material effects of racism as stemming from a history of biology being shaped and *managed* by social systems, rather than the other way around.[37]

This conception of race as biology-managed-by-culture is also helpful for analyzing the results of genetic anthropological studies into contemporary American populations. For instance, Y-chromosome (Y-DNA) and mitochondrial DNA (mtDNA) analyses conducted among Black and "mixed" American and Caribbean populations have revealed a preponderance of European Y-DNA haplotypes (passed down from father to son), on the one hand, and African and Native American mtDNA haplotypes (passed down from mother to child), on the other.[38] This phenomenon, known as "sex-biased mating," reflects the sexual power dynamics of plantation societies: in particular, the privileged access of White male colonists to enslaved and indentured women, as well as the concerted efforts to prohibit sexual relations between White women and Black or Indigenous men in order to maintain the racial "purity" and social dominance of White families. In some cases, these genetic portraits can also reveal evidence of how individuals attempted to escape the fate imposed on them by racial systems. For instance, a recent population genetic study of the United States, carried out by researchers from the DNA ancestry-testing company 23andMe, found that 3.5 percent of 35,524 self-reported European Americans in the cohort had 1 percent or more African genomic ancestry.[39] The authors propose that this ancestry may be biogenetic evidence of Black ancestors who "passed" into White communities, a feat that involved disguising telltale "African" phenotypic traits and cutting oneself off permanently from Black kin and acquaintances in order to assume a White identity that could be passed on to future generations. Through careful analysis, genetic studies have the potential not only to reflect the impacts of racial worldviews on population structures, but also to reveal genealogies that have been obscured by those very racial dogma.

The social effects of genetic studies do not end with what they can tell us about how racial schemas (among other cultural forces) have shaped population structures and histories. Another dimension is how the results of genetic studies and personal ancestry tests feed back into discourses about race, ethnicity, and nationhood. Stuart Hall famously argued that race operates discursively, "like a language," and I find this concept useful for envisioning the multiple possibilities for how DNA ancestry data may be translated into cultural repertoires of meaning, depending on who is reading (or "writing") them, and in what context.[40] Hall's notion of the body as a "script" resonates with the popular and scientific imaginaries of DNA as "code" or "book of life."[41] Whereas these analogies are usually meant to underline the universal, a priori character of the information contained in DNA, Hall claims that it is the acts of *reading* and *interpretation* that inscribe bodies with racial signification. A similar argument, I think, can be put forward to understand how genomic data become linked to different regimes of racial thought.

Perspectives on DNA Ancestry

Context and perspective are key to defining how individuals and societies read DNA ancestry data, and they are dynamics that operate on multiple and intersecting scales. At various points, this book compares the cultural meanings and political significance given to genomic data in Brazil and the United States, two nations known for their contrasting hegemonic racial schemas.[42] Whereas the United States is known for developing laws of ancestry that organized "racial" mixture through the production of a "color line," which notionally separated Whites from non-Whites, Brazil has styled itself "the country of miscegenation" (*o país da miscigenação*), to reflect its history of intense and supposedly indiscriminate sexual and cultural mixing, principally among male European settlers and Indigenous and African women. "Racial" mixture and separatism therefore offer different cultural lenses through which people in Brazil and the United States might read and comprehend their personal genomic ancestry data.

Claiming that Brazil and the United States are "naturally" racial opposites as a result of their demographic histories, however, obscures the fact that the two nations' elites have been in almost constant dialogue about race since at least the nineteenth century, and at many points have fashioned their countries' racial doctrines in direct counterposition to one another.[43] One arena in which this dialogue has played out is international scientific production. During the nineteenth century, for instance, scholars in Europe and the United States believed "miscegenation" was a slippery slope toward racial degeneracy (an assertion confirmed, for some, by their visits to Latin American countries). These accusations inspired Brazilian elites to develop their own doctrines of racial improvement. Like other Latin American nations, they sought to attract waves of European migrants, hoping the latter would "Whiten" the national body by mixing with or outcompeting their Black and Indigenous counterparts.[44] By the end of the Second World War, however, the scientific consensus around the long-term effects of "racial" mixture was undergoing a radical shift. In 1951, an international committee of scientists brought together by the UNESCO upheld the idea that "amalgamation" was not only biologically harmless but a potentially positive force.[45] This evaluation was significantly influenced by scholars who contrasted the racial violence afflicting the segregated United States with what they saw as relative racial harmony in unsegregated Brazil.[46]

The belief in the potential of genetic and cultural mixture to soften racial tensions and produce "postracial" societies remains an influential and widespread myth in both countries today, and scholars in the United States continue to look to Brazil as a model in this respect. For Brazilians, on the other hand, this image has been marred in recent decades by sociological data demonstrating that these ideologies of mixture have failed to dismantle— and, according to some, have even compounded—systems of entrenched racial inequalities and prejudice in the country.[47] Yet, attempts to address these structural problems through the introduction of race-based affirmative action have raised concerns, in Brazil and abroad, that the country's unique, autochthonous approaches to "race relations" are being ousted by a hegemonic North American racial worldview.[48]

Accepting this dichotomy of a racially segregated, unmixed north versus a fluid, harmonious, racially mixed south can be a trap, leading observers to see only a "natural" opposition between the two and concealing numerous potential similarities in how race and racism are experienced and conceptualized in both societies.[49] In this book, I attempt to temper the polarizing effects of comparison by drawing attention to the transnational dimensions of scientific, political, and activist discourses about race and showing how various racial schemas tend to overlap and interact in any given reading of genomic data. I am aware that social scientists studying conceptions of race and ethnicity are always "faced with an ever-moving target which [we ourselves] are partly propelling in an open-ended journey."[50] Instead of normatively affirming which readings of genomic data are most scientifically "correct" or politically promising, I take stock of how different interpretations are mobilized and play out in various social contexts, showing how circumstances, practices, and power dynamics combine to condition the emancipatory and/or oppressive effects of these technologies. My findings echo the observation of geneticist Charles Rotimi, who called DNA ancestry testing a "double-edged sword":[51] while helping to deconstruct racial ideologies in one context, these technologies may be used to reinforce them in another. While undoing the dehumanizing, roots-severing work of slavery and racism *here*, DNA ancestry-testing practices may contribute to instating different kinds of hierarchies and bio-colonial tendencies *there*. By uncovering the power dynamics at play in the writing and reading of genomic ancestry data at various levels of society, this book aims to shed light on the stakes and processes that influence how DNA is made to visualize the past in the present, and which worldviews it conjures up or banishes in the process.

Scientists and academics are key actors in this book, both for their work in creating and shaping genomic ancestry data in the lab and as interpreters of this knowledge for the general public, who attempt (with varying degrees of success) to set boundaries for how this information may or may not be applied to existing conceptions of race and identity. Some of the geneticists interviewed in this book work for DNA ancestry-testing companies, which I treat as key actors in their own right for their impact in shaping public understandings of the relationship between genetics and identity over the past two decades. Many of these large corporations are founded and based in the United States, and although their products project an image of DNA ancestry as a universal tool for parsing human genetic variation, their worldviews are often markedly U.S.-centric and Eurocentric. Whereas academic discussions about genetic ancestry tend to be fraught with moral concerns about the role of science in reproducing or eliminating racial worldviews, DNA ancestry-testing companies are driven by a market logic that seeks to replicate modes of understanding ancestry that feel familiar and enticing to the public, in order to attract a broad customer base for their products. They have popularized the concept of genetic "ethnicity" as an alternative paradigm for imagining collective biocultural identities, albeit one that has a tendency to fix and naturalize connections between genes, people, and geographies.

Another important set of actors who have sought to shape and reappropriate racial worldviews are groups that have been targeted by racism historically. African-descendant activists throughout the Atlantic World have long sought to repurpose Blackness, turning it from a racial category into a collective political identity, founded in a common genealogy of forced migration and enslavement and oriented toward fighting racial and colonial oppression. These movements are both local and transnational in their dimensions and influences. For example, in recent years Afro-Brazilian activists have devised strategies to strengthen Blackness as a political identity to gain popular support for public policies aimed at redressing the historic exclusion of Black Brazilians from elite levels of society. These groups have found inspiration in the tactics of African American civil rights activists in the United States, whose work to dismantle legal segregation in their own country engendered a new form of group-based politics.[52] As I discuss in chapter 4, test-takers who identify with Black political discourses typically bring a host of sociological knowledge—what France Winddance Twine has dubbed "racial literacy"[53]—to bear on their readings of genomic data. At the same time, the definitions of race and cultural meanings attached to Blackness differ between Afro-Brazilians and African Americans, as a result of the historical dynamics of racism and racial ideology in each country. As I explore in chapter 1, these differences condition each group's perspectives on DNA ancestry tests and their potential as a conduit for collective identity formation—whether in the service of deconstructing biological notions of race, reclaiming African ethnic links, or helping (re)define the contours of Blackness. Activists, like scientists, are in the business of trying to set boundaries for how genetic data may or may not be mobilized socially and politically, and they are typically attentive to the potential of these technologies to relieve or perpetuate forms of racism and colonial oppression. However, the relationships that activists and scientists (and activist scientists) imagine between DNA ancestry, race, ethnicity, and personal identity are not always the same, and these groups can find themselves in conflict.

The final category of actors who appear in this book are those that I class broadly as DNA test-takers: a heterogeneous group whose members bring various perspectives and intentions to their readings of genetic ancestry data. In Brazil, where no national DNA ancestry-testing market existed until very recently, most of the test-takers I interviewed were students and university staff who had taken a DNA test as participants in an international research project on the genetic dynamics of *mestizaje/mestiçagem* in Latin America.[54] In the United States, the participants were people who had taken one or more tests provided by commercial DNA ancestry companies. Some were genealogists interested in using genetic tools to further their family history research, while others were attracted to these technologies out of a general curiosity or to answer specific questions about their personal origins. These individuals read and assessed the validity of their DNA ancestry tests as a source of information about their family histories and personal identities through multiple lenses. National narratives of race and ethnicity were a key reference, and many test-takers also drew on scientific discourses (both current and anachronistic) to conceptualize the relationship between their genetic results and personal identity. Some were fluent in activist discourses about the political nature of racial identity, and others less so. Significantly, test-takers also read their genetic ancestry data in the light of other forms of ancestral and racial knowledge: family stories; observations on the inheritance of physical traits and personal characteristics within family lineages; feelings of cultural or political affinity to particular ethnic and racial collectives; and concrete experiences of how others had categorized or miscategorized them racially in the past, based on racialized phenotypic markers. In some cases, genetic results give accounts of ancestry that contrast with these other forms of knowledge, and the question of how subjects negotiate this tension is explored in detail in chapters 4 and 5.

Bodies, Markers, Origins

The book's title, *Permanent Markers*, is a reference to the ways that racial distinctions bind to our bodies through the overlaying of historical, scientific, political, and cultural discourses about difference and otherness. It is also meant as a question about the fixedness or fluidity of these scripts across time and changing societal contexts: Will there come a time when race is no longer a salient marker of inequality or identity? What would need to happen for this to be the case? At the turn of the millennium, some observers predicted that the new "genomic era" would spell the decline of skin color and other visible phenotypic distinctions as primary "racial" markers, as scientists began to scrutinize our differences and similarities on a molecular scale. Some hoped this shift in perspective would make race seem less socially meaningful and relevant, either as a basis for discrimination or as a mode of collective identity.[55] What I observed during my research was that DNA ancestry markers have not simply replaced those epidermal markers, nor has race lost salience in the last twenty years as a way of understanding social divisions and inequalities. Instead, DNA markers often function as a parallel script alongside—or in contradiction to—embodied experiences of racism and identity.

In large part, this book focuses on the debates surrounding attempts to reconstruct the ethnic identities of enslaved Africans using DNA, projects that aspire to emancipate Black bodies from the racial schemas produced by slavery and colonialism. According to Hortense Spillers, the capture and export of Africans to the New World "marked a *theft of the body*—a willful and violent (and unimaginable from this distance) severing of the captive body from its motive will, its active desire."[56] Inscriptions of different kinds performed the dual work of systematically erasing the ethnic identities of captive Africans—dehumanizing them and divesting them of their individuality, their sense of attachment to a family or community—and fixing them within racial hierarchies. These violent acts of effacement were wrought simultaneously on the body and in the abundance of texts produced by the colonial bureaucracies.[57] Upon boarding the slave ships, the captives' flesh was branded with the initials of the slave company;[58] their names were entered into ledgers, or sometimes they were simply recorded as numbers of "heads." Those that survived the grueling voyage were made to answer to new names whose meanings were often cruel and degrading, or else they were forced to take Christian names through baptism.[59] These new identities were once again inscribed in account books, plantation lists, and church records. Occasionally other identifying details were included, such as the individual's native language, African "nation," and distinctive physical traits. Rather than being intended to preserve these aspects of the individual's identity, this information was collected for the purpose of marking out the enslaved to colonial authorities in the event of runaways.

While enslaved Africans resisted these injuries against their personal identities in various ways—for instance, maintaining their native names, tongues, and memories of their former lives in secret—the trauma of the Middle Passage and the plantation irrevocably reoriented the way they defined their sense of attachment and community. African-born slaves could often be identified in the colonies by their "country marks": ritual scarifications or dental modifications that, in their native lands, had designated their social status or membership of a particular community. However, these practices no longer held the same meaning in the Americas and were eventually abandoned. Their languages, too, underwent changes, as they learned European and Creole lingua franca to communicate with one another and with their American-born children.

Engaging in what were frequently coercive and enforced sexual relations with enslaved women proved another effective way for slaveholders to sow divisions and create hierarchies among the enslaved, producing new castes of "mixed race" children, who were often chosen to work as house slaves, away from their mothers. Once again, the evidence of racial difference was held to be legible on the bodies of these "mixed" individuals: in their skin tone, hair texture, eye color. Perversely, in many American societies, acculturation and "racial" mixture could become routes to social ascension, even freedom, leading some enslaved Africans to strategically "exchange their country marks" in a bid to gain a higher place in the caste system.[60] Even so, many harbored desires to return to their homelands, beyond the ocean. In the most extreme cases, some enslaved Africans practiced suicide as a means of "flying" back to their homelands and freeing themselves and their unborn children of the ignominy of slavery.[61] Nevertheless, those that made the return journey during their lifetimes often found themselves marked out from the local populations by their language, customs, religion, and appearance. Some assumed a sense of superiority over the African "natives" by dint of these hard-acquired qualities and installed themselves as slave merchants or missionaries.[62]

Whiteness—which is often erroneously thought of as an "unmarked" identity—was also a product of these processes, defined in opposition to the condition of the enslaved.[63] In a seeming paradox, efforts to attribute racial inferiorities to Africans (among other populations labeled as "non-White") intensified in the context of the abolitions of the Atlantic slave trades and slavery itself. From the late eighteenth century onward, social scientists in Europe posited race as a major organizing factor in human development, suggesting that natural hierarchies—rather than centuries of colonial exploitation—were the cause of "innate" inequalities between the different "types of man." Numerous scientific techniques, including anthropometry, the cephalic index, photography, color charts, and fingerprinting were developed in the dual aim of discovering the "natural" frontiers separating the various "races" of mankind and permitting the accurate classification of individuals into these groups. Skull shape, skin color, facial traits, hair texture, and other physical attributes became clues that, when quantified and compared, were intended to reveal the body's underlying racial essence. As Jean-François Véran has noted, if transatlantic slavery was "probably the most radical of the many attempts through modern history to reduce people to bodies that cannot speak," then nineteenth-century anthropologists "used these bodies, dead or alive, to produce the knowledge confirming that they were indeed inferior and primitive."[64]

From Deconstructing to Reconstructing Ethnic Identities

From the early twentieth century, biological-deterministic theories of race were being progressively deconstructed by an "egalitarian" school of thought, influenced notably by the voices of African-descendants, Jews, Indigenous Americans, and scholars from the Global South. Influential scholars like Franz Boas and W. E. B. Du Bois in the United States, and Gilberto Freyre in Brazil, argued that many of the negative stereotypes attributed to so-called inferior races were not innate characteristics but the consequences of colonial domination, racism, and Eurocentric ideologies.[65] They proposed that culture and biology were governed by separate systems of inheritance, and argued human capacities were not primarily determined by biology but rather by upbringing, cultural and environmental contexts, political ideologies, and the uneven social opportunities these conditions afforded. In some cases, they used anthropometric and newly emerging genetic methods to expose the instability of racial structures that were meant to be solid and natural, and worked to reveal the political and ideological motivations behind the historical attempts to force humans into social hierarchies that were then designated as natural.[66]

While the origins of this deconstructionist trend are well known, this period also saw the beginnings of a *reconstructive* anthropology, whose pioneers proposed to use their scientific tools and techniques to recover the African cultural identities and kinship links effaced by slavery and processes of racialization in the Americas. From the 1930s onward, anthropologists and linguists like Melville Herskovits, Lorenzo D. Turner, and Pierre Fatumbi Verger framed their work as a means of restituting a sense of dignity and identity to Black American populations still struggling with the social and psychological legacies of slavery and construed as culturally "pathological" in American societies.[67] In recent decades, the reconstructive paradigm has gained political salience thanks to international decolonial movements, whose advocates have demanded reparations and restorative justice programs for African-descendant and Indigenous peoples throughout the Americas and the Caribbean. Attempts by states to accommodate these demands have led to the institutionalization of new roles for scientists, such as guaranteeing the authenticity of groups' claimed ancestral links to the victims of slavery and colonization. In Brazil, for instance, where the post-dictatorship 1988 constitution conceded special collective rights to Indigenous groups and the "remainders" of maroon communities (*remanescentes de quilombos*), groups must have their identity claims validated by certified anthropologists and historians through the production of official reports and certificates (*laudos*).[68] This trend has always been controversial. For one, researchers have been challenged on their interpretation of key clues used to recover "original" cultures and identities. The long-standing debate between Herskovits and sociologist E. Franklin Frazier over the interpretation of matrifocal structures among Black American and Brazilian families is well known. What the former took to be survivals of West African kinship structures, preserved throughout slavery, the latter diagnosed as a sign of cultural anomie and social disorganization originating *in* slavery.[69] Elsewhere, social scientists have felt ambivalent about the idea of "authenticating" identities, given the current disciplinary consensus that identities are not stable, enduring structures but mutable, polyvalent, and subject to social negotiation. Multicultural policies have been criticized for trapping communities within a declared ancestral culture, forcing them to constantly perform an "authentic" identity and maintain links to their designated homeland in order to retain their legal status.[70] Nonetheless, this risk is often outweighed by scientists' desires to help communities gain the much-needed rights and resources that this special status may afford.

In recent years, parallel developments in genetics have seen the body take center stage once more as a source of evidence for ancestral origins and identities that are no longer preserved by paper records, cultural and linguistic traces, or living memory. The first major attempt to use genetics to reconstruct the identities and origins of historically enslaved individuals was by researchers of the New York African Burial Ground Project (NYABGP) in the 1990s, an initiative that arose after construction works in lower Manhattan revealed the remains of a site identified in eighteenth-century maps as a "Negroes Burying Ground." Aware of the symbolic as well as the scientific significance of the burial site, the leaders of the NYABGP—for the most part researchers from Howard University, a historically Black institution—engaged with the self-designated local "descendant community" to produce a research agenda reflecting the concerns and interests of African American citizens and scholars. In particular, the team shunned standard forensic approaches that focused on "racing" the remains, instead developing a multidisciplinary and biocultural approach that focused (among other things) on shedding light on the "populational and geographic origins" of the Burial Ground population.[71] While the scope of the resulting genetic study was limited by technical issues, the team succeeded in analyzing forty-eight mtDNA samples from among 400 disinterred individuals, linking forty-five of them to groups found currently in West and Central Africa.[72]

An unanticipated corollary of the NYABGP was the founding in 2003 of a DTC genetic ancestry-testing business, African Ancestry, Inc., which adapted some of the techniques developed through the Burial Ground research studies to estimate the ethnic origins of living descendants of enslaved Africans.[73] Like other early DNA ancestry companies, African Ancestry provided its results to customers through letters and printed certificates, which affirmed their genetic ancestry with impressive levels of statistical confidence. The company is well known for organizing emotive "roots reveal" ceremonies, in which its founders, medical geneticist Rick Kittles and entrepreneur Gina Paige, confer on test-takers an African ethnic affiliation in the presence of a supportive public. The company has also received criticisms over the methodology and epistemic limitations of its DNA tests and the extent to which it encourages its customers to incorporate their genetic identity into their social lives and practices (these issues are explored further in chapter 2); others have raised questions about the ethics of profiting from the desire of African-descendants to recover the identities of their enslaved ancestors.[74] Nonetheless, it is clear that the work of African Ancestry and other commercial DNA-testing companies has helped introduce new forms of *biosociality*, defined by Paul Rabinow as the "formation of new group and individual identities and practices arising out of [genetic] truths."[75] In this case, modes of biosocial identification are oriented toward reworking notions of kinship, ethnicity, and racial affiliation based on the evidence of a shared genomic inheritance.

Like other reconstructive efforts, using DNA to explore personal and collective ancestries presents scientists with important ethical dilemmas and raises fundamental questions about the objectivity of the knowledge they offer. The assumed authority of genetic data stems both from the impersonal rigor of the statistical processes involved and the portrayal of the scientist's role as simply making visible an identity contained within the very genetic *code* of the human body. Not long after Crick, Watson, and Wilkins were awarded the Nobel Prize for their studies on the double-helix structure of

DNA, anthropological geneticists began to refer to the molecule as a "document" or "archive," containing "reflections" or "records of the past." These were thought of as being inscribed in DNA in the form of characteristic mutations or "markers," pertaining to ancient migrations, encounters, and divergences among populations and offering potentially more complete accounts of recent demographic events than oral or written histories.[76] In the words of philosopher Georges Canguilhem, the genome was regarded as "meaning inscribed in matter" and studying it became "a work of discovery" in which, "once the key is found, the meaning is found and not constructed."[77] Yet, ethnographic studies of genetic practices have shown that geneticists do not merely decode the clues to identity held by the body, but actively interpret and edit these scripts.[78] The producers of DNA ancestry data must make key scientific and ethical decisions about which areas of the genome to "read"; what geographic regions, populations, and historical time depths to focus on; how to categorize and display results; what constitutes an acceptable error margin, and so on. Nonetheless, much of this interpretative work, as well as the political and economic interests that underpin it, are concealed in the products delivered to users.

In this book, I am interested in foregrounding the processes of interpretation that go on behind the scenes in research and commercial laboratories, including debates among scientists about differing ways to represent genetic human variation and how these practices vary according to the anticipated uses of this information. As I show in chapter 1, genetic expertise is not only used in a reconstructive sense, but also brought to bear on moral questions about how to interpret DNA ancestry results—for instance, in the context of debates about how to designate the beneficiaries of university quotas and other measures to tackle the effects of racism. In chapters 2 and 3, meanwhile, I focus on the different ways that DNA ancestry is constructed and presented to users by scientists working for research laboratories and DTC testing companies. How do the economic dynamics of the genetic ancestry market influence the way that data are shaped and made available to consumers, and how do scientists position themselves within these processes?

Ancestries and Subjectivities

A primary concern of this book is how personal uses of DNA ancestry technologies connect to broader societal understandings of race, as well as ideas about the potential and limitations of genetics as a tool for reconstructing transnational family histories and ethnic identities. As a White British researcher with no (known) African ancestry, I approach this subject as a "racial outsider,"[79] and I think it is important to comment here in some detail on my own subjectivity as a researcher and how this has influenced my research scope and analysis.

My racial positionality has had an inevitable impact on the methodological and practical aspects of my research, for instance, conditioning my access to certain spaces (physical and virtual) and my interactions with informants. This point was emphasized to me early on through an exchange with the administrator of an online group aimed at African-descendant DNA test-takers. Having requested access to the group, and not wishing to "lurk" without the members' consent, I posted a message stating my identity as a British researcher studying uses of DNA ancestry data and inviting anyone interested in discussing their experiences to contact me directly. I was promptly ejected from the group. In a direct message, the administrator firmly explained the members' desire that the group should be kept exclusively for its original intent, since "learning about our ancestry is a private matter." The administrator informed me, moreover, that my presence in the group had made some members feel very uncomfortable. In her words, "Imagine being at home and feeling safe . . . then you realize that someone is in your kitchen that you do not know and they have started going through your laundry, possibly taking what they want. This is how some feel right now." I apologized to the administrator and asked her to reassure the members that I had not recorded any details posted in the group.

Further down the line, when embarking on my fieldwork in earnest, I adjusted my sampling approach, seeking out potential research participants through personal acquaintances and contacting people who had posted their DNA results publicly on social networking sites like Instagram, rather than in closed networks. I am aware that some Black and African-descendant test-takers I approached may have decided not to participate in my study because of doubts about my motivations in researching this particular topic; some individuals (particularly in the United States) openly questioned why I was interested in *their* stories. Given the grievous history of medical abuses, psychological harm, and expropriations of personal data to which Black populations have been subjected through research led by White scientists,[80] I fully understand these concerns and, of course, respect these choices. While other African-descendant test-takers seemed eager to talk to me about their DNA ancestry-testing experiences and were generous with their time and the stories they shared, I am aware that some topics, particularly relating to memories of slavery and experiences of racism, may be less easy to share with a White interlocutor. I have therefore sought to place my research findings in conversation with those of Black scholars, who have studied these phenomena in depth from an "insider" standpoint.[81]

Nevertheless, the impact of researchers' racial status on their interactions with research informants is not always predictable. In Brazil, it is possible that my status as a White, foreign researcher gave me certain advantages: I did not experience, for instance, the suspicion or accusations of racism described by France Winddance Twine, a Black U.S. researcher asking questions about race and prejudice in rural Brazil.[82] Indeed, I was rarely questioned about my choice of research topic and found that Brazilian interviewees (most of whom were participants in an international genetic study on the dynamics of admixture in Latin American populations) generally had few qualms about sharing details of their ancestry and family histories with me—although these genealogies were notably thinner in qualitative detail than the ones shared by test-takers in the United States. The sense of personal and political value attributed to ancestry and family histories, on the other hand, was much greater among the Brazilians I met who were involved with Black movements and Afro-Brazilian cultural associations. These individuals were attuned to the ways that ideologies of racial Whitening and mixture have been used to efface memories of African ancestry in Brazil and challenge the articulation of antiracist movements based on an oppositional Black identity.

In the interests of gaining a sufficiently large research cohort, I decided to broaden my sampling strategy in both countries to include test-takers who did not identify a priori as Black or African-descendant. One advantage of this strategy is that it allowed me to capture a broader range of perspectives on what it means to "have" African ancestry or to "be" African-descendant. In Brazil, for example, where the national identity is based on the concept of "racial" mixture, a large majority of people may assume or claim they have African ancestry without identifying with the labels Black or *afrodescendente*. In the United States, meanwhile, DNA ancestry testing has been used to reveal traces of African ancestry among families who believe their genealogies to be entirely of European descent. Including these additional perspectives allowed me to give a more rounded assessment of the impacts of DNA ancestry testing on modes of racial identification in both countries, in particular the effect of these technologies in articulating the imaginary frontier between Blackness and Whiteness—an issue I explore in detail in chapter 4.

My racial positionality also shapes my subjectivity as an interlocutor in ongoing debates about the DNA ancestry industry and the role genetics can or should be afforded to inform conceptions of identity, kinship, race, and ethnicity. Going into this project, like many of my geneticist and social scientist colleagues, I was critical of projects that portrayed DNA as a place to look for clues about one's personal identity. I did not have a prior interest in genealogy or family history research and was doubtful that such activities could substantially inform my own sense of self or belonging. Nonetheless, during my fieldwork I decided to send my own DNA for analysis to various companies, to gain an "insider's" view on how different enterprises present genetic ancestry results to their customers. As someone who has always had the privilege of feeling secure in my own ethnic and national identity, I was aware of feeling little of the catharsis, revelation, and sense of empowerment professed by many African-descendant test-takers after receiving my own genetic "ethnicity" results. I realized that, unlike some Black and Indigenous test-takers, I had the privilege of not worrying overly about the risks I might incur by handing over my DNA to private companies or whether the resulting data might be used against me, my family, or my broader community.[83] Comparing my own experience of DNA testing with the stories of other users also highlighted for me the ways in which personal experiences of racism, exclusion, and cultural trauma can condition the social value and significance placed on these data. What can seem trivial or "just a bit of fun" to one person may turn out to have life-changing consequences for another. Furthermore, these experiences allowed me to perceive the Eurocentricity of the DNA ancestry industry—a fact that contradicted my initial assumption that these technologies were primarily of interest to members of racial and ethnic minority groups who are the inheritors of various forms of cultural and historical trauma. As I examine further in chapter 3, the DNA ancestry-testing market's predominant focus on Euro-descendant and U.S. clients has implications for the way genomic ancestry is constructed and for how effectively these technologies are able to estimate the genetic origins of users of different national and ethnic backgrounds.

As part of my research process, I also set up a blog site on which I discussed my results, and I soon began to be contacted by genealogists and curious members of the public, seeking help interpreting their results or advice on which companies I considered to be "reliable" or "trustworthy." Initially, I struggled with these requests, which I found hard to reconcile with my critical stance toward the DNA ancestry-testing industry. Nonetheless, I took this as an invitation to better understand the interests of diverse stakeholders and publics who are affected in different ways by these technologies. The DNA test-takers I interviewed were often well aware of the academic debates surrounding the genetic ancestry industry and were keen to put forward their own views. One U.S. genealogist, who at the time was engaged in reconstructing the links between a group of his ancestors who were separated through a plantation sale, voiced his fears that the criticisms of well-meaning scholars like myself could deter members of the public from using these services, in turn diminishing the chances for African Americans to recover this important heritage.

At the same time, these interactions highlighted the desires felt by many test-takers to verify the authenticity of their genetic identities in order to "activate" them socially, investing them with personal meaning.[84] Chapter 5 explores these issues through cases of individuals who seek to connect with their family origins in Africa. Verifying the objectivity and precision of DNA results becomes a fundamental issue in terms of knowing how to identify the *right* kin and legitimating these genetic identity claims in different social and official contexts. My analysis examines the clues that come into play in contextualizing these data, including oral and regional histories, on the one hand, and subjective elements such as intuition, choice, and "family" likenesses, on the other. Among these accounts, the body comes back into view as a site of memory, yet on its own it is rarely sufficient to guarantee an "authentic" connection between diasporic and African individuals. In West African contexts, where painful memories of slavery are still yet to be fully exorcised, the kinship bonds hinted at by DNA markers must be negotiated alongside the knowledge of certain groups' historical complicity in the transatlantic slave trade. Can DNA testing help heal the wounds of the past in these cases, and if so, how?

Structure of This Book

This book is arranged around three key scales of analysis for understanding how genetic data become linked to issues of race and personal identity: (1) mediatized discourses and representations of DNA ancestry; (2) the construction of genomic data among scientists; and (3) personal uses of DNA ancestry technologies by members of the public. Chapter 1 compares the divergent cultural impacts of two media features, released one year apart in the United States and Brazil, respectively, which aimed to use DNA testing to shed light on the African origins of groups of African American and Afro-Brazilian celebrities. The chapter situates these two features in relation to local myths of identity and contemporary antiracist politics that have shaped popular imaginaries about how particular identities, kinship links, and historical narratives are read onto genetic ancestry and how the latter may (or may not) be used to tackle diverse forms of racism. In examining the prominent role played by geneticists and other scientific experts in narrating these two features, the chapter also introduces the question of who has the power to interpret DNA markers and to determine what they "say" about our identities and our pasts.

Chapters 2 and 3 focus on the scientific debates and processes that contribute to shaping how DNA ancestry data are presented to different publics. Chapter 2 examines the strategies used by groups of research scientists in Brazil and the United States to find "objective" and scientifically robust ways to convey personal DNA ancestry reports to members of the public, while guarding against "ideological" or divisive uses of these data. In chapter 3, I turn to the world of commercial DNA ancestry testing, drawing on the case of AncestryDNA (currently the leading global ancestry test provider) to examine the social, scientific, and economic factors that have influenced the construction of a new generation of high-resolution genetic "ethnicity" tests. Despite these technologies' reputation for "pinpoint accuracy," I argue that their ahistorical approach to recovering ancestry, combined with a strong Eurocentric bias within the industry, limits their relevance and reliability as tools for shedding light on African diasporic genealogies.

Chapters 4 and 5 center on personal uses of DNA ancestry tests by Brazilian and U.S. roots-seekers. Chapter 4 examines how DNA ancestry data are being brought to bear on existing conceptions of ancestry and identity in both countries and explores various hypotheses about how these technologies may be shaping racial boundaries. It also looks at the relative social salience that is given to DNA ancestry data vis-à-vis other "racial" markers such as skin color—particularly when the two appear to give differing accounts of identity. In chapter 5, I explore the influence of DNA ancestry technologies on contemporary conceptions of kinship and ethnic identity through the lens of U.S. and Brazilian individuals who are seeking to connect with their African roots. The analysis focuses on how test-takers assess the historical authenticity of their African ethnic matches in the absence of solid genealogical evidence and against prevailing beliefs that a majority of African cultural inheritance was lost through slavery. Finally, in the epilogue I circle back to Momondo's "DNA Journey" and ask, in light of the book's findings: What, if any, is the antiracist potential of DNA ancestry testing?

1 Geno-Myths

Henry Louis Gates Jr. leans one elbow against the upper balcony of the Ellis Island Immigration Museum, his body turned toward the camera. The hall below is empty, but the microphone captures the echo of the voices of hundreds of visitors who have come to pay their respects to the ancestors who disembarked here decades ago, alongside millions of other European immigrants, ready to start their new lives as U.S. citizens. In the background, a U.S. flag hangs stolidly over the quiet hall. Gates's expression is somber as he announces to his viewers: "I envy my friends who can come here and celebrate their ancestors' journey and trace them through the records so diligently compiled here. They can even type the name of their ancestor into a computer and access the record of the day of their arrival. Unfortunately, there is no Ellis Island for those of us who are descendants of survivors of the African slave trade." For generations, Gates explains, African Americans have been unable to gain such information about their African ancestors, who were forcibly transported to the Americas and stripped of their histories and identities by slavery. "But what if we *could* trace our roots?" continues Gates. "What if we could even travel through time, across the Atlantic Ocean, and find where our ancestors came from in Africa? Now, thanks to miraculous breakthroughs in genealogy and genetics, we can begin to do just that."[1]

The PBS documentary miniseries *African American Lives* began with these lines and aired on U.S. television over the course of two weeks in February 2006. In four episodes, the Harvard professor of African American literature accompanied eight distinguished African American guests on an exploration of their family lineages, beginning with the recent history of the civil rights movement, Jim Crow segregation, and the Harlem Renaissance and traveling back in time through the Civil War to the era of chattel slavery. In the final episode, once the paper trails had been exhausted, each guest, including Gates, was presented with two sets of personalized DNA ancestry test results. The first examined their autosomal DNA (genetic material inherited from all recent direct biological ancestors),[2] which conveyed their genomic "admixture" percentages in relation to three continental populations ("European," "West African," and "Native American"), a technique that Gates claimed was "turning ideas of racial purity upside down." The second relayed the names of the African countries and, in some cases, ethnic groups to which each guest had been matched, based on analyses of their maternally inherited mitochondrial DNA (mtDNA) and paternally inherited Y-chromosome DNA (Y-DNA). The show reached its climax as one guest, comedian Chris Tucker, traveled to Angola to meet a community with whom he had been genetically matched. The episode's title, "Beyond the Middle Passage," conveyed the symbolic significance of this knowledge. It was, according to Gates, a way to help African Americans find the identities of their ancestors, allowing them to heal the wounds of the Middle Passage and hence "to stake our claim ever more deeply within the American tradition."[3]

The following year, a group of Brazilian journalists working for BBC Brasil launched a special feature entitled *Raízes Afro-Brasileiras* (*Afro-Brazilian Roots*). The project was intended to explore and celebrate the history of Brazil's African-descendant populations in commemoration of the 200-year anniversary of the abolition of the British slave trade. The content was published in two parts on a dedicated page of the BBC Brasil website. A first round of articles, published during the first week of May 2007, introduced the special feature and presented a discussion of recent historical and genetic studies into Brazil's African heritage. Readers were also informed that nine Black Brazilian celebrities had agreed to trace their personal genetic profiles using DNA ancestry tests, and their results would be revealed, one by one, during the last week in May. Like the guests of *African American Lives*, each celebrity was presented with two sets of results: an estimate of their regional ancestral origins based on mtDNA and Y-DNA analyses, and a description of their genomic admixture, divided into "African," "European," and "Amerindian" percentages. Whereas the emotional climax of *African American Lives* revolved around the revelation of each guest's African ethnic origins, *Raízes Afro-Brasileiras* dramatically foregrounded the contrast between the participants' mixed genetic heritage and their assumed Black identities through headings like "Neguinho da Beija-Flor has mostly European genes," "Result 'wrestles' with what I feel, says Djavan," and "No one knows how to define me, says actress who is Black and '70% European.'"[4]

If the format and inspiration behind these two projects were similar, their reception and impact in their respective countries was markedly different. Viewers attending an official webinar hosted by the creators of *African American Lives* joined TV critics in complimenting the series for its thought-provoking content on the topics of race and identity.[5] As one viewer stated, "I thought the coolest lesson was that one's 'heritage' or 'cultural identity' is based not on 'race' . . . but rather one's own and others' perceptions."[6] Others enquired eagerly how DNA could help them learn more about their own African origins. As the first major U.S. television program to present DNA testing as a means of tracing family histories, Gates's formula was successful enough not only to be revived for a second season (2008) and a spin-off special (*Oprah's Roots*, 2007), but to inspire an entire franchise of celebrity family history shows, the latest of which, *Finding Your Roots*, is currently in its seventh season. These and other successful genealogy documentary series like The Learning Channel's *Who Do You Think You Are?* have helped familiarize the U.S. public with the concept of genetic ancestry testing; they also endorse the products of particular DNA-testing companies that act as sponsors and scientific consultants for these series. In turn, the rising popularity of the genre has mirrored the growth of the DNA ancestry-testing market itself: while still a cottage industry in 2006, it has since been transformed into a multimillion-dollar international market oriented toward informing customers about their unique "ethnic makeup."

In Brazil, on the other hand, the initial aim of *Raízes Afro-Brasileiras*, which was to shed light on the African origins of Black Brazilians, eventually gave way to scrutiny of the relationship between the guests' genetic ancestry results, their physical appearance, and affirmed racial identities. On the same day that the first profiles were published, the BBC Brasil website opened a web forum that stated that "recent genetic research has shown an intense degree of miscegenation in the Brazilian population" and asked readers whether, based on this information, they felt that the concept of race still made sense in Brazil. Among the more than 400 posts received over the following four months, the largest proportion of respondents replied "no," with many reasoning that "Brazilians are all mixed," and some declaring that "racial categories are racist."[7] In the context of an ongoing national polemic about the introduction of racially targeted quotas at prestigious federal universities, meant to tackle the systemic exclusion of dark-skinned Brazilians from the upper echelons of society, some critics seized on the DNA profiles as evidence of impossibility of dividing Brazil into "Blacks" and "Whites." Many commentators drew special attention to the participants whose genetic profiles appeared to contradict their affirmed racial identity. In particular, the news that Neguinho da Beija-Flor, a dark-skinned Afro-Brazilian samba artist from Rio de Janeiro, had "more European than African" genomic ancestry was used by some pundits to denounce the quotas initiatives.[8] In anticipation of these attacks, representatives of the country's

Black movements—including one activist who took part in the feature—branded the BBC Brasil feature an attempt to sabotage the quotas campaigns and questioned the legitimacy of the science used.[9] Such was the level of controversy that within a week of the feature's publication, BBC Brasil editor Rogério Simões released a post on the site's editorial blog, clarifying that "the BBC has not entered into any the debate over the establishment, or not, of quotas for Blacks, nor any other social policy based on 'racial' characteristics, because this was not the aim of the reports." Nevertheless, Simões remarked, "The genetics carried a surprise: many individuals that seemed to belong to a specific race are also a combination of the various peoples that formed the Brazilian nation. For some, it is a fact to be celebrated, for others it is a source for polemic. But, undeniably, it is a fact."[10]

Does DNA testing simply convey "the facts" about ancestry? The radically different interpretations detailed above—relating to two similar sets of genetic data, produced under the same pretext, a year apart in the United States and Brazil—suggest that DNA ancestry information do not simply speak for themselves. Donna Haraway has written of the necessity of treating scientific knowledge as "situated"—that is, as information that draws sense from interwoven histories, myths, and political relations, rather than holding an inherent and irreducible meaning. For Haraway, readings of scientific data are necessarily "engaged and produced: they do not flow naturally from the text," so that even "the most straightforward readings of any text are also situated arguments about fields of meanings and fields of power."[11] When interpreting DNA ancestry data, family and national histories tend to form our immediate frames of reference. Yet, as Michel-Rolph Trouillot signaled, historical narratives are themselves the fruit of power struggles, involving "the uneven contribution of competing groups and individuals who have unequal access to the means for such production."[12] These two parallel examples offer a starting point for exploring how the cultural and political authority of particular myths and historical narratives of race and national identity stack the odds in favor of particular readings of the links between DNA ancestry and identity, while making other interpretations difficult or impossible to access.

Unequal Ancestries and the Problem of Traceability

As Gates tells it, the inspiration for *African American Lives* came to him in the small hours, one night in 2003.[13] A prominent expert in African American literature who had previously created documentaries about African history and culture,[14] Gates had recently taken a DNA test from the newly established company African Ancestry in the hopes of learning about his own African family origins. As it was for many African Americans of his generation, this was a lifelong dream that Gates could clearly trace back to his memories of watching Alex Haley's *Roots* as a young man. Both novel and miniseries (released in 1976 and 1977, respectively) recount the story of Haley's ancestor, Kunta Kinte, a young Mandinka man who grew up in present-day Gambia and was captured and sold into slavery, shortly before the American Revolution. The narrative traces the lives of Kunta Kinte's descendants from the eighteenth century to the present day, ending with Haley himself learning his family history from an elderly aunt and setting out to locate the origins of his ancestor based on a handful of names and African words passed down within the family for generations. With the help of two Africanist scholars, Haley was able to trace his family origins to a village called Juffure in the Gambia. The community's historical link to Kunta Kinte and his forebears was confirmed by a local *griot*, and Haley was welcomed back by the villagers as their long-lost kin.[15] The book, which Haley referred to as a work of "faction" (fiction based on fact), was an instant bestseller. It won a Pulitzer Prize in 1977 and was adopted as a course book at 276 colleges and universities over the next decade. A TV miniseries, released in January 1977, attracted a record number of viewers, with an estimated 130 million individuals tuning in to watch the final episode.[16] Today, the story has achieved mythical status in U.S. culture.

Roots challenged what anthropologist Melville Herskovits dubbed the "myth of the Negro past": the idea that African American populations had no history or original culture, having lost their traditions through slavery. In his 1941 book of the same title, Herskovits argued that this was not a social fact but a myth used widely to confirm the inferiority of people of African descent and to justify treating them as degenerative elements within American societies. Contrary to portraits painted by leading sociologists of Black families as "pathological" and "rootless,"[17] Haley's tale chronicled the efforts of the enslaved to maintain kinship ties with their loved ones, as well as a sense of connection to an African origin, even in the most adverse conditions. As suggested by the book's subtitle, *The Saga of an American Family*, Haley offered up his family's account as an example of the "bootstrap" narratives used to embody the core U.S. values of hard work, struggle, and social ascension. At the same time, he predicted, his own ancestors' story would become "a symbolic saga of all African-descent people—who are without exception the seeds of someone like Kunta who was born and grew up in some Black African village, someone who was captured and chained down in one of those slave ships that sailed them across the same ocean, into some succession of plantations, and since then a struggle for freedom."[18] In fact, *Roots* inspired a wave of public interest in genealogy, motivating thousands to take to the archives in pursuit of their own family histories—an activity that has only gained popularity in U.S. society ever since. Aside from posing the tantalizing possibility that others might be able to uncover their own African origins in a similarly miraculous manner, many African Americans found that the popularity of the show made it easier to broach the silence around slavery within their families, by alleviating the shame associated with this episode in their collective history.[19]

Although he had already been conducting his own genealogical research for several years by the time Haley's narrative was published, Gates claims that ever since watching the miniseries he was gripped by "a serious case of *Roots* envy" and longed to trace his family origins back to Africa.[20] However, in his book *In Search of Our Roots*, which narrates the stories explored in the two series of *African American Lives* (2006, 2008), Gates explained the difficulties he and many other African American genealogists had encountered in making this connection:

> The problem was slavery; the institution of slavery—more correctly, the people who created it so perversely, designed it to destroy any possibility of maintaining the family ties necessary to tracing one's ancestry, through the deviously brilliant act of obliterating our family names, our surnames. . . . This seemingly simple act of naming—or not-naming—interrupted the continuity of family that last names ensure; surnames signifying, as they do, common bonds of blood and tradition and heritage, as veritable links in a chain, a traceable familial chain of being. For us, for those of us descended from the 455,000 Africans who arrived in this country directly from Africa and indirectly from the Caribbean as slaves . . . it was this "traceability," as it were, that the evil genius of slavery sought to take away from us on both sides of the Atlantic, making us fragmented and not whole.[21]

Gates hoped that *African American Lives* could help Black Americans solve this problem of "traceability." In the opening scenes to the documentary, outlined at the beginning of this chapter, he framed the uneven access to ancestry in the United States as symptomatic of an entrenched inequality still separating White and Black Americans. Historically, the founding of genealogical societies, the maintenance of archives, and the production of pedigrees and other genealogical memorabilia have been oriented toward White elite families.[22] Since the 1950s, and more markedly after the publication of *Roots*, the field of family history has undergone a process of relative social leveling. However, as Gates noted in the opening scenes to *African American Lives*, disparities continue to exist, conditioned by structural issues such as the access to, organization, and funding of archives. For instance, the Ellis Island database featured in the documentary was gifted to the United States in 2001 by the Church of Jesus Christ of Latter-day Saints, an organization that has been cataloging genealogical data since the late nineteenth century as part of its evangelical mission. In contrast, similar resources for African American family historians, such as the Freedman's Bureau Records database (now hosted by the National Museum of African American History and Culture) and the International African American Museum's Center for Family History in South Carolina have only been unveiled in the last five years.[23]

The feeling of *not knowing* one's ancestry, and the sense of disparity it engenders, is also made tangible in contrast to the apparent ease with which other groups are able to name their "founding fathers" or cultures of origin. For instance, Charles Blockson, coauthor of the seminal manual *Black Genealogy*, recalled feeling ashamed by his "ignorance" of his own family history "because some of my White friends could trace their families back to William the Conqueror."[24] Some of the African American DNA test-takers I interviewed over the course of my research mentioned the dread they felt at being asked to complete family history assignments at school. This bitterness was often more keenly felt in relation to classmates of other minority ethnic backgrounds, such as Latino or first-generation African immigrants, who, despite being considered racial "allies" in many social contexts, often seemed able to recount their family history in envy-inspiring detail. In the words of Fatimah, who attended middle school in Colorado in the early 1960s, "A lot of the kids that I went to school with were Latinos, Mexican Americans. . . . And they could trace [their names] to particular conquistadors—at least in their minds, that's what they did, or that's what they told us. And we didn't have any of that. And it left a rancor, and a feeling that you had been cheated out of your ancestry. I remembered when the Black Power movement came in, and I told my grandmother, 'You know we came from Africa,' and she said, 'Yeah, that's what they said.' And I thought, 'we don't know.'"

Other African American roots-seekers pointed to the disparity between what they knew about their European versus their African ancestral origins.

Jarreau, who went to middle school in New Jersey in the mid-1990s, remembered being given the task of coloring in his countries of ancestry on a map of the globe. Enlisting the aid of his grandmother, he colored in several European countries: England, Scotland, Ireland, Italy. When it came to the family's origins in Africa, however, Jarreau's grandmother told him that they would never know where exactly they came from, saying it was "almost impossible to tell." His schoolteacher, meanwhile, instructed him to color the entire continent—a solution that Jarreau remarked "didn't sit well with me." As if to make matters worse, Jarreau remembered that the only other two Black students in his class were the children of Nigerian immigrants who seemed to have no issue filling in their own ancestry maps. Indeed, for Latino and African immigrants to the United States, the stigma of "rootlessness" attached to Black Americans may offer a lesson in the importance of cultivating a family history and retaining links to the "Old World." For instance, a first-generation Nigerian American who grew up in Maryland in the 1990s described to me how his parents strove to forge in him a sense of knowledge and pride in their birth country and ethnic group, precisely to prevent him from suffering the same sense of inadequacy and rootlessness as his "American Black" friends.

These anecdotes underline the fact that ethnicity is not something that people automatically "have," but rather an identity that must be worked at and reproduced, particularly in contexts of migration and displacement. According to Matthew Frye Jacobson, the U.S. focus on ethnicity came to prominence in the 1960s, with the culmination of the civil rights movement. Intense public discussions about the historical injustices inflicted on Blacks, Native Americans, Mexicans, and other minorities in the name of White racial supremacy prompted the descendants of recent European immigrants to distance themselves from the "White Anglo-Saxon Protestant" (WASP) identity to which their parents and grandparents had aspired.[25] The rhetoric of Black Power advocates like Charles V. Hamilton and Kwame Ture (then known as Stokely Carmichael), who argued in favor of the recognition of group rights and group power (a notion that contrasted sharply with the historical focus on *individual* liberties in the United States), provided a useful basis on which numerous White ethnic groups could stake a claim to their own collective identities. Hence, U.S. citizens of Polish, Italian, Greek, Slavic, Irish, and Jewish descent, among others, who had previously experienced immense pressure to assimilate culturally and linguistically to the WASP norm, began to disavow the category of Whiteness in favor of a range of ethnic denominations. This shift gradually saw the reintegration of the "hyphen" (i.e., Italian-American, Chinese-American, and so on)—used pejoratively since the early twentieth century to mark recent immigrants' status as not yet "100 per cent Americanized"[26]—as a fully accepted facet of the modern, multicultural U.S. identity.

The "ethnic turn" of the 1960s and 70s marked the move toward a new politics of cultural pluralism. Advocates of this social change encouraged U.S. citizens to attempt to resurrect elements of the cultural identities that had been painfully cast off by their parents and grandparents, popularizing the idea that all citizens should be able to align themselves with a dual, if not multiple, identity, amalgamating one or more ethnic identities (relating to Old World countries of origin) with their U.S. nationality. In his 1971 book *The Rise of the Unmeltable Ethnics*, philosopher Michael Novak argued that all U.S. citizens have an ethnicity "developed in us not only by our individual effort, but also by the social and cultural traditions in which we were reared,"[27] and consisting of "a cast of mind, a set of cues, an historical memory, a set of approved stories to live out."[28] The exceptions were those who "have suffered historical amnesia; consciously, at least, they are rootless, without cultural memory, loyal to no tradition or project."[29] For Novak, this distinction marked a chasm between "White ethnics" and Black Americans, since, although both groups had suffered the trauma of displacement and subsequent prejudice at the hands of WASPs, the latter were unable to leave behind their racial category because of their inability to recover their familial origins prior to their arrival in the United States.

Contemporary DNA ancestry companies present their products as a way for customers to recover these ancestral ethnic identities, regardless of their background or family history knowledge. For instance, a video commercial for African Ancestry, the company that provided some of the DNA analyses for *African American Lives*, informs viewers that "there are 56 countries in Africa. Don't you think it's time you knew which one you were from?"[30] The business specializes in matching customers to a particular African ethnic group and country, based on the analysis of two parts of the genome (mtDNA and Y-DNA) known as uniparental markers. These areas of the genome contain large quantities of polymorphisms (randomly accumulated genetic mutations), which vary among human populations in a way that roughly correlates to geography, reflecting migration patterns dating from the early expansion of modern humans into different world regions. They are transmitted without recombination, so the same DNA sequence can be shared over numerous generations, making it a useful marker of a particular genetic lineage. The mitochondrial genome is inherited matrilineally, from mother to child, so that its genetic transmission mirrors a single maternal lineage in a genealogical tree; the Y-chromosome is inherited from father to son, mirroring a single paternal lineage. A shared sequence of mtDNA or Y-DNA between two individuals is therefore deemed to be indicative of a common ancestry, while the strength of the match and the age of the ancestral connection can also be evaluated, based on the number of consecutive matching DNA base pairs found between two sequences. The analyses rely on the assumption that the inheritance of distinctive mtDNA and Y-DNA sequences correlates with ethnic group membership—for instance, due to the effects of selective mating (e.g., culturally prescribed endogamous practices) and isolation by distance (the theory that people are more likely to mate with individuals who are geographically close by rather than far away). In this sense, ethnic groups are imagined as both cultural entities *and* extended genetic kinship groups, so that by indicating the existence of a recent shared ancestor between two individuals, an mtDNA or Y-DNA match may also suggest a shared cultural origin.

Back in 2003, Gates was delighted when Rick Kittles, the company's cofounder and scientific director, informed him that based on his mtDNA analysis, Gates was likely "descended from a Nubian person." Enthused by this experience, Gates began to imagine a television series that would bring together his passion for family history with the new "DNA searches." He contacted his friend, musician and composer Quincy Jones, to help him enlist a group of high-profile African American celebrities for a project that would trace their family trees back to slavery and ultimately present them with their African "tribal" origins. As Gates recalls, he had little problem recruiting the show's all-star lineup of guests who were "all on board" with the concept. Shortly after, he secured $6 million funding for the project from Johnson & Johnson and Coca-Cola, after pitching them the chance to associate their products with "the whole world finding out Oprah Winfrey's roots."[31] For Gates, the ability to (re)connect to an African origin was a crucial element to what he saw as the beneficial effects of genealogical research for Black Americans. In an interview with *Ancestry* magazine in 2006, just before the show's release, he explained: "My goal is that children, especially inner-city black school children, will realize the wonders of archival research and their own family histories *and* where they came from in Africa— something they can actually touch and something that affects them directly." Jeanie Croasmun, the article's author, continued: "Gates wants [the audience] to see the origins of some of their role models, and understand that their family histories don't end when the first of their ancestors was enslaved. He wants them to know that through technological advances, they may, for the first time, be able to discover the specific African culture from which their families stem."[32]

Against the Color Line

Gates sees DNA testing and genealogical research as heuristic devices that, particularly for African Americans, can open up new possibilities for self-improvement and taking pride in an identity that is not exclusively racial. Yet he does not advocate for an exclusive focus on African ancestry. In our interview, Gates told me of another important memory that informed his vision for *African American Lives*. The anecdote relates to the moment Gates first felt an interest in researching his family tree; it was on the day he attended his grandfather's funeral, at the age of nine. Standing over the casket, Gates told me, he was struck by how pale his grandfather's skin looked and how White he had looked even when he was alive. Later that evening, after the burial, Gates's father brought out a copy of the obituary of his great-great-grandmother, Jane Gates, dated January 6, 1888. The obituary referred to her as "an estimable colored woman," and Gates's father told Henry and his brother that Jane had been a slave and a midwife, a fact that he never wanted them to forget. The next day, Gates asked his father to buy him a composition book and he proceeded to interview his parents about their family history—in his words—"to find out how it was possible that my ancestor could be a slave, and yet that my grandfather could turn out looking so White."[33]

By his own account, Gates's first brush with genealogical research was inextricably entwined with the enigma of the foundational racial fiction in the United States: the "one-drop rule." Genealogical pedigrees and fractional quotas of ancestry have been used since colonial times to classify individuals racially. For instance, at different moments between the eighteenth and early twentieth century in the state of Virginia, having "one-fourth Negro blood," "one-sixteenth or more of Negro blood," or "any ascertainable Negro blood" (the classic definition of the "one-drop rule") were the benchmarks for legally defining an individual as "colored" and therefore excluding them from the privileges of Whiteness, defined in contrast as having "pure" European ancestry.[34] The rule's logic allowed Whites (and, given the patriarchal structure of colonial society, White men in particular) to maintain legal, economic, and sexual power over other groups. Sexual relationships between White men and enslaved women were frequent and typically coercive. Perversely, sex become a tool for slaveholders to increase their enslaved population, since any children born to enslaved women were automatically classed as unfree. It is worth underlining that the categories "colored" or "Black" and "White" ultimately had little to do with skin tone or physical appearance; rather, the rule created a system in which individuals of "racially" mixed ancestry might continue reproducing with individuals with lighter skin and greater proportions of European ancestry, without their descendants ever legally crossing the color line (see figure 1.1).[35]

When planning the content of the DNA-testing episode, Gates felt that admixture testing could provide a useful tool for deconstructing these traditional notions of U.S. racial groups as discontinuous and "pure," revealing them instead to be socially constructed. African American genomes were ideal for demonstrating this message, Gates claimed, because so far he had never tested an African American on one of his shows who did not have some proportion of European ancestry—something Gates viewed as "amazing." Upon receiving his own admixture test results in the episode "Beyond the Middle Passage," the show's host appeared surprised to be attributed 50 percent European ancestry, making him, in his words, "half White." This label, which would be an oxymoron under the strict logic of the one-drop rule, seemed to be used provocatively by Gates to open up new racial possibilities, posing the idea that one might recognize simultaneously one's European and African ancestries without the latter negating the former. At the same time, during the series Gates put across the unequivocal message that identity should not simply be dictated by genetics. In one scene, Gates asked his colleague, Harvard sociologist Sara Lawrence-Lightfoot (who was attributed 45 percent European genetic ancestry, the second highest proportion within the group) whether this result made her "less African American than someone who, say, would be 100 percent sub-Saharan African?" Lawrence-Lightfoot refuted the idea, stating, "I care less about these figures than I do about one's sense of identification with a cultural group, or a racial group." Her answer clearly denoted to viewers that genetic ancestry, while potentially useful as a genealogical tool, should not be used to deny the reality of Blackness as a collective political and cultural identity.

Not all African Americans share Gates's view of European genetic admixture as something to embrace. In her study of the company African Ancestry, Alondra Nelson observed that many clients preferred to use their uniparental testing services because they were perceived as giving them greater chances of receiving *only* African results. Asked whether she was

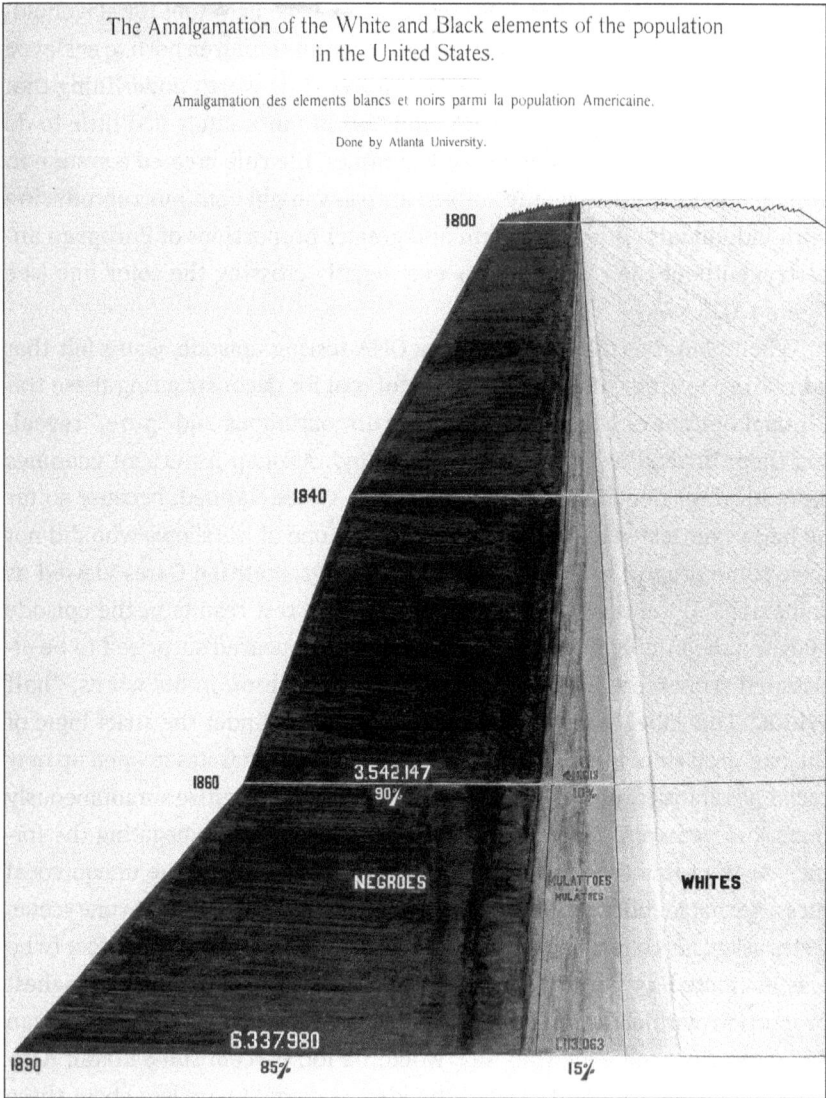

The Amalgamation of the White and Black elements of the population in the United States.

Amalgamation des elements blancs et noirs parmi la population Americaine.

Done by Atlanta University.

1800

1840

1860   3.542.147   393.615
        90%   10%

NEGROES   MULATTOES   WHITES
           MULÂTRES

1890   6.337.980   1.113.063
        85%   15%

FIGURE 1.1 Estimate of U.S. "racial" mixture by W. E. B. Du Bois and students from Atlanta University, ca. 1900. The "color line" is represented by the solid line between "Whites" and "Mulattoes." The shading to the right of the line represents individuals of Black ancestry who have "passed" as White, indicating that in reality the line was permeable. Daniel Murray Collection, U.S. Library of Congress.

interested in taking an admixture test, one genealogist told Nelson, "I don't need to take that test. We're all mixed up. We know that already."[36] Although African Ancestry offered an admixture testing product for a number of years, it has since been discontinued. For some, receiving genetic proof of one's European ancestry is to be reminded of the histories of sexual violence inflicted on African-descendant women under conditions of slavery and the habitual disownment of "mixed" children by their White fathers.[37] For his part, Gates has championed what he sees as the profound social value of admixture tests: namely, to alert White and Black Americans to the extent to which their family trees became entwined through the history of slavery, resulting in the sharing of a common genetic heritage that is now coming to light through DNA ancestry testing. He has been particularly encouraging of attempts by White Americans to investigate traces of African ancestry revealed by their DNA results, while criticizing Black Americans who attempt to ignore or deny their European genetic ancestry.[38]

Gates's vision for the potential of DNA ancestry tests to undo racial myths by revealing ancestral mixtures extended beyond the United States. In 2008, when the BBC Brasil journalists were beginning to publicize their feature *Raízes Afro-Brasileiras*, they included extracts of an interview with Gates in which he expressed his enthusiasm for the project and what it could reveal about the country's history of "racial" mixture. Gates was cited as claiming, "In Brazil, no one is pure. That's why Brazil has the face of the future."[39] In recent decades, scholars in the United States have frequently looked to Brazil and other Latin American societies as examples of the capacity of "racial" mixture to lessen the tensions and distance between racial groups, even offering an antidote to U.S. legacies of the one-drop rule and the color line.[40] Brazil's political leaders, for their part, have long sought to cultivate this image on an international stage, portraying the country as a paragon of "racial democracy." On the other hand, for several decades Black activists in Brazil have sought to challenge the hegemony of these national narratives of mixture, redefining them not as an antidote to racism but as seductive myths that have long supported systems of White supremacy and prevented the country from coming to terms with the reality of its entrenched racial inequalities. Despite Gates's confident declaration that Brazil was "the face of the future," by the time *Raízes Afro-Brasileiras* was published the country was in the midst of a national debate about its problems with racism, how to tackle them, and what racial narratives would shape Brazil's future identity.

Mixture: Between Fact and Myth

Mixture has never been a simple fact of Brazil's history. Rather, it has attained a mythical quality, often being used less to talk about the past than to make claims about the nation's future.[41] The meanings of mixture have changed radically over time, and they have also been powerfully shaped through continuous comparisons with the United States, a country typically construed as Brazil's racial opposite.[42] For instance, whereas in the nineteenth century, the concept of "racial" mixture was used to account for the country's social and economic backwardness in comparison to "racially pure" Europe and North America, under populist dictator Getúlio Vargas (1930–45, 1951–54) the term was appropriated to describe the unique conditions that primed Brazil to become the world's first "racial democracy." The inspiration for this new national myth was Gilberto Freyre's 1933 sociological treatise on Brazil's history, *Casa-grande e senzala* (published in English as *The Masters and the Slaves*). In his account, Freyre proposed that Brazil's Portuguese forefathers, themselves the mixed descendants of Christians and Moors, were unique in the colonial Americas in displaying a total "lack of feeling or awareness of race superiority," a fact made evident through their obvious sexual preference for Indigenous and African women.[43] According to Freyre, centuries of cultural mixing (*mestiçagem*) and indiscriminate "racial" mixture (*miscigenação*) had provided the conduit to the formation of the modern *mestiço* nation, marked by its shared attitude of racial tolerance. The success of Freyre's account derived partly from its positive portrayal of Brazil's *mestiçagem* as the amalgamation of three founding populations that each contributed—albeit unequally—to the country's development. The narrative also contrasted the genial, "tropical" character of the Portuguese with the notorious cruelty and puritanism displayed historically by nations like the British, whose ex-colonies continued to struggle with outbreaks of racial violence, exacerbated by regimes of segregation. In Brazil, Freyre argued, racial hatred was anathema since all Brazilians knew themselves to be linked by a common, mixed heritage.

Initially, the belief that progressive cultural and "racial" mixture could lead to the neutralization of racial inequalities was widely embraced in Brazil, including by Black activists who had campaigned since the 1930s to improve the situation of the country's Black populations.[44] In 1950, Abdias do Nascimento—a pioneer of Brazil's contemporary Black movements—declared optimistically that "through the inspiration and imposition of recent advances in biology, anthropology and sociology," the country's historical "racial" mixture was fast becoming "a well-defined doctrine of racial democracy, to serve as a lesson and model to other peoples with complex ethnic formations like our own."[45] Under the military dictatorships (1964–85), however, the idea that Brazil had already achieved a state of "racial democracy" became political dogma. Groups that tried to protest the continued existence of color prejudice and discrimination or to organize politically to challenge these issues under the banner of Black activism were labeled "un-Brazilian" or "reverse racists" and accused of spreading false ideas imported from the United States.[46]

Nonetheless, social scientists continued to provide compelling empirical evidence of the existence of entrenched racial inequalities in Brazil, rooted in the hierarchies produced by slavery and perpetuated by forms of "veiled racism." Their studies found that *negros* and *pardos* were disproportionately represented among low-earning occupations in comparison to *brancos*, with lower life expectancies and literacy rates and fewer years of schooling. Despite the fact that Brazilian governments have never pursued de jure regimes of racial segregation, the overrepresentation of dark-skinned Brazilians in shantytowns and *favelas* in cities like Recife, São Paulo, and Rio de Janeiro pointed toward de facto residential segregation along lines of race and class.[47] By 1978, Nascimento had revised his position, describing racial democracy as a myth and *mestiçagem* as a tool used by Brazil's dominant classes to bring about the genocide of Afro-Brazilians.[48]

The transition to democracy presented new political opportunities for activists like Nascimento, some of whom acquired government positions and sought to use their influence to advocate for legislative change. The 1988 Brazilian constitution embraced some multicultural measures—for instance, awarding special legal rights and recognitions to Indigenous communities and *remanescentes de quilombos* ("survivals" of communities of runaway slaves). In the 1990s, President Fernando Henrique Cardoso (who trained as a sociologist under Gilberto Freyre and specialized in the topic of "race relations") became the first Brazilian president to officially recognize racism as a national problem requiring official legislative and bureaucratic action.[49] He also broke the mold in a landmark presidential address in 1995 by referring to Brazil as a "multiracial society" composed of "distinct races"—a significant departure from the traditional view of Brazil, popularized by Cardoso's former mentor, as a "mixed-race society," characterized by a continuum of "colors" and devoid of discrete racial categories.[50] One of the main initiatives proposed by Cardoso's government to tackle issues of racial inequality and exclusion was the implementation of affirmative action schemes in the public sector and higher education, among other spheres. In preparation for the 2001 Third World Conference on Racism, held in Durban, South Africa, a Brazilian delegation consisting of state officials and representatives of Black activist groups presented a report in which they requested, among other things, the introduction of affirmative action initiatives in communities of primarily African descent, as well as the promotion of new educational curricula highlighting the history and contributions of Africans and the African diaspora.[51] These recommendations were further strengthened by the expert advice offered by the Durban committee, which, following the conference, released a report that explicitly endorsed affirmative action by governments around the world as a means to promote "equality, equity, social justice, equal opportunities and participation for all" and to address the racism routinely suffered by the "descendants of Africans, Caribbeans, indigenous peoples, and other discriminated peoples."[52]

The Racial Quotas Polemic

The progressive rhetoric and policies of the Cardoso government seemed largely in tune with the mood of a nation whose citizens overwhelmingly agreed, by the mid-1990s, that racism was a national problem.[53] Nonetheless, the adoption of the first racial quota schemes at public universities in the early 2000s inspired a nationwide polemic and provoked almost a decade of debates among academics, legislators, and the media over the very definition of race and the future of Brazil's antiracist politics. Although they dominated public debate and came to be synonymous with the term *ações afirmativas* in Brazil, it is worth stating that the university quota schemes were far from the only affirmative action scheme introduced in Brazil during this period with the aim of tackling various types of poverty and promoting racial inclusion.[54] However, unlike other approaches (e.g., providing scholarships for Black and other underprivileged students or offering special preparatory courses to ensure that these groups had a better chance of competing in the university entry exams), the quotas were deemed particularly contentious because they entailed reserving a certain number of places for target groups, thereby making race "a primary determinant of admission."[55]

Criticisms of the quotas were various, hailing from different segments of society and commentators of different political stripes. Some expressed doubts about the effectiveness of affirmative action at the university level as a way to tackle the country's racial inequalities (rather than addressing deficiencies in the public school system, for example) and questioned whether focusing on racial inclusion at this educational stage might have the undesirable effect of overburdening quotas students, who were likely to be less academically prepared, increasing the chance of dropouts.[56] Some argued that the schemes would have a stigmatizing effect on Black students, diminishing the merit of their academic achievements if it was suspected that they "only got in through the quotas." Others raised concerns that the initiatives would further disadvantage poor White students (despite the fact that most universities also reserved quotas for public school students who did not identify as *negro/a* or *pardo/a*).[57]

Another line of argument, put forward by a number of social scientists specializing in studies of race and racism, held that the quotas necessarily functioned on a binary racial logic that risked for the first time imposing an official color line in Brazilian society between those who were deemed admissible under racial quotas and those who were not.[58] Supporters of this view alleged that the Black movements were attempting to import a new "biracial" order, inspired by the example of the United States, but which was unsuited to the particular dynamics of Brazil's social and racial issues and would only serve to exacerbate racial tensions.[59] They questioned whether such a biracial regime could be dismantled once the quotas had accomplished their goals and drew ominous parallels between the antiracist proposals of Brazil's Black movements and the racist rhetoric of U.S. segregationists and Nazi Germany.[60] These claims were refuted by supporters of the quotas, who pointed out that even if they were not officially mandated or recognized, clear divisions already existed between the socioeconomic conditions and life chances of *brancos*, on the one hand, and *pardos* and *negros*, on the other. Rather than aggravating racial tensions, they suggested that the quotas could promote mixing and mutual understanding among students of different social and racial backgrounds, offering a chance for White students to better understand the discrimination suffered by their Black peers and, in turn, to reflect on their own privileges.[61]

Perhaps one of the thorniest areas of debate, even among supporters of the initiatives, was how to define who was eligible for quotas. How could universities ensure that the initiatives would reach those most likely to suffer from discrimination or disadvantage while avoiding the risk of "fraud" (i.e., the possibility that White students might claim they were Black to gain access to quotas)?[62] The Universidade de Brasília (UnB), which had opted for a system of solely race-based quotas, made headlines in 2003 after deciding to assess candidates' eligibility based on their physical appearance.

Each candidate had to submit a photograph taken in controlled conditions, and these pictures were sent to a panel of referees, including a student, a sociologist, an anthropologist, and three Black movement activists, who decided whether they qualified as Black.[63] The UnB's photo verification process became the target of renewed critiques in 2007—just days after the publication of *Raízes Afro-Brasileiras*—when the panel classified a pair of identical twins differently, accepting one as a quotas student and categorizing the other as *branco*.[64] The notion that two siblings—who grew up in the same context and shared the same physical traits (and presumably, the same experiences of discrimination)—could be judged differently by the UnB panel was taken as a damning testament of the process's fallibility; under significant media pressure, the university overturned the decision, classifying both brothers as *negro*.

Color, Ancestry, Identity

Although *Raízes Afro-Brasileiras* was published in the heat of these debates, the feature's organizers later claimed they did not anticipate the links that some commentators would draw between the participants' genetic profiles and the legitimacy of race-based quotas. Silvia Salek, who was assignments desk editor for BBC Brasil in 2007, told me that she had recently become interested in the theme of genetic ancestry, and she proposed to her colleagues the idea of offering DNA tests to famous Brazilians of different *cores* ("colors," a concept that describes not only skin tone but a combination of physical traits, including hair color and texture, eye color, nose shape, etc.) and publishing the results together as a feature. After learning that a similar piece had been conducted a few years earlier by another Brazilian magazine, Salek and her colleagues decided instead to focus exclusively on Afro-Brazilian celebrities, linking their piece to the upcoming bicentenary of the abolition of the British slave trade in 1807. Their aim was twofold: to celebrate the historical impact of African cultures on Brazilian society and to show that Brazilians' ancestry did not necessarily correspond to their physical appearance—a theme that Salek believed could surprise Brazilian readers, challenging their concepts of race in a positive way and thus contributing to the fight against racism. To this end, the journalists recruited a group of nine Afro-Brazilian musicians, athletes, and activists and launched a competition inviting members of the public to have their own DNA results revealed alongside the celebrities, picking two winners from among some 3,000 entries.[65]

The team approached Sérgio Danilo Pena, professor of medical genetics at the Universidade Federal de Minas Gerais (UFMG), to process the DNA ancestry tests for the feature through his genetic-testing company Laboratório GENE. The collaboration seemed apt since Pena had written about the disjunction between "color" and ancestry in a series of popular science articles aimed at deconstructing the biological validity of race. His argument—which is elaborated in full in numerous popular and academic texts—consists of two main points. First, the phenotypic traits used popularly to distinguish between different human "races" (Africans, Asians, Europeans, etc.) are controlled by a mere handful of the roughly 25,000 genes that make up the human genome—meaning that, overall, humans are much more genetically similar than this superficial variation would suggest. Second, in Brazil, centuries of admixture among human groups have meant that the small proportion of genes that control phenotypes like skin color have become dissociated from the DNA markers used by scientists to estimate an individual's genetic ancestry.[66] Pena's claim is that "color" is meaningless as a marker of race (which, in turn, he regards as a genetically invalid concept) and that all Brazilians share a similarly mixed ancestry, regardless of their appearance. As he wrote in 2000 for the popular science magazine *Ciência Hoje*, "If the many White Brazilians who have Amerindian or African mitochondrial DNA markers became aware of that, [we hope that] they would value more the exuberant genetic diversity of our people and, who knows, build a more just and harmonious society in the twenty-first century."[67] Pena's perspective is therefore staunchly antiracialist. He argues against the validity of race as a taxonomic concept in genetics and regards social and political conceptions of race and "color" to be relics of scientific racism, which, he hopes, will eventually fade from use. Brazil's unique history of genetic mixture, Pena argues, makes it the epitome of a raceless society. In his words, "the only way to conceptualize each Brazilian is in relation to their individuality as a unique human being, by virtue of their singular genome which is a genealogical mosaic, and of their life story."[68]

In fact, Pena had been a leading voice in the racial quota debates for the previous few years. In 2004, he coauthored a paper with Maria Cátira Bortolini, professor of genetics at the Universidade Federal do Rio Grande do Sul (UFRGS), in which they responded to the idea, floated by some public commentators, that DNA ancestry tests could offer an objective method for deciding who should be termed eligible for the quotas. Pena and Bortolini's answer was unequivocal: DNA tests should *not* be used to classify affirmative action candidates. However, they argued, "modern genetics can provide support for political decisions and . . . the genetic profile of the Brazilian population should be taken into account for political decisions." In particular, they raised the point that, as a result of the nation's historical admixture, "[Brazil's] Afro-descendants are much more numerous than they appear based on their physical characteristics, attaining the impressive number of 146 million people . . . [while] many of those who identify as Black have a significant proportion of European ancestry."[69] Quotas that attempted to divide the country into notionally "pure" racial groups, the authors implied, were at odds with the country's very genetic makeup.

Since the DNA ancestry results formed the main substance for the *Raízes Afro-Brasileiras* profiles (unlike Gates, the journalists did not attempt to conduct a genealogical investigation into each participant's family roots), Pena's approach was influential for shaping the feature's narratives around ancestry, race, and identity. At the time, Laboratório GENE was one of the only Brazilian companies offering commercial DNA ancestry testing, and Pena had provided these services for several media features of this kind in the past.[70] For *Raízes Afro-Brasileiras*, he offered to conduct both admixture and uniparental tests, to give a range of results for each participant. Unlike African Ancestry, which provided the uniparental tests for *African American Lives*, Pena did not offer to match the participants to a specific African country or ethnic group. When I interviewed him in 2013, Pena explained that the tests were extremely labor intensive for the scientists at the laboratory: "You do mtDNA sequencing, and you have to go searching for the haplogroups, and it's a headache." In his view, unlike the United States, where society was more of a mosaic and people sought to acquire various additional identities, in Brazil, most Black people did not feel such an "allegiance" with Africa: "Brazilians just want to be Brazilian." Moreover, based on previous studies, Pena anticipated that the participants would not have exclusively African mtDNA and Y-DNA haplotypes—rather, they would be a "mish-mash" of Amerindian, European, and African lineages.[71]

In fact, in both *Raízes Afro-Brasileiras* and *African American Lives*, eight of the nine celebrities were found to have mtDNA haplotypes characteristic of African populations, while four of the Brazilian participants were attributed "African" Y-DNA lineages as well.[72] Whereas *African American Lives* featured scenes of geneticists and historians working together to pinpoint which of the matches were most likely to reflect the guests' ancestral origins at the time of slavery, based on historical data of shipping routes and the internal African trade, in *Raízes Afro-Brasileiras* participants were presented with names of *all* the ethnic groups and regions with which Pena had found matching haplotypes, based on his laboratory's database. Sometimes, the quantity and range of the matches seemed overwhelming. In the case of Olympic gymnast Daiane dos Santos, the list of mtDNA matches included over twenty groups, of which it was reported "the only one that Daiane recognizes are the Yoruba—a group famous in Brazil for its predominance in Bahia. The list [also] contains less well-known names like Bakaka, Fula, Futa-Fula, Mansonca, Pepel, Chuabo, Serer and Wolof, among others." In the headline to her article, Santos was reported to be "the prototypical Brazilian," based on her admixture results (39.7 percent African ancestry, 40.8 percent European, 19.6 percent Amerindian), which, among all the participants, showed the most even distribution between the three continental groups. Santos declared herself proud to "have a bit of each" and confirmed that what she knew of her own family composition reflected the makeup of the entire country: "There are cousins who are blond, *índio*, ginger, *negro*. It's all mixed. It's like Brazil, no one is purely from any one place, it's a mixture of races."[73]

The idea of genetic mixture as a legacy of slavery and colonialism was presented in *Raízes Afro-Brasileiras* in terms that echoed Freyre's classic narrative of *mestiçagem*. In one article, readers were told that a recent genetic study into the ancestry of Black Brazilians in São Paulo offered "genetic confirmation of the historical clues that in colonial times the most common sexual relationships were between European colonizers—who came in groups of many men and few women—and native (Amerindian) women or those brought as slaves from Africa." Manolo Florentino, professor of history at the Universidade Federal do Rio de Janeiro (UFRJ), who acted as a consultant for the feature, was quoted as saying that "Brazilian racial mixture is much more a case of poor Portuguese men interacting maritally and sexually with Black women than of elite men maintaining sexual relations with poor enslaved Black women. . . . It's much more a history that brings together poor lovers of different colors than it does violence and rape, as a certain camp would have us believe."[74] Florentino's statement offers an example of how "molecular portraits" of Brazil have often been treated, "more than a reconstruction of Brazil's history through genes, as a proposal of sociability mediated by genomics."[75] This tendency to regard love and family relations as the antithesis of racism has been challenged in recent years in Brazil, as well as in other Latin American societies marked by national narratives of mixture. Feminist scholars have pointed to historical and contemporary evidence that romantic love does not preclude violence and coercion, while families bound together by fraternal love can—and do— internalize racist attitudes, inflicting prejudice on their close kin.[76] More- over, the focus on "cordial" mixture as the defining pattern of Brazil's colonial sexual relations detracts from other stories—for instance, the ef- forts of enslaved communities to maintain ethnic links and seek stable family attachments among themselves; the unequal power dynamics that underpinned the relationships of concubinage between White men and mixed-race women, setting the bases for Brazil's current "pigmentocracy"; and the systemic and lethal racial violence meted out to Black populations (a legacy that continues in the present day).[77]

Not all of the participants joined Santos in expressing pride at their mixed ancestry. Singer-songwriter Seu Jorge, for instance, expressed anger at learning he had 12.9 percent European admixture and a characteristically European Y-DNA haplotype, stating that he would have applied for "indem- nification" if he was "100 percent Black." He also challenged the character- ization of this admixture given by historian Manolo Florentino, saying, "Miscegenation was barbarity. It wasn't a love story, it was barbarity. I'm glad to know that part of my people resisted and they make up 85 percent of my genes."[78] Seu Jorge's reaction reflects the concern shared broadly among Black activists—both in Brazil and in other societies marked by sim- ilar patterns of "racial" mixture—about how to shore up an *exclusive* Black identity that can form the basis for political demands of reparation for the legacies of slavery. As Stéphanie Mulot has written regarding the French An- tilles, the conundrum is as follows: "In a mixed society, where physical appearance bears witness to a nuanced mix of tangled Black and White ori- gins, how can we be recognized as descendants of the victims or the au- thors of a foundational crime? Is it possible to hide a part of one's ancestry in order to declare one's affiliation to a sole lineage, which will become the basis for implementing strategies of memorialization—and if so, how? Doesn't the process of creolization prevent, in fact, any univocality of iden- tity, of genealogy, and memory?"[79]

Nonetheless, some of the *Raízes Afro-Brasileiras* guests saw in their DNA results the legitimation of an ancestral African cultural heritage. For in- stance, musician Sandra de Sá expressed her excitement at discovering she had 96.7 percent African ancestry and that her family's mtDNA and Y-DNA haplotypes were of African origin. She described her belief that music was "rooted" in her family as a result of this African ancestry, stating, "This gives me every reason to love my family even more, to tell them this. My mother has amazing pitch, my father is a musician, my uncles and aunts are musicians. I often say I have a slave's feet, that I've even got marks from the chains. I believe that our soul has memory and that I carry a lot of Africa in me. You can't imagine how happy I am."

The remark, however, was juxtaposed with a comment by Francisco Salzano, professor of human evolution at UFRGS, who opined: "It's debatable. To this day there is no formal indication that musical preferences or styles or sporting abilities are specific to any ethnic group."[80] Salzano's comment may have been aimed at deconstructing the myth that the overrepresentation of Black individuals in areas like music and sport in Brazil is the result of innate genetic differences between racial groups. Yet it also seems to dismiss the idea that any recognizably African traditions could be passed down from generation to generation, whether in the genome, as Salzano assumes, or through alternative mechanisms of memory ("in the soul"), as Sá suggests. This stance was notably different from that of Gates in *African American Lives*, who purposefully highlighted the shared "musical genius" between composer Quincy Jones and the Tikar ethnic group, gesturing toward the possibility that cultural inheritance *can* mirror the transmission of genetic markers. The commonsense notion that we resemble the people to whom we are related (whether in a physical sense or in terms of shared interests and talents)[81] was used in that case to reinforce the idea of a long-distance ethnic affiliation, uncovered by the DNA test.

In contrast, Seu Jorge and Sandra de Sá's desire for a stronger affiliation to their African origins was criticized by readers in the BBC Brasil online forum. One commentator wrote, "It's clear there is only one race, and that's why I don't understand statements like the one made by Seu Jorge, who seemed disappointed to have European ancestry, or by his fellow artist Sandra de Sá who 'feels proud to be nearly 100% Black'; if she was 100% Black would she still feel proud? It seems like reverse racism to me. I'm mixed-race, a Brazilian of planet Earth." The statement is symptomatic of what Alexandre Emboaba da Costa has called the "affective character" of Brazilian identity discourses, which condition citizens who suffer racism to silence their feelings of pain and despair, instead reasserting their commitment to the principle of conviviality and the promise of a race-free future.[82] By the same token, any affirmation of a competing attachment to another community is regarded as a threat to national cohesion and must be discredited in the strongest terms. Hence, the guests' avowed affection for Africa was interpreted as "reverse racism," a rejection of mixed-race Brazil.

Unmasking the Politics of DNA

Among the various profiles, the results that most caught the imagination of the media and public were those of Neguinho da Beija-Flor. A samba artist regarded in Brazil as unambiguously Black based on his physical appearance and self-identification (his stage name translates as "little Black guy"), Neguinho was reported to have 67.1 percent European genomic ancestry, compared to "only" 31.5 percent from Africa.[83] The result was commented on in various other Brazilian newspapers, including an article for the conservative magazine *Veja* by an outspoken critic of the university quotas, Reinaldo Azevedo. Referring to the recent scandal surrounding the UnB's so-called "race verification" panel, Azevedo asserted that "the result of [Neguinho da Beija-Flor's] DNA test demoralizes the well-intentioned racism some are attempting to implant in Brazil at all costs, and which only serves to meet the expectations of some tricksters, professionals of the cause, in search of authority and notoriety."[84] News of Neguinho da Beija-Flor's DNA results even traveled beyond Brazil. The story was reproduced in English on the BBC News website under the title "BBC delves into Brazilians' roots"[85] and was soon picked up by the North American White supremacist web forum Stormfront. Posting the BBC article for other forum members to read, one commentator wrote, "His DNA test result must be an error. This man does not look like he's almost 3/4th European. Is this pro-multiracial propaganda? Or could he be a rare phenotype anomaly?" For many Brazilian observers, rather than being an anomaly, Neguinho da Beija-Flor's DNA profile was concrete proof of Brazil's unique genealogical disorder. Along these lines, his example was cited in a 2011 Supreme Court case that argued for the quotas policies to be declared unconstitutional, as evidence that some Black Brazilians were "more likely" to be descended from a slaveholder than an enslaved individual.[86]

The case ultimately failed, and in 2012 a decade of debate was brought to a close when a national quotas law was sanctioned by President Dilma Rousseff. However, the repeated uses of DNA ancestry as a tool to publicly discredit the quotas programs damaged the confidence of Black activists in the potential of genomics to help consolidate a collective Afro-Brazilian identity. In many cases, activists felt that the data had been used to challenge the reality of their own experiences of discrimination or to downplay the importance of the racial inequalities affecting Brazilian society, on the grounds that "we're all equal."[87] As a colleague of Frei David dos Santos—Franciscan friar, Black activist, and founder of EDUCAFRO, a network of university preparatory programs for "Blacks and people in need"[88]—explained to me in 2013 when I asked whether he would ever consider taking a DNA ancestry test: "We have to think about that information so that it is used for the good of the community. We have to think really hard about what it's going to be used for. Depending on how the information is used, yes, I might take [a genetic test], if it was used in such a way so that we could not generalize everything according to genetics. Because what discriminates, what humiliates, what hurts, what keeps our people out of spaces of circulation, what forms an opinion of you—it's phenotype, not genotype."[89]

Among the *Raízes Afro-Brasileiras* participants, Frei David was the only one to publicly question the role and motivation of scientists in interpreting the DNA ancestry data; indeed, in a later interview with the Bahian newspaper *A Tarde*, he explained that he had taken the DNA test precisely "to unmask its use."[90] At the time, the BBC Brasil journalists reported Frei David's frustration at learning that his mtDNA and Y-DNA haplotypes both matched Indigenous American populations, "given that the target of the project was to dig deeper into [my] African origin[s]." He was quoted as saying, "I don't accept that science has no technical instrument to look deeper into [our] African heritage, considering that Africa was and is the cradle of civilization. He [Sérgio Pena] simply boycotted the result on purpose."[91] Pena denied this allegation and responded that his analysis was undertaken "with the same care and high quality as the others." He also sent Frei David further details explaining the results—a gesture Frei David later rebutted while continuing to demand more information on his African origins. Asked for a second opinion by the BBC Brasil journalists, Professor Francisco Salzano asserted that although in theory it would be possible to attempt to pinpoint Frei David's African ancestry by studying his autosomal DNA, this would be "much more complex and [would] possibly involve a higher margin of error."[92]

It is interesting to compare Frei David's experience with that of Gates, who was the only guest on *African American Lives* whose mtDNA and Y-DNA results were both matched to European populations. Expressing his disappointment at this result, Gates asked Mark Shriver, professor of biological anthropology at Penn State University, to use a "revolutionary new" analysis to estimate the exact origins of the 50 percent West African ancestry revealed by his admixture test. Shriver complied, and in the final scenes of the documentary he revealed that Gates's DNA most closely resembled sequences taken from Mende individuals in Sierra Leone. The scene drew to a close with Gates confidently informing viewers that "as DNA databases grow . . . we'll be able to find with ever more accuracy the identities of our ancestors and the roots of our family trees."[93]

In their respective countries, Gates and Frei David are both light-skinned Black men. Yet, unlike Gates's father, who impressed on him the importance of knowing his Black origins, during his own childhood Frei David's family avoided mention of their African roots, and it was not until he left home that he came to recognize and embrace his Black identity.[94] Until very recently, this experience was typical in Brazil, where cultural and racial Whitening has long been a strategy of social "betterment" and inequalities are typically thought of as caused by class rather than racism.[95] In the United States, on the other hand, generations after the abolition of slavery and the achievements of the civil rights movement, African American parents continue to encourage their children to strongly identify with their Black heritage. These identity practices stem partly from a sense of pride and recognition of the collective struggles African Americans have gone through historically, but they can also serve as a protective strategy in a society where violent and institutionalized forms of anti-Black racism continue to be rife. Hence, although Pena's observation that Black Brazilians tend to be less interested in their African ancestry than in just "being Brazilian" has been confirmed by sociological surveys,[96] we should be wary of assuming that this is a "natural" consequence of contrasting demographic and biological histories (i.e., the United States as multiracial "mosaic" versus Brazil as raceless "mixture"). As I explore further in chapter 5, many Afro-Brazilian activists are intensely interested in the possibility of recovering their African ancestries and Black family histories, although some have sought alternatives to genetics and genealogical methods for doing so. Similarly, while the UnB twins scandal and other similar cases were used throughout the quotas debates to reinforce the idea that Brazil's history of mixture has made it "naturally" impossible to draw a clear line between "Black" and "White," critics have pointed out that such racial distinctions are made on a daily basis by the country's law enforcement, to lethal effect. In the words of anthropologist Jaime Alves, "The Brazilian ambivalence to identify one's race is called into question in the *favelas* by the police's ability to not only locate racial difference, but also to reaffirm that difference through and in death"—an observation that is routinely evoked by Black activists in the saying, "If you want to know who is Black and who is not in Brazil, just ask the police."[97]

The story is similar in the United States; indeed, in 2009, after returning home from a filming stint abroad for one of his genealogy series, Gates himself was racially profiled by police and arrested in his own house in a wealthy suburb of Cambridge, Massachusetts.[98] As a conciliatory gesture, he later invited Sergeant James Crowley, the White police officer who confronted and arrested him, to take a DNA test. Gates revealed on *The Oprah Winfrey Show* that the two men shared the same Y-DNA lineage, believed by scientists to have originated in Ireland some 1500 years ago, making them, in his words, "distant cousins."[99] Gates's genial approach to deconstructing the United States's racial myths through genetics and family history have won him admirers from a cross-section of U.S. society. During our interview in 2014, he mentioned that he could no longer walk through an airport without people (including "older, White conservatives") constantly thanking him for his work on the series, something he identified as one of the most gratifying parts of his career. The future that Gates envisions for the United States is not one in which ethnic and racial identities are meaningless and irrelevant; rather, he imagines a multiracial and multicultural society in which everyone is able to recognize and celebrate all aspects of their ancestral mixture without fear of prejudice.[100] DNA ancestry testing, he seems to suggest, can help with this vision by revealing beyond doubt how interconnected U.S. society really is, beyond the fiction of the color line.

Yet we must question the effectiveness of genetic data, like those offered by Gates to Crowley, for tackling the various forms of systemic and structural racism seen today in the United States and Brazil. Studies like Alves's into the racial dimension of police brutality in Brazil, for example, highlight the deficiency of conceptualizing racism as a mere misunderstanding of the facts of biology or as an issue that can be resolved by members of society becoming more racially tolerant and "open-minded." Alves reports, for instance, how spending on police forces and prison systems increased massively under the "progressive," neoliberal governments of Cardoso and his successor, Luiz Inácio Lula da Silva—as did the scale of killings by undercover death squads and on-duty police officers in places like São Paulo.[101] Similarly, the scale of racially motivated police brutality and incarceration of young Black men in the United States has been brought to the fore numerous times in the past decade, most recently (at the time of writing) with the Black Lives Matter protests in the summer of 2020, sparked by the killings of George Floyd and Breonna Taylor, among others.[102] Most forms of present-day racism cannot merely be "unthought," for they are perpetuated by material inequalities with complex structural and institutional roots.[103] Moreover, the ideologies that underpin behaviors such as racial profiling do not require individuals to believe in race as *biologically* encoded difference. Forms of cultural and environmental determinism (the idea that a person's character and behavior is ineluctably molded by the conditions in which they grew up) can offer effective conditions for prejudice and discrimination to thrive, with the same fatal consequences. Indeed, in Brazil it is universally accepted that everyone is mixed, but this does not prevent citizens' chances of social mobility being strongly influenced by how they appear racially to others.[104]

Between the U.S. and Brazilian cases, we can see the dangers inherent in assuming scientific certainty about race. DNA ancestry should be viewed not as presenting universal truths about race and identity, but as *situated* information that gains different meanings through the lens of various myths of identity, and in the light of local power struggles that revolve around genealogies of violence and inequality. In the cases described above, the reputed objectivity of DNA was used by actors as a discursive resource to alternately reinforce and call into question particular identity projects. In Brazil, genetic evidence of the country's historical "racial" mixture was used by some to argue against the imposition of race-based redistributive policies, while reinforcing a traditional narrative of a nation whose collective identity is, "by nature," hybrid and raceless. The interpretation in the United States went in a different direction, presenting DNA markers as a tool for African Americans to reclaim an "authentic" ancestral origin preserved in the genome, therefore (re)converting a racial identity into an ethnic one. Both sets of actors demonstrated a kind of strategic essentialism,[105] treating their readings of DNA not just as indicative of their ancestors' historic identities but also of what their own identities *should be*. The populations with whom we share DNA, it was suggested, demand love and allegiance— even if, in practice, certain connections were brought to the fore while others were muted.

The culturally ingrained myths of the past provided by Haley's *Roots*, on the one hand, and Freyre's *Casa-grande*, on the other, also opened up different visions of what identities the genome can yield. In *African American Lives*, the desire to reconnect with a lost African identity led Gates to lobby his geneticist colleagues to push the boundaries of ancestry analysis, an impulse that has since been taken up by numerous DNA ancestry-testing companies. Pena and Salzano, meanwhile, rejected this option as technically unviable and privately questioned the social value of going to such lengths to pinpoint individuals' African origins. DNA ancestry tests, nonetheless, are an evolving technology with multiple uses, and the directions in which they are developed are mediated by various economic, epistemic, and ethical considerations. As we shall see in chapter 2, the extent to which

DNA ancestry technologies should cater to the identity projects of the public, or aim to disseminate a more scientifically "pure" vision of human origins, remains an object of intense debate among geneticists. As international companies increasingly position themselves as the primary mediators and curators of genetic knowledge, who has the final word on what DNA can—or should—say about human identities?

. . . .

On a cold and blustery day in February 2013, I stepped out of Hammersmith Tube station and joined a throng of people heading purposefully for the London Olympia arena. Our destination was Who Do You Think You Are? Live, at the time the largest annual genealogy convention in the United Kingdom. All around me, excited Brits—for the most part, retirees—were striking up conversations and swapping notes about their train journeys down to London. Some were just here for the day; others had decided to "make a weekend of it," buying a three-day ticket that would give them access to technical seminars as well as guest talks by renowned genealogy experts from the United Kingdom and abroad. Walking five abreast through the arena's double doors, we were greeted by an immense hall, filled wall-to-wall with a maze of stands, poster displays, and cordoned seating areas. Officially appointed volunteers (many of them also retirees) welcomed us in with cheery greetings, flyers, and free candy.

The first row of stands was dedicated to some of the most established names in the global genealogy industry: Ancestry.com, offering computer and internet points for visitors to test out the company's extensive online archive database; FindMyPast, set up as a mock courtroom and advertising its stock of criminal records; and FamilySearch, providing free consultations with genealogy experts from the Church of Jesus Christ of Latter-day Saints. The surrounding labyrinth of stands and poster displays was principally occupied by small companies, charities, and regional genealogy groups. The booths of these regular attendees appeared modest next to the flashy global giants. Interspersed among them, I found what I had come looking for: pioneers of the rising trade in personal DNA ancestry tests, here in London hoping to gain a foothold in the thriving family history market. At pride of place in the center of the convention hall, a group of young, smiling blonde assistants stood handing out information leaflets for BritainsDNA, a company promising to "trace your early ancestry over many thousands of years, revealing stories only DNA can tell"—and, for a limited time only, offering free tests to inform customers if they were carriers for "the red hair gene." In the opposite corner was another large stand hired by FamilyTreeDNA, whose information board offered tips to prospective test-takers about conducting family history research into particular ethnic roots. A few aisles down, a lone representative of the company DNAme was attempting to garner interest in his firm's unique selling point: a DNA vending machine ostentatiously named "the ultimate Time Machine," which dispensed genetic ancestry-testing kits to the public at "only" £50 apiece.

This was my first foray into the world of direct-to-consumer (DTC) genetic ancestry testing. As the director of one U.S. company told me, over the previous decade ancestry testing had evolved from a "cottage industry" that shifted a few hundred kits a year to a booming market attracting thousands of test-takers per month. With their promises to sell customers access to their own "ancient" and "ethnic origins," the firms at Who Do You Think You Are? Live seemed to exemplify what John and Jean Comaroff have labeled "the identity economy[, where] the corporeal meets the corporate, where essence becomes enterprise."[1] Yet, despite their plush display boards and professional appearance, these companies were far from secure in their status as purveyors of genetic science. On the third day of the convention, a confrontation broke out between Alistair Moffat, CEO of BritainsDNA, and two geneticists from University College London (UCL), Mark Thomas and David Balding. The three men had already been embroiled in a private dispute since the previous year, when Thomas and Balding issued email complaints about Moffat (a journalist by training) for disseminating "outrageous" scientific claims and "misleading" comments about his company's genetic products and funding during BBC radio interviews and television programs. Moffat, in turn, raised the stakes by threatening the scientists with libel action if they persisted in portraying the company as "fraudulent" or its science as "'wrong' or untrue."[2]

The following day, Thomas published an article in the *Guardian* newspaper warning members of the public against companies like BritainsDNA, whose services he likened to "genetic astrology." In it, he reminded readers that "nobody is pure this, or pure that, and a substantial proportion of human ancestry is common to all of us. Ancestry is complicated and very messy." While Thomas affirmed that geneticists could compare the Y-DNA or mtDNA of two individuals and make reasonable, albeit potentially imprecise, estimates about how long ago they shared a common ancestor, he stated that "saying where, and in what ethnic group, that common ancestor lived is considerably more speculative. In the hands of 'genetic ancestry testing' companies this speculation almost invariably comes from the murky world of interpretative phylogeography—an approach to 'reading' our genetic history that is easily steered by subjective biases, has never been scientifically shown to work and, in some forms, has been explicitly shown not to work."[3]

Throughout my fieldwork stints in 2013 and 2014, I heard similar complaints from the Brazilian and U.S. research scientists I interviewed—namely, that DNA ancestry-testing businesses were peddling "junk science" and delivering results that went "beyond what the science can tell us" about personal origins. At first glance, these objections seem like a straightforward example of what Thomas Gieryn has called "boundary work," the "ideological efforts by scientists to distinguish their work and its products from nonscientific intellectual activities."[4] Thomas and Balding, for instance, were concerned that prominent public figures like Moffat (who has no formal genetic training) were misrepresenting scientific findings and giving a false idea of the technical and epistemic scope of genetics to produce knowledge about human identities. Hence, allowing such companies to dominate headlines and public debate on genetics could ultimately be damaging to the public's trust in the field. Others objected to the idea of customers being swindled out of their money for a product that was not as scientifically robust as they assumed. Digging a little further, however, I found that underlying many of these complaints were deep concerns about how genetic ancestry data may be used to fuel ethnic prejudices and racist political agendas—issues that clearly connect to the still recent history of atrocities committed in the name of "race science."

As I conducted my fieldwork, I was therefore surprised to find that some geneticists who were openly critical of commercial DNA ancestry-testing companies were producing what seemed to be rather similar personalized ancestry reports through their own work, as recompense for participants in research projects or as part of nonprofit ancestry-testing initiatives, envisioned as alternatives to DTC companies. What was it, then, that made commercial DNA ancestry vendors scientifically suspect, and how did research scientists demarcate their own practices as more objective, ethical, and robust?

In the pages that follow, I look to debates among U.S. scientists about using DNA to estimate the ethnic origins of the descendants of enslaved Africans, alongside the work of Brazilian scientists who produced personalized DNA ancestry tests as part of a nationwide project into the genetic dynamics of *mestiçagem*. What emerges are the choices made by research scientists about how best to present ancestry data to particular user groups, and their efforts to position themselves and their science in relation to particular societal discourses regarding race, ethnicity, and mixture. How do geneticists negotiate their responsibilities as providers of scientific knowledge vis-à-vis their agency in broader struggles against racism and for social justice?

Controversies around African Ancestry

Established in 2003 in Washington, D.C., African Ancestry was among the first DTC genetic ancestry-testing companies to emerge worldwide, and the only commercial entity to focus specifically on recovering customers' African genetic roots. Similar to Thomas and Balding's reactions to Britains-DNA, among geneticists who work on the population histories of the African diaspora, African Ancestry's approaches have inspired passionate critiques and in some cases outright opprobrium. The virulence of these criticisms, in turn, are matched by the enthusiasm the company's products have inspired among its clients, including numerous prominent African American celebrities who have given glowing endorsements of the company's services after receiving their personal DNA ancestry results in one of African Ancestry's unique "roots reveal" ceremonies.

The business's MatriClan and PatriClan tests are based on mtDNA and Y-DNA analyses. As Alondra Nelson has described in *The Social Life of DNA*, these tests were developed by the company's scientific director, Rick Kittles, during his time spent working on the New York African Burial Ground Project (NYABGP) in the 1990s.[5] Although they represent only a small proportion of an individual's overall genomic heritage (each equivalent to a single lineage in a family tree), these analyses are understood by scientists to be particularly useful for inferring "biogeographical" ancestry because of the structured way haplotypes are distributed among modern populations throughout different geographic regions.[6] Finding that a person's mtDNA haplotype matched those of individuals currently living in West Africa, for instance, could allow scientists to say with a good degree of certainty that one of their distant maternal ancestors originated in the region. Given the lack of comprehensive population reference databases in the early 2000s, however, many scientists were reserving judgment on just how precisely or robustly these markers could trace an individual's ancestry to a specific geographic area or ethnic group.

As Nelson notes, some of the most strident critics of Kittles's project were his former colleagues from the NYABGP. While these scientists (most of whom are African American) uniformly acknowledged the existence of a strong public interest in searching for one's ancestral origins in Africa, and the desirability of helping communities gain insights into this aspect of their family histories, they nonetheless signaled what they saw as potential scientific and ethical issues with the process. First, they pointed to caveats in the uniparental testing method—which they believed might not offer users the level of accuracy they assumed or hoped for—and the impossibility of verifying the company's results independently since it kept the contents of its reference database private. Second, they drew attention to the means by which the company transmitted its results to the public, pointing out the importance of conveying the limitations of these procedures to test-takers. While some suggested these weaknesses could be mitigated—for instance, through the development of more comprehensive reference databases—overall the scientists remained divided in their opinions about whether these shortcomings were justified by the potential benefits the tests could offer to users.[7]

This ethical dilemma was summed up neatly in a section from a 2003 BBC documentary called *Motherland: A Genetic Journey*, which followed three British Afro-Caribbean roots-seekers as they traced their African origins using uniparental tests. The documentary included interviews with Kittles—who used his private reference database to search for the participants' genetic matches in Africa—and with Fatimah Jackson, a biological anthropologist and ex-colleague of Kittles from the NYABGP. In one sequence, Jackson and Kittles responded separately to a question about the reliability of the ancestry inferences. First, viewers heard Jackson give the following reply: "It just happens that the mitochondrial DNA and the Y-chromosome are good markers into the past. But they're just markers. They're like an arrow pointing to the past. But they're not the past! They're not the entirety of the past. They're stepping stones, they're flashing lights, but they're not all of who we are." Immediately, the film cut to Kittles, who remarked: "Well, that's better than nothing, that's what I say! It's sort of like walking in a very dark room and looking around for the light switch. And in this situation, maybe you find a flashlight, and that flashlight is enough light for you to maneuver in the room. And it's . . . I feel it's a tremendous feeling when you do connect and find a potential ancestor."[8]

When I was conducting my fieldwork in Washington, D.C. in 2014, Jackson had recently been appointed professor of biology at Howard University, and we met several times during my stay to discuss my research. As one of only a handful of Black women professors of physical anthropology in the United States until very recently, Jackson's academic career has been oriented by her attempts to confront and challenge the Eurocentrism and, more broadly, the racism and sexism of her discipline. In the 1990s, Jackson spoke out against the Human Genome Project's overwhelming focus on Euro-descendant populations, and she argued for the inclusion of African Americans in the Human Genome Diversity Project, despite prevailing attitudes that they were not "a real population" given their relatively recent history and origins.[9] A specialist in African population genetics, Jackson has conducted research in Tanzania, Liberia, Nigeria, Uganda, Rwanda, and Burundi, and she was a professor at the University of Khartoum in Sudan. In addition to her academic interest in genetics, heredity, and the relationships between people, Jackson has delved into her own family roots, first through the oral histories passed down by her grandmother and later through documentary research. Growing up, she told me, "it was just taken for granted in my family that not everyone was African—that some of the people were Native American and some were European American . . . it wasn't seen as odd or unusual." Having her own mtDNA tested as part of a research collaboration with geneticist Deborah Bolnick only confirmed this impression, as Jackson was matched to "two hunter-gatherer tribes in Siberia." These experiences had also influenced Jackson's outlook on the possible social and humanitarian applications of genetic knowledge. During one of our conversations, Jackson told me that she was in favor of DNA ancestry testing, stating: "I think it should become one's patriotic duty to be genetically tested, and to find the links, and then to go find . . . all your people, and connect with them." In her opinion, one of the important lessons that genetics can teach us is to reassess the ways we categorize people, disassociating "language, ethnicity, culture" and encouraging us to create "more meaningful categories" that allow people to connect in different ways.[10]

This broad, humanist outlook also shaped Jackson's attitudes toward African Ancestry, of whose products she remained critical. One of the things she was critical of was the company's decision to present its results in the form of a Certificate of Ancestry (figure 2.1), which is mailed to customers as physical proof of their DNA test results. The certificates bear the DNA test-taker's personal name and usually the names of one or two ethnic groups located in a particular geographic region, with which they "share maternal/paternal ancestry." Alondra Nelson has observed that some African Ancestry customers refer to their Certificates of Ancestry as a "birth certificate," signaling their symbolic recuperation of a "preslavery" identity.[11] On the African Ancestry website, one customer writes: "In 2006, I made my first trip to the Motherland. When I returned to America, I decided that I needed to know where I came from. This was truly one of the greatest

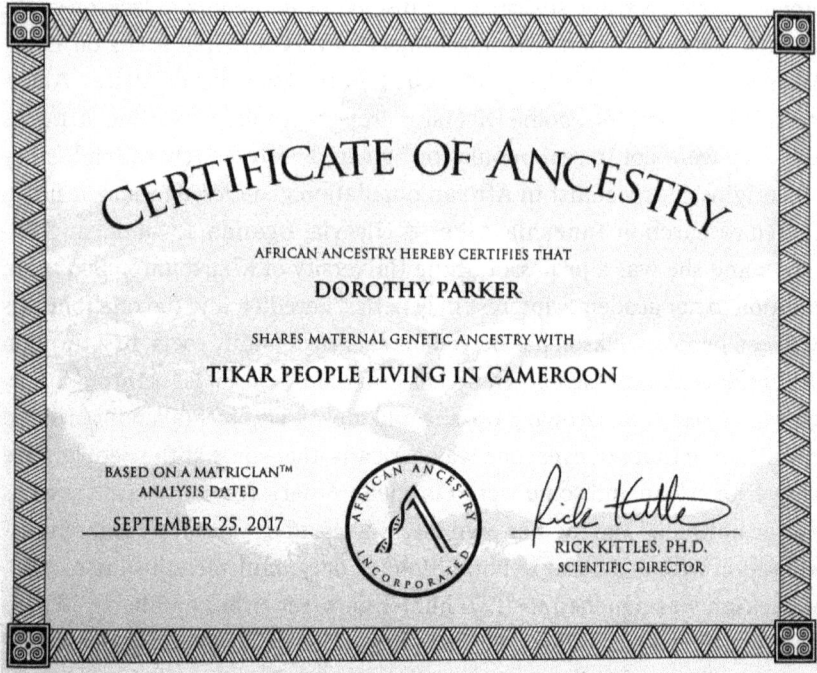

FIGURE 2.1 Example of personalized mtDNA ancestry results by African Ancestry.

and proudest moments of my life. I made copies of the certificates and laminated them to show my family and friends—I walk with my copies every day. Thank you for affording myself and others the opportunity to get to know our '*Roots*.'" Displaying the results in this way makes them seem definite, permanent, giving clients a sense of certainty that they have recovered their ancestors' "true" origins. However, as Jackson pointed out, very often these ethnic results are picked out from a whole list of DNA matches that might represent a much wider geographic spread—including matches found outside Africa. The rather broad geographic dispersal of many uniparental haplotypes among modern populations, as shown in figure 2.2, is a vestige of the way that humans have migrated and intermixed over the course of our species' history. To single out one or two haplotype matches found in particular ethnic groups or countries is therefore to constrict the range of interpretations that test-takers may draw from these data. This, for Jackson, does customers a disservice since it veils the broader message she believes genetics can offer to users: namely, that "all of humanity is connected. We're just too dumb to see it."[12] This view was shared by Henry Louis Gates Jr., who, despite being thrilled in 2003 when African Ancestry

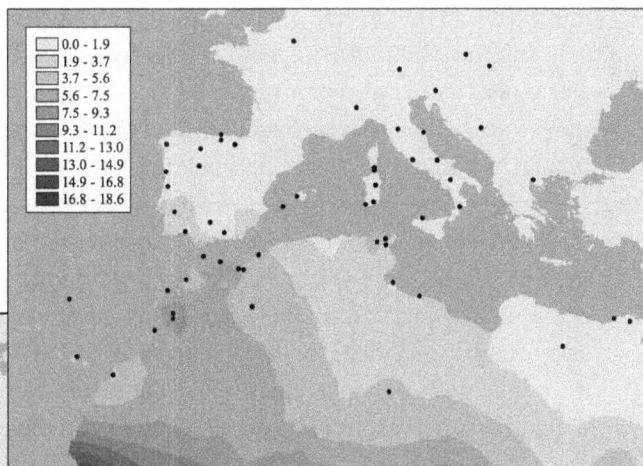

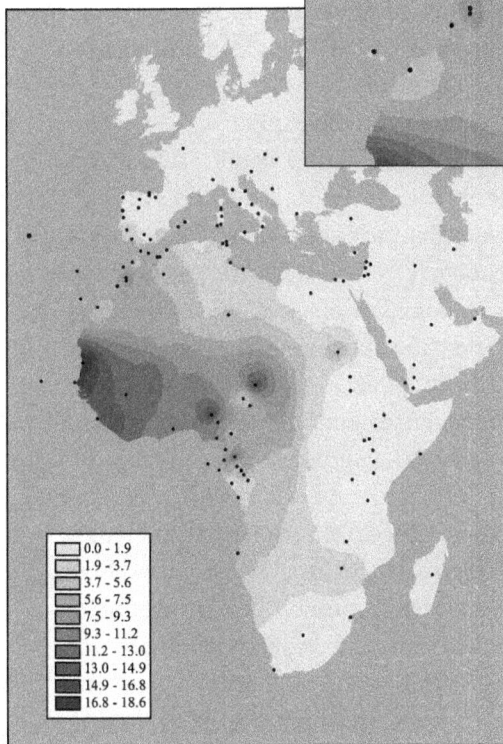

FIGURE 2.2 Contour maps of mtDNA L1b sub-haplogroup, showing differing frequency distributions throughout populations in continental Africa and the Mediterranean Basin. Hernández et al. "Early Holocenic and Historic mtDNA African Signatures in the Iberian Peninsula." Distributed under a CC-BY-2.5 license.

informed him that he had a "Nubian" mtDNA haplotype, was later shocked to be informed by another genetic testing laboratory in 2007 that his mtDNA was more likely European rather than "Nubian."[13] While Kittles denied Gates's accusation that the company had simply given him the result "they thought I wanted to hear," the geneticist stated that the case had been "a learning experience for me . . . I had a very poor European database."[14] While the company claims to have since improved its reference databases, some of the research scientists I interviewed seemed convinced that African Ancestry was still unduly prioritizing customer satisfaction and business profits over a more "objective" approach, which should aim to educate the public and challenge ideas about the extent to which genetic kinship structures align with racial and ethnic group membership.[15]

As an alternative to African Ancestry's DNA-testing model, Jackson recommended I find out more about the African American DNA Roots Project, a nonprofit venture and independent scientific program founded in 2000 by Bruce Jackson, director of biotechnology at Massachusetts Bay Community College, and Bert Ely, professor of biological sciences at the University of South Carolina.[16] The project's scientific aims were to collect genetic samples from North American, Caribbean, and African populations and to conduct analyses of the mitochondrial genome, Y-chromosome and X-chromosome, to understand how specific haplotypes had evolved in different populations since the transatlantic trade in enslaved Africans. The public dimension of the Roots Project was developed in parallel and aimed to deliver personalized ancestry results to participants. As Jackson and Ely's database grew, they hoped to gain a better picture of the distribution of mtDNA and Y-DNA variation among African regions and populations and assess the precision with which these haplotypes could produce regional and population-specific genetic matches within Africa. As Ely explained, this approach was congruent with their own principles of how science should be done, namely, "You go in with an open mind, and let the data lead you."[17] While they hoped to help members of the public pursue their genealogical research, the group did not set out a fixed rubric for what results they aimed to deliver to participants.

Initially, Jackson and Ely opted only to provide volunteers with the broadest and most confident inferences—for instance, whether their genetic haplotype was of African or European origin, a distinction they believed could be confidently made based on published datasets of world haplogroup phylogenies.[18] At the same time, they began to search for patterns in the distribution of specific haplotype sequences among different ethnic groups, to ascertain whether these markers could indeed be used to infer a more specific origin. In particular, Jackson and Ely were searching for evidence of whether the distribution of certain haplotypes mirrored the boundaries of ethnic groups in Africa. The results, however, were disappointing. When comparing 171 African American mtDNA haplotypes to a database of 3,725 African mtDNA sequences, about half of all the African American sequences yielded multiple matches, with only around 5 percent being matched to a single ethnic group and the remaining 40 percent finding no match at all. Furthermore, the haplotypes performed poorly when used to estimate the identity of people who knew their African origins. Out of ten mtDNA sequences donated to the project by individuals from Senegal, Nigeria, Cameroon, Ghana, and Sierra Leone, five were identical to at least two other countries as well as the donor's country of origin, sometimes with matches as far-flung as Mozambique, Kenya, or Ethiopia. Three samples found no matches in the database, and the other two found identical matches in countries that were not the donor's country of origin, yielding "false positive" results.[19]

By the time Ely and Jackson had the results of these studies, the Roots Project had stopped accepting new participants because of funding limitations and already had a long waiting list. The group posted a message on their website recommending that anybody still interested in having their DNA tested should send their sample to the Genographic Project (a nonprofit run by National Geographic), which was offering mtDNA and Y-DNA tests for around $100 at the time. The Genographic Project provided customers with the name of their haplogroup (expressed as a combination of numbers and letters, such as "E3b" or "L2a1," designating their place on a phylogeny of world "lineages") along with a map showing its geographic distribution among contemporary populations. For Ely, this was preferable to the ethnic affiliation approach used by African Ancestry since, rather than arbitrarily narrowing the range of results to one or two population matches, it widened the scope of genetic affiliation to a large geographic area comprising diverse national and ethnic groups.

Bruce Jackson, meanwhile, maintained the Roots Project until 2014. He opted to carry on conducting uniparental analyses but provided participants only with the information he saw as scientifically robust. A significant proportion of his clients, he informed me, were African Ancestry customers who were unsure of their results' accuracy and wanted a second opinion. Jackson's response was invariably to reject the validity of the ethnic labels provided by the company: "You're not Mandinka . . . we don't know what you are!" Instead, he provided users with their haplogroup, details of the regions in which it was predominantly found, and notified them of *all* genetic matches in the project database, providing updates as the reference data grew. Jackson explained to me that although it may not be as satisfying for test-takers to learn they had not been matched to a specific ethnic group, this in itself constituted an important lesson: namely, that genetics "can't tell us everything about a person's identity."[20]

Toward More Complex Genetic Histories

The African American scientists I interviewed were concerned with the idea that the DNA ancestry-testing model used by African Ancestry could perpetuate notions of "purity" among users. It was not the idea of *racial* purity they worried about; indeed, many felt that most African Americans were aware enough of examples of "mixture" in their own family trees to be wary of such discourses. Rather, it was a concern with ethnocentrism: the idea that test-takers might believe the ethnic group written on their Certificate of Ancestry accounted for *all* their African ancestry—a fact that, as Fatimah Jackson pointed out, did not fit the demographic history of slavery in the Americas, which was shaped by mixture with European and Native American groups, but also *between* African groups of diverse cultural and genetic backgrounds. Whereas African Ancestry actively espouses an Afrocentric philosophy, encouraging clients to identify strongly with the African group(s) named in their test results, Jackson voiced concerns that this could serve to fragment the collective Black cultural identity and the sense of political solidarity among African Americans that has been so hard-won in the United States.

Some of the researchers I interviewed also raised questions about the ability of the tests to accurately estimate a person's ancestry dating to the period of slavery, based only on contemporary reference populations. As Shomarka Keita—a physical anthropologist associated with the National Human Genome Center (NHGC) at Howard University, who also worked on the NYABGP—explained to me, such inferences rely on the premise that ethnic groups have remained stable for the past three centuries or more, and that the African individuals sampled for these databases likewise have ethnically "pure" ancestry. The reality is likely much more messy. Ethnic groups and their borders in Africa have both been shaped by and changed over time because of colonialism and the slave trades.[21] Moreover, ethnic affiliations do not necessarily reflect genetic relatedness. To illustrate this point, Keita told me an anecdote about a Senegalese man he met in Washington, D.C. The man declared himself Wolof (the largest ethnic group in Senegal), but said he was on his way to pray for Ramadan, since his grandfather had been a Qur'anic scholar of the Fulani people. His mother, on the other hand, came from Lake Chad—some 2,000 miles east from Senegal. The label Wolof, Keita explained to me, described the man's language but not his religious affiliation, nor his immediate ancestry. As this example suggests, identities as a rule do not tend to be "pure" and rigid; rather, they are multifaceted and changeable—qualities that can sometimes be masked by ethnic designations.

For some academics, the technical and epistemic difficulties in locating an "authentic" historical identity should not be a barrier to customers treating their results as personally significant. Thus, Africanist historians Linda Heywood and John Thornton of Boston University, who both consulted for the show *African American Lives*, have argued the following:

> For people seeking their roots, it is probably not as important to link
> to a long-lost political group or try to locate the 18th-century name
> of genetic ancestors. The real contribution of the results provided by
> DNA is that they connect an African American living in, say, Boston or
> New Orleans with an African who identifies himself by a name—say,
> Asante or Wolof—and who lives in Ghana or Senegal. The African
> American who shares genetic sequences with that person can link
> himself to that modern ethnic group. By matching genetic anomalies
> in an African American and an African, one can establish that these
> two individuals had common ancestors two centuries ago.[22]

Heywood and Thornton suggest that many members of the public may not demand such a high standard of historical accuracy as scientists, since their motive for taking a test is fundamentally different: it is about finding a *contemporary* connection, rather than pinpointing a given ancestor's *historical* origin. In their reading, a positive genetic match speaks for itself, automatically according an authentic and socially significant relationship between two individuals. The question of how test-takers evaluate the "authenticity" of DNA matches is explored in depth in chapter 5. For the moment, it should be noted that the claim that these links "speak for themselves" is problematic. For instance, it is rare that mtDNA and Y-DNA matches can confidently be attributed to an ancestor who lived just two centuries ago; more often, the shared "anomaly" arose hundreds or even thousands of years earlier. In the latter case, an individual is likely to have many contemporary genetic matches owing to the antiquity of the lineage: Will each be granted the same significance? When I spoke to Thornton in 2014 he recognized this shortcoming and advocated for using historical data to corroborate genetic matches wherever possible. At the time, Heywood and Thornton were listed as consultants on the website of AfricanDNA, a DNA ancestry-testing service set up by Gates in 2007 as an alternative to African Ancestry.[23] The historians' contribution had been to produce a set of stock narratives that could provide historical context for specific uniparental matches, based on their knowledge of the shipping patterns and routes of the transatlantic trade, while broadly ruling out DNA matches pertaining to groups or regions that were unlikely to have been directly implicated in the trade. Thornton acknowledged that the methodology did not yield truly personalized results, which would involve the labor-intensive work of tracing each customer's individual family history and assessing the DNA matches accordingly. Despite these limitations, he was glad that genetics was finally allowing African Americans to think about their ancestry in more than a vague way. In his words, "DNA gives people that extra sense of fact because, supposedly, it's not just statistics; it's *personal*."[24]

What Makes a Genetic Marker?

In the United States, the vehemence of the debates surrounding African Ancestry seemed proportionate to the scientists' sense that genetics had an important role to play in helping redress the legacies of racism and the erasure of family history knowledge caused by the transatlantic trade in enslaved Africans. Many were critical of the idea that DNA tests could offer simple and definitive answers to the identity quests of African Americans, but none doubted the social importance of these genealogical endeavors. In contrast, Brazilian scientists' commentaries on African Ancestry highlighted different concerns. In 2006, a paper in the journal of the Universidade de São Paulo, written by social scientists Ricardo Ventura Santos and Marcos Chor Maio and geneticist Maria Cátira Bortolini, remarked on the new "fever" for DNA testing in the United States. They cited a piece in *The New York Times* that described the varying reactions of African Americans who had taken a DNA test and unexpectedly been matched to European lineages. As one of the leading DNA ancestry-testing companies at the time, the authors argued, African Ancestry may be misleading test-takers into thinking that the DNA analysis would confirm the "purity" of their African lineage—an impression given by an illustration of a four-generation family tree on the company's website, in which each ancestor was represented by brown-colored faces, "as if the expectation was that all [the person's] ancestors were phenotypically Black/African." Although they believed genetic ancestry results were liable to become culturally resignified to support essentialist conceptions of race, the authors claimed that genetics itself remained on the front line in questioning the acceptance of biological conceptions of race. With the new trend in commercial DNA testing, Santos and colleagues signaled that "genetics, race and identities, with their diverse intersections, are walking along a knife edge."[25]

In chapter 1, we saw how, during the first decade of the 2000s, public debate in Brazil about issues of race and national identity was dominated by the introduction of racially targeted university quotas, a move that some people saw as heralding a shift from the old narrative of *mestiçagem* toward a new "biracial" project, modeled on the United States. It is hardly surprising, then, that when interpreting this DNA-testing trend for a Brazilian audience, the authors foregrounded concerns about the technologies' potential to emphasize narratives of racial purity or mixture.

I met one of the paper's authors, Maria Cátira Bortolini, in 2013, when she welcomed me to the Universidade Federal do Rio Grande do Sul (UFRGS) in Porto Alegre, southern Brazil, to conduct interviews with the scientists and volunteers of an international genetic study of which she was one of the principal investigators. The Consortium for the Analysis of Diversity and Evolution in Latin America (CANDELA), was launched in 2011 and received funding from the Leverhulme Trust in the United Kingdom, as well as from scientific councils in various Latin American countries.[26] Led by the Colombian geneticist Andrés Ruiz Linares, then based at UCL, the project was carried out simultaneously in five countries (Brazil, Chile, Colombia, Mexico, and Peru) and proposed to shed light on the consequences of the historical admixture between the region's three main ancestral populations: Europeans, Indigenous Americans, and Africans. The first large-scale study of its kind in Latin America, the CANDELA project aimed to gather extensive genetic, morphological, and sociological data on admixed individuals from each of its participating countries, to understand how this mixture manifested through genotype, phenotype, and social perceptions of ancestry.

The Brazilian branch of the project, entitled "Phenotype, Genotype, Dynamics of *Mestiçagem* in Brazil," was led by Bortolini, along with a team of geneticists and physical anthropologists at the UFRGS, with support from Brazilian research promotion agencies: the Conselho Nacional de Desenvolvimento Científico e Tecnológico (CNPq), Coordenação de Aperfeiçoamento de Pessoal de Nível Superior (CAPES), and Fundação de Amparo à Pesquisa do Estado do Rio Grande do Sul (FAPERGS). Over the course of 2011 and 2012, a total of nearly 1,600 Brazilian participants were recruited from universities and hospitals based in three different geographic areas: Rio Grande do Sul, in the south; Rondônia in the northwest; and Bahia in the northeast. These three regions were selected pragmatically, primarily on the basis of particular researchers' links to the locales and access to laboratories where sampling could take place. Although the sample was not meant to be representative of Brazil's overall genetic makeup, due to their differing demographic histories these regions were also seen as offering potential insights into the varying dynamics of migration and admixture among the country's "founding" populations.[27] Participants were asked to donate a blood sample for DNA extraction, as well as a range of anthropometric data, including weight and height; hip, waist, and head circumference; a skin spectrometry reading (a means of quantifying skin color, based on levels of melanin pigmentation); eye color; and hair color and texture. Each participant also filled in a sociological questionnaire that gathered quantitative and qualitative data about their known ancestry, self-attributed racial or ethnic identity, as well as other socioeconomic indicators.

I became interested in CANDELA after learning that the project had conducted personalized DNA ancestry tests for its participants. These were intended as a means of attracting volunteers to the project and thanking them for donating their genetic sample and other data to the study. In contrast to the projects described in the previous sections, CANDELA chose to offer admixture tests, rather than uniparental analyses, to its participants. Posters were put up, principally around university campuses and university hospitals, offering volunteers the chance to learn their "percentage of European, African, and Indigenous genetic ancestry" (figure 2.3). Initially, the personal reports were to be generated using the same technology chosen for the scientists' genomewide association study. This meant conducting an admixture analysis, whose results would be produced using a microarray chip designed to assay some 50,000 single nucleotide polymorphisms (SNPs, pronounced "snips"), which are positions found across the genome at which the DNA sequence varies among humans.[28] A subsequent genotyping of the samples involved more than 700,000 SNPs.

As the project got underway, however, the organizers realized it would take well over a year to deliver the results to participants using this approach, by which time many might have become frustrated or forgotten about their involvement in the project. Instead, they allocated a portion of their budget to a separate analysis, this time using a much smaller set of thirty "ancestry informative markers" (AIMs), which would allow for a rapid turnaround in the results. The SNPs used in the analysis were selected from

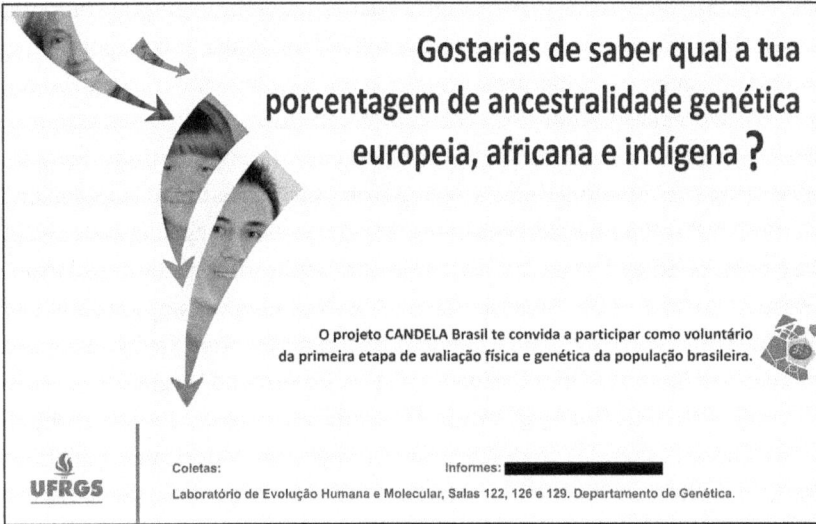

FIGURE 2.3 "Would you like to know your percentage of European, African, and Indigenous genetic ancestry?" CANDELA Brasil volunteer recruitment poster, 2011. Used here by permission.

a published list of DNA markers, known for being highly informative at distinguishing between Indigenous American, European, and African continental ancestry. The AIMs were chosen on the basis of two main optimization criteria. The first was high differentiation in allele frequency between continents—for instance, a SNP variant intended for inferring African ancestry should be found consistently among contemporary African populations but not (or at least rarely) among Europeans or Indigenous Americans. The second was low differentiation in allele frequency among reference populations *within* continents—which is to say, for example, that the same "African" marker would ideally appear with the same degree of consistency among populations living today in Senegal and South Africa. After producing a shortlist of markers that fit these criteria to the greatest possible extent, the scientists tested their accuracy in correlation with the original larger panel of 50,000 AIMs. In order to remain within the project budget, their objective was to determine the smallest number of markers that would still give reliable estimates for the three continental ancestries. They eventually settled on a set of thirty markers, whose ancestry estimates coincided around 70 percent of the time with the larger panel.[29]

The CANDELA volunteers' individual ancestry estimates were created using a program called ADMIXTURE, which apportioned test-takers' DNA, based on the thirty AIMs surveyed, to a maximum of three putative parental populations (African, European, and Amerindian). Since it is impossible to access the genomes of the historical ancestors of Latin Americans, the scientists used contemporary reference populations as a proxy—a standard procedure in "admixture mapping." In this case, the populations were defined using DNA reference data selected from the International HapMap and HDGP-CEPH cell panels and published Indigenous American datasets,[30] and they comprised 169 samples from five sub-Saharan African populations (mostly "Yoruba" from Nigeria, as well as "Mandenka" populations and "Bantu" from South Africa and Kenya); 299 samples from seven European populations (mainly "Utah Residents with Northern and Western European Ancestry," "Tuscan Italians," "French," "Sardinian," and "Basque" populations); and 408 samples from forty-eight Indigenous American populations (mostly from Mexican, Central American, and Andean groups). Like the AIMs, these references were chosen to reflect a broad cross-section of populations from each continental group. As is often the case with such studies, however, the comparison was limited by the contents of existing public databases, in which certain regions (in particular Africa) are typically underrepresented so that a handful of groups (in this case, mainly "Yoruba" from Nigeria) stand in for a much broader pool of regional genetic diversity.[31]

When I heard about the admixture tests offered to participants by the CANDELA project, my initial thought was that they reproduced a conventional, racialized vision of Brazil's population history. Yet, being familiar with Bortolini's earlier work (e.g., the 2006 paper with Santos and Maio, mentioned previously, and her coauthored paper with Sérgio Pena about whether genetics could help determine the beneficiaries of university quotas, discussed in chapter 1), I was aware of her strong antiracialist stance and attempts to publicly deconstruct biological conceptions of race. I learned through interviews with the CANDELA Brazil scientists that the decision to focus on these three continental ancestry categories stemmed from the project's aim to produce results that could lend themselves to comparisons among (as well as within) the admixture histories of the various Latin American countries under study, which were viewed as sharing a common heritage of European, Indigenous American, and African ancestry, albeit with differing genetic contributions and degrees of mixture. As one of the postdoctoral researchers on the Brazilian CANDELA project explained to me:

> From a technical point of view, there exist [genetic] markers that
> infer European, Amerindian, and African frequencies. They exist

because of the history of the environment to which they have become adapted, their evolutionary history. . . . And that creates a specific "background" among populations. [Among] Asians as well, there exist specific Asian genetic backgrounds. From a Latin American point of view, we know that Native Americans, and the Africans and Europeans that arrived here, were populations that came together, and they created that dynamic of mixture that is our people. Those different frequencies between populations—those markers—are useful to find out how that mixture came about, over generations—a hundred, two hundred generations—how that mixture between those three populations came to shape the ancestry of the Brazilian population and the Latin American population as a whole.[32]

The idea that DNA markers "exist" by themselves has been challenged by social studies of genetics. According to anthropologist Amade M'charek, "in order to be a marker, a DNA fragment [has] to be aligned to various technical procedures and components. . . . A marker is, therefore, a hybrid. It is both an object and the technology to confirm its presence."[33] In the context of admixture testing, "good" markers are alleles (in this case, nucleotides—DNA bases) that show very different frequencies between particular human populations (e.g., continental groups selected as ancestral genetic "stock") as well as similar frequencies *within* each population category. The labeling of an AIM as "Amerindian" is contingent on the distinctions scientists wish to draw with other categories under study (in this case, "African" and "European"). The chosen markers are those that discriminate most successfully and consistently *between* the three "parental" groups—even though the borders of the groups may overlap, and within them we may also find substantial genetic heterogeneity. These criteria present an ideal standard, which very few AIMs actually meet. In reality, DNA markers are rarely exclusive to a given human group and will not be shared by all members of the population in question. Ancestry tests therefore include an error margin (in this case, ±10 percent) to reflect that AIMs are found in higher frequencies among some populations than others, making the results probabilistic rather than definitive.

Imagining Admixture

One of the guiding questions of the CANDELA project was to understand how regional differences in the degrees and intensities of admixture among particular ancestral groups had shaped the genetic and phenotypic characteristics of various Latin American populations. This was a line of investigation that had been pursued for some time by researchers at the UFRGS, in particular by the laboratory's founder, Francisco Salzano, who since the 1960s had conducted various genetic studies into the regional dynamics of admixture in Brazil.[34] Within the field of population genetics, a broad, current definition of "admixture" could be "the outcome of matings between individuals from two or more genetically differentiated populations,"[35] or "a sudden increase in gene flow between two differentiated populations."[36] In my interviews with members of the CANDELA project, I noticed that terms like *mistura*, *mestiçagem*, and *miscigenação* were often used interchangeably to refer to genetic admixture. Whereas *mistura* may refer to any type of mixture, *mestiçagem* in Brazil refers specifically to the cultural and biological mingling among the country's "founding" populations, beginning in the colonial period. *Miscigenação*, too, has overtly racial connotations. The term originated as a loanword from the English "miscegenation," which was coined in the United States as part of a Civil War–era hoax meant to spread alarm among White liberals about the impacts of "racial blending" among Black men and White women should slavery be abolished.[37] Ironically, even after the term's pseudoscientific origins were revealed, it nonetheless became absorbed into vernacular and scientific language to refer to the process of biological mixture among "racially" distinct groups. Today, the term's peculiar history has largely been forgotten. Nevertheless, *mestiçagem* and *miscigenação* continue to maintain coherence as genetic *and* lay concepts, since they convey a phenomenon that all Brazilians know to be true: Africans, Europeans, and Indigenous Americans *did* meet and reproduce in the Americas, and in the process of mixing their descendants became changed, both biologically and culturally. In this respect, Peter Wade has argued that the "specification of biogeographical ancestry (African, European, Amerindian) can be considered racialized—despite the rejection of race as a valid category by the geneticists . . . because it relies on familiar, racelike categories, which are refigured in an idiom of genetic ancestry."[38]

By focusing on the "founding" Latin American populations of Indigenous Americans, Africans, and Europeans, then, the CANDELA project relied on a specific conception of "admixture" that bore resemblances to traditional "racial" groupings, although it was not conceptualized in this way by most of the researchers. Indeed, among the CANDELA researchers I interviewed, Salzano was the only one who affirmed to me that humans could be divided genetically into "racial" groups. Salzano, one of the founding figures of Brazilian population genetics, was one of the signatories of the 1964 UNESCO

"Proposal on the biological aspects of race" and a lifelong opponent of scientific racism. His definition of "racial" groups was taxonomic: categories comprising groups of populations, or single populations, proposed on the basis of hereditary physical traits.[39] As he explained to me:

> There is no doubt that if you bring me the blood of someone who currently lives in Europe, the blood of someone who lives in China, and of another person who lives in Africa . . . if I extract their DNA, and if I have the laboratory conditions for it, I will tell you for certain—practically certain, with a nearly 100 percent guarantee—who is who. So we are able to pinpoint in a very specific way—although that depends, of course—in diverse contexts like Brazil, where there was a lot of miscegenation, mixture, between the three large groups. . . . But there is a difference between them.[40]

For Salzano, the validity of "racial" groups as a biological concept became clearest as one compared individuals who embodied the extremes of evolutionary divergence among humans: individuals who, because of their own (and presumably their ancestors') geographic isolation, had no recent history of mixture and likely shared the least possible genomic heritage. His argument echoes one made by Leslie Dunn, one of the founders of population genetics, in the 1951 UNESCO Statement on the Nature of Race and Race Differences: "The physical anthropologists and the man in the street both know that races exist; the former, from the scientifically recognizable and measurable congeries of traits which he uses in classifying the varieties of man; the latter from the immediate evidence of his senses when he sees an African, a European, an Asiatic and an American Indian together."[41] Dunn's definition conflates social and genetic conceptions of race—the first relying on racialized visible traits (skin color, hair, facial morphology, etc.) and the latter referring to underlying structures of genetic diversity, suggesting that they are essentially one and the same. Yet scientists have since shown that genetic diversity is *not* evenly distributed in a way that would reflect classic "racial" taxonomies—for instance, studies have shown present-day African populations alone to hold a disproportionate share of the world's genetic diversity, due to the antiquity of our species' origins in the region.[42] For many geneticists, this is seen as an important argument against the usefulness of race as a genetic concept.

Other members of the CANDELA project described this contrasting effect between continental genetic "backgrounds," conversely, as a *consequence* of admixture testing. Tábita Hünemeier—a biologist and one of the main coordinators of the Brazilian branch of the study—explained that "humans are shaped by a large gradient, and that gradient is only broken, generally, when we need to carry out a study, and in those cases, we create a category because we plan on analyzing that category mathematically. But it's an artifice that is used by researchers."[43] Following Hünemeier's explanation, using AIMs to differentiate among genetic "backgrounds" has the effect of making these abstract, overlapping entities appear sharp, discontinuous, and fixed. It also temporarily obscures a bigger picture of genetic continuity among human populations, whose histories in turn contain multiple, complex layers of mixture.

Framing the study based on conventional understandings of *mestiçagem* as a trihybrid mix between Indigenous Americans, Europeans, and Africans necessarily had the effect of limiting the conclusions that could be drawn about participants' ancestry and about Latin American population histories in general. For example, the project's organizers decided not to include Asian markers in the analyses, since these groups were considered to be a minority in the region, having little overall genetic impact. This did not deter some Asian-descendant Brazilians from wanting to participate. Virginia Ramallo, a biological anthropologist who coordinated the project's communications with its participants, recalled telling some volunteers: "[The test] is based on a series of markers that won't consider your ancestry—which you know you have, because you've met your four grandparents and they're Japanese—because we're not interested in recovering ancestry, we're interested in this model of three different continents: European, African, American." Their response: "Oh no . . . but I still want to."[44] The assumption that Latin America's Asian-descendant populations are minority groups, mainly consisting of recent migrants who remain relatively unmixed with the general population, has been challenged recently by historians, who argue that the erasure of these groups' long-standing presence in the region since the colonial period has actually been one of the consequences of national ideologies of *mestiçagem/mestizaje*.[45] Including additional reference groups and markers in the admixture test might have allowed the project to challenge conventional wisdom about the ancestral composition of Latin American populations, revealing the influence of groups whose contributions have historically been minimized or obscured.

There are other ways that admixture can be envisioned that do not invoke conventional "racial" groupings. For example, María Fernanda Olarte Sierra and Adriana Díaz del Castillo H. have described how a group of Colombian population geneticists, committed to practicing "nonhegemonic" forms of science, chose to eschew the traditional categories of "mestizo, Afro, and Indigenous," instead coming up with alternative categories for their study of inhabitants of the Guajira region. Their model—which accounted for the existence of various distinct Indigenous groups as well as the effects of internal migration in the region—appeared to capture patterns of genetic variation that would have been missed by the use of conventional "racial" categories. Nonetheless, when the researchers came to publish their study in an English-language journal, they found themselves under pressure to present their categories in terms that would be comprehensible to international audiences, and ultimately they opted to refer to their sample populations using racial terms (e.g., "mixed-race," "native," "white"). This observation highlights how far both racialized sampling approaches and commonsense ideas about the ubiquity of "racial" mixture have become a convention for genomic research into Latin American populations, to the extent that alternative methodologies are discouraged over concerns about their limited "translatability" and scope of comparison in relation to other research studies on the region.[46]

In a similar way, the economic and practical conditions imposed by the CANDELA project clearly shaped and limited the possibilities for how the participants' DNA ancestry tests were constructed. As Ramallo suggested, the tests were not intended as a tool for volunteers to "recover" their personal family history but rather as a measure of their genomic composition based on a limited set of reference populations. While the analysis was not based on the most cutting-edge technology available, it did fulfill certain other important practical requirements: affordability, speed of processing, and comparability of results across the five participating countries. Nonetheless, given Bortolini's earlier characterization of genetic, race, and identity as "walking along a knife edge," I wondered how the Brazilian CANDELA team regarded their own role in terms of guiding interpretations of the data they were providing to volunteers.

Walking the Knife Edge between Genetics, Race, and Identity

During my fieldwork among the CANDELA scientists, I began to perceive a disconnect between the public-facing discourses of figures like Sérgio Pena, who tends to emphasize the statistical *insignificance* of genetic differences among humans,[47] and the everyday work of geneticists, which involves magnifying and delving into the genetic variations among human groups. When I brought this up with Bortolini, she stated that "anyone who studies biological diversity studies differences. Anyone who studies the role of natural selection, the role of genetic drift in history, the evolutionary trajectory of any species, studies differences. . . . So if you . . . were to try and make out that biological differences don't exist, well, no geneticist would say that, because that's ridiculous, that's not a geneticist."[48] Bortolini categorically rejected the idea that "pointing out that diversity exists means you are feeding prejudices." On the other hand, through personal experience, she was keenly aware of the potential for genetic knowledge to become reinterpreted in public debate in ways that could play into discourses about "racial" difference. During the 2000s, Bortolini intervened actively in public and scientific debates about affirmative action, based on her expertise as a geneticist.[49] However, by the time the national quotas law was passed in 2012, she began to decline interviews with journalists on the topic: "I said 'look, [the quotas] are a political decision, about public policy, and what I have to say is of no interest. . . . I'm a scientist and that's it.'" Once again, Bortolini portrayed her science as balancing "on a knife edge": wanting to inform understandings of human history and biological diversity, but without weighing in on sociopolitical questions about racism and inequality. As a result, she said that the CANDELA Brazil project did not actively seek out media attention for its findings.

Nevertheless, the project did involve an aspect of knowledge exchange, integrated through the planned delivery of DNA ancestry results to volunteers, which also required the Brazilian team to think about how they would frame this information and respond to questions from participants, particularly regarding sensitive issues such as racial identification. When I asked Bortolini about these interactions and whether the CANDELA volunteers seemed to differentiate between the concepts of genetic ancestry and race, she paused before answering: "Well, yes . . . the issue of race is very complicated because even while [the term] is preserved in part of social discourse . . . elsewhere there's the idea that 'there is no race' and so on, so people are afraid, not knowing if they should say it or not say it, and they come to us asking 'can I say I'm Black or . . . ?' So it's a pretty confusing thing, you know." Bortolini's solution was to clarify the technical workings of the genetic analysis, so that participants could understand as far as possible the epistemic origins and limitations of their DNA report, while pointing out that identity formation was primarily a *social* process that could not be arbitrated by geneticists. In addition to the information sheet that accompanied each volunteer's genetic report, the team devised a standard email response for volunteers who asked whether their DNA ancestry results could inform their racial identification, telling them that if they wanted to reconstruct their own identity based on their genetic ancestry information, this would have to come from "an individual and personal decision."

This effort to limit the authority of geneticists to strictly biological matters is another example of scientific boundary work. Gieryn has observed that this work often functions not only to separate "scientists" from "pseudoscientists" (discrediting the work of the latter while reinforcing the authority of the former), but also to disengage the production of scientific knowledge from its consumption, thereby protecting the autonomy of scientists' work in the face of criticisms regarding broader applications of their technologies.[50] For Bortolini and her team, this seemed the most practical way to deal with the potential dilemma of how participants might decide to use their DNA reports once they left the lab. To an extent, the researchers attempted to guide volunteers' perceptions of what their results meant and how they could "legitimately" be used—for instance, by including a "frequently asked questions" section in their genetic report, which advised test-takers on how to interpret potential disjunctions between their DNA ancestry and their known family history, among other issues. In some cases, the researchers were confronted with volunteers who stated openly their intention to use their DNA report for legal or official purposes. One of the CANDELA researchers recalled being approached by a man who stated he needed a "legal certificate" to prove that he was 100 percent European. When she questioned him further:

> [He] entered into a discourse about White supremacy . . . racism, antisemitism, and [said] "I need to know." And I said, "Look, first of all, you're not going to receive a certificate" . . . and I explained all the error [margins]. I said, "You can't say that, because there are all these things that are important for the interpretation of the test." And he said, "So you mean you all simply don't know what you're doing? You can't say who's who?" So I said, "No, it's not like that," and he said, "But there are studies that separate Celts from . . ." and I said, "It's not that simple, if you look you'll see that those studies are all based on percentages of error."

Ultimately, while the researcher felt she could not turn away a volunteer, she tried to emphasize to him the possibility that he would not receive his desired result. She did not see him return for the sampling sessions.

While the CANDELA researchers were careful not to try and influence individual test-takers about the meaning they ascribed to their results, they nonetheless held clear ideas about what constituted "appropriate" or "good" interpretations of DNA ancestry. Ideas about the unity and long-standing genetic mixture of human populations, for instance, were clearly privileged over notions of purity. By requiring participants to complete questionnaires about their racial self-identification, family history, and expectations regarding their DNA results, the project also invited volunteers to reflect on how this genetic knowledge might compare with or impact their sense of identity and ancestry. This introduced a potential learning moment, in particular in cases where genetic ancestry did *not* coincide with personal expectations. In Hünemeier's view, this knowledge could have an important impact on Brazil's collective process of identity construction, "not as something that segregates [people], but as something that shows that at the end of the day everyone has points of intersection within that ancestry." For this to happen, though, she suggested, participants would have to not only take into account their own results but see how they compared with those of other volunteers—something the organizers were considering achieving by producing a summary of the project's survey data to send around to all volunteers. In this sense, to offer some broader genetic truth about ancestry, DNA testing could not be an individualistic pursuit but rather a comparative, communal exercise. Hence, even if a volunteer received an estimate of "100 percent European" or "100 percent African," they would have to recognize that this result was part of a continuum, and that they shared ancestry with other Brazilians of different "colors" and backgrounds.

Science at the Service of Society

Like other historical disciplines, population genetics draws on various technologies, reference datasets, and scales of analysis to bring to the fore different stories about human histories. During their "normal" scientific work, geneticists are able to delve into the fine-scale variations between particular populations, without losing sight of the broader picture that *Homo sapiens* is a rather genetically homogeneous species, whose members are much more similar than different on a genomic scale. When working with DNA ancestry tests, however, it is the diversity and contrasts between populations that are brought to the fore.

In the case studies described above, researchers struggled to reconcile the specific, "artificial" narratives of ancestry conveyed by personalized DNA tests with the broader messages they felt genetics had to offer to the public. In the CANDELA case, participants' personal identity projects were largely seen as secondary to a broader scientific project, which was framed by a specific paradigm of ancestry and admixture. Scientists were ambivalent about the social relevance of the data they produced for volunteers, working on the one hand to reduce the possibilities of DNA ancestry data being used to support political identity claims, while encouraging participants to reflect on the idea that they (and Brazilians on the whole) shared underlying genetic connections that belied their superficial phenotypic differences. In contrast, the African American scientists I interviewed were convinced of the social value of catering to the desires of members of the African diaspora to uncover their family histories prior to slavery, but they were uncomfortable with the idea that genetics should be used to support ethnocentric political agendas. When I interviewed Fatimah Jackson in 2014, for instance, she referred back to the statement she had given for the *Motherland* documentary a decade earlier. Ultimately, she conceded, Kittles had been right. For African Americans who had long been deprived of a sense of their own history, "lighting a candle *is* better than standing in the dark. I just wish that the interpretation of the light was more comprehensive."

In general, the researchers I interviewed in both countries were wary of commercial initiatives that appeared overeager to "tell the public what it wants to hear." A pragmatic solution offered by many of the scientists I interviewed was to educate public users about the limitations and uncertainties of these technologies, equipping them to make more "informed," *impersonal* judgments about what the data mean and how they may legitimately be used. Nonetheless, even among scientists, the question of legitimate uses remains contentious. What, for instance, is the significance of a genetic match? Is it an arrow pointing to an ultimately inaccessible past, as Fatimah Jackson suggests, or a means to "reverse the Middle Passage," as Henry Louis Gates Jr. has proposed?[51] Or, as Shomarka Keita pointed out: What gives people from faraway countries the right to claim African ethnic identities based on DNA samples, with apparent disregard for the autonomy of the groups concerned?[52] Indeed, what is the authority of scientists, or of DNA-testing companies, to arbitrate over personal identities at all?

Among the researchers I interviewed, Maria Cátira Bortolini showed the greatest resistance to the idea that scientists should impose their authority over individuals' racial or ethnic identification. Her stance was influenced by the introduction of quotas at her own university, the UFRGS, and the internal conversations about how to determine the eligibility of candidates. Bortolini, like many Brazilian scientists, was familiar with the case of the Universidade de Brasília (UnB), which was excoriated by the media after instating a panel of "experts" to verify applicants' self-reported race. Critics at the time noted the uncomfortable parallels this method drew with the activities of "race scientists" in the late nineteenth and early twentieth century and the irony of these methods being used now to benefit the cause of Black Brazilians.[53] For Bortolini, such activities constituted a dangerous abuse of scientific authority, which was to be avoided. What made CANDELA's DNA-testing initiative acceptable, it seemed, was the team's resolute refusal to validate or intervene in participants' decisions about how to relate the results to their own identity.

This desire to disengage genetic research as far as possible from issues of "identity politics" was not shared by all of the CANDELA scientists I interviewed. Ana Angélica Leal Barbosa, professor of biology at the Universidade Estadual do Sudoeste da Bahia (UESB), was one of the few tenured geneticists I met in Brazil who identified as Afro-descendant. While Barbosa was completing her studies in the 1980s, she told me, the research projects she was involved in were oriented primarily toward analyzing the degrees of "racial" mixture (miscigenação) within Brazilian populations. Since qualifying as a professor, she has chosen to focus her research instead on the population histories of quilombos—communities composed of the descendants of runaway slaves.[54] Barbosa recalled instances when she had been questioned by other geneticists about her research focus: "Why work with the Black population? Why not another population?" For her part, Barbosa stressed the importance of situating genetic research in relation to the historical and contemporary social dynamics of racism. In her view, this meant expressing to the public that humans are simultaneously genetically similar and different, while also recognizing the reality of how sociopolitical forces produce inequalities among citizens, based on racialized physical typologies. In her words:

> We need to understand that [racial problems] exist, that we are
> really all one species, but also that those differences exist in the case
> of Brazil, and that they're social differences, so if you say "no,
> everyone is the same," you're minimizing . . . a difference that is
> important for us Afro-descendants, [a difference] that's not only
> maintained by genetics, but which is maintained by the social and
> political context. And we need to recover that [difference], because
> to recover Black culture is to recover our people. . . . So, I think
> within genetics, we need to broaden our political vision of that issue,
> because sometimes we see ourselves as only scientists, and we think

"oh no, everyone's the same," and then [you ending up saying that] Neguinho da Beija-Flor is White.[55]

In a roundabout way, the issue of affirmative action policies may have broader implications for how ancestry and population histories are conceptualized by geneticists. In *Race Decoded: The Genomic Fight for Social Justice*, Catherine Bliss charts the emergence of a "race-positive" trend in genomic research in the United States from the late 1990s into the 2000s, which was propelled primarily by scientists who identified as members of racial and ethnic minority groups.[56] Such individuals often bring to their engagements with genetics a broader toolkit of sociological knowledge about the way race and racism continue to shape societies—dynamics that can be invisible to scientists who have not had firsthand experiences of racial discrimination.

There is currently a greater plurality of approaches to population genetics and ancestry testing in the United States than in Brazil—a fact that may, in part, be a consequence of affirmative action initiatives that have opened up the discipline to scientists of diverse knowledge backgrounds, who in turn bring different questions and ideas about how to use DNA to shed light on the past. As we have seen with the debates around African Ancestry, this diversity of perspectives can also be a source of tension among practitioners. Nonetheless, even the scientists I interviewed who criticized the company's products recognized its broader social contributions. For example, part of the appeal of African Ancestry has been the confidence its clientele places in the company's scientific director, Rick Kittles—a sign that his community-oriented practices have helped assuage a long-standing mistrust of biomedical research within these communities caused by multiple cases of abuse and exploitative conduct toward African American participants.[57] Similar forms of community engagement have been practiced by some Brazilian medical geneticists, who have worked with Black movement activists to mobilize research into conditions that have historically been associated with Afro-Brazilian populations.[58] Such relationships can potentially open up avenues for communication between scientists and members of the public, providing a forum for fostering broader and more nuanced understandings of genetics and human histories. At the same time, in the context of contemporary multicultural societies where claiming a coherent racial or ethnic identity can be an important means of gaining political resources and recognition, it is perhaps logical that groups will seek to use genetic data strategically to try and strengthen their collective identity discourses.[59]

Such is the geneticist's dilemma. Although they may try to put forward certain perspectives and narratives about the past, scientists can never fully anticipate or control the uses and interpretations of the data they produce. At the same time, demonstrating other ways of imagining human origins and histories may simply not be enough to counter the sociopolitical salience of racial and ethnic categories in contemporary societies that continue to grapple with deep structural inequalities put in place by slavery and colonialism.

But we must look beyond academic debates to grasp the societal impact of these technologies. Chapter 3 explores how interactions between genetic-testing companies and customer groups—particularly in the United States—have further shaped the evolution of a global DNA ancestry market that is increasingly centered on the production of "ethnic" admixture tests. These developments have pushed the boundaries of what seemed to be "scientific." Whereas many of the researchers I interviewed in 2013 claimed it was "speculative" or even "impossible" to pinpoint an individual's ancestry to particular ethnic groups, within a couple of years the market was saturated with companies offering to uncover customers' unique "ethnic mix" with unparalleled precision. How do these companies reinforce their claims to objectivity while aspiring to create ancestry estimates that are simultaneously personal and global in scope?

3 Technologies of the Self

. . . .

> One of the most common questions we get asked all the time is,
> "What's my ethnicity?" or "Where am I from?" And it turns out,
> the answer is in your DNA.
>
> —Promotional video, AncestryDNA homepage

The first months of 2014 were an exciting and turbulent time for the world of DNA ancestry testing. AncestryDNA—a subsidiary of the Utah-based genealogy giant Ancestry.com—and the Californian biotech company 23andMe had unveiled major updates to their DNA ancestry tests, offering to link customers to over twenty "genetic regions" by analyzing not just a handful but hundreds of thousands of positions across their genome, using cutting-edge genotyping technologies. Sales figures for both companies were growing steadily, no doubt boosted by their new, lower retail price of $99 per test.[1] Other businesses were fast following suit. Houston-based FamilyTreeDNA— one of the first companies to begin selling DNA tests to the public for genealogical purposes in the early 2000s—rolled out its new autosomal analysis, myOrigins, in May 2014. Shortly after, 23andMe expanded its market to the United Kingdom and Canada, a move that was mirrored in 2015 by AncestryDNA, which made its tests available for online purchase in the U.K., Ireland, Canada, Australia, and New Zealand. That same year, both companies genotyped their one millionth customer. The U.S. genetic ancestry industry, in other words, was on the verge of going global.

Against this backdrop, as the epigraph to this chapter indicates, "ethnicity" was fast becoming a buzzword in the industry, with both AncestryDNA and FamilyTreeDNA branding their new autosomal products as a means for customers to find out their "genetic ethnic origins." In their book *Ethnicity, Inc.*, John and Jean Comaroff have signaled that in the present age of the global "commercialization of identity," ethnicity is often experienced, paradoxically, "as a precipitate of inalienable natural essence, of genetics and biology, and . . . as a function of voluntary self-fashioning, often through serial acts of consumption."[2] This apparent contradiction is clear in the context of the thriving DNA ancestry market, in which companies—each one boasting its unique reference panels, modes of analysis, and private customer database—jostle to tell potential customers "who they *really* are." Depending on where they decide to submit their DNA, members of the public can end up with differing portraits of their ancestral heritage; if they are not convinced by one company's estimates, they may opt to have their results reanalyzed by a competitor. Likewise, the menu of ancestral populations offered by each company opens up possibilities for clients to explore and try on different "ethnic options" within the scope of their own results. Identity, in this sense, becomes "*both* ascriptive and instrumental. *Both* innate and constructed. *Both* blood and choice."[3]

It may be tempting to dismiss this market of ancestry as a phenomenon that both essentializes the concept of ethnic identity and voids it of any meaningful content—or to condemn the industry for merely preying on the narcissism and ingenuousness of customers in order to extract profit from their biomatter. In a recent work, science writer Adam Rutherford draws parallels between the DNA ancestry-testing industry and the Anthropometric Laboratory set up by Francis Galton (commonly considered the father of eugenics) in London in 1884. In exchange for fourpence, members of the public could be "accurately measured in many ways, either to obtain timely warning of remediable faults in development, or to learn their powers." Within a year 9,337 people had voluntarily submitted themselves to the process—a testament, in Rutherford's analysis, to "our fascination with ourselves, and willingness to reach into our purses to satisfy those egos."[4]

It is perhaps telling, though, that the DNA ancestry-testing industry has its roots in a broader trend in direct-to-consumer (DTC) advertising and services, which has been particularly influential within the U.S. pharmaceutical sector. In that context, drug companies have set up websites encouraging patients to take an active role, alongside medical professionals, in researching and choosing pharmaceuticals to regulate their program of care. The result is a form of "biological citizenship" in which patients "engage in self-techniques to speed the process of recovery."[5] Along similar lines, Gísli Pálsson has suggested that DNA ancestry tests may likewise be considered a kind of Foucauldian "technology of the self," a tool that permits individuals to perform operations on their "own bodies and souls, thoughts, conduct, and way of being, so as to transform themselves in order to attain a certain state of happiness, purity, wisdom, perfection, or immortality."[6] While to some extent regarding them as inseparable from regimes of domination and biopower, Foucault specified that such technologies are fundamentally concerned with practices of self-care: with cultivating and acquiring a sense of identity through forms of introspection.

The concept of DNA ancestry testing as a service tailored toward clients' self-care also resonates with recent ethnographic studies that portray family history research as a mode of kinship work and care for the dead—a topic that I explore further in chapter 5.[7] Indeed, the gradual merging of DNA ancestry-testing services with global genealogy companies such as Ancestry.com and MyHeritage has been key to the rising popularity of these technologies and has allowed providers to brand them not as crude "racial" mixture tests, but as a way of getting in touch with one's cultural heritage, retrieving lost kinship ties, and generally learning more about one*self*. Yet this commercial arrangement has also given rise to new technical developments. By combining large sets of genomic and genealogical data, scientists are able to test and stabilize the results produced by their admixture algorithms, attempting to fix them within a given historical time line. Similar to the pharmaceutical sector, citizens (in this case, experienced genealogists) assume an active role in this process, using their own research to assess the reliability of these tools and in some cases lobbying for product alterations and service improvements.

Nonetheless, the mode of "biological citizenship" that emerges from these practices risks being—in the words of Nikolas Rose and Carlos Novas—a "citizenship of brand culture, where trust in brands appears capable of supplanting trust in neutral scientific expertise."[8] What is the scope for objectivity in the results produced by these companies, guided as they are by questions of profit, consumer interest, and market competition? What role do consumers play in helping calibrate the tests, by delivering feedback on their capacity to accurately describe their "ethnic" makeup? Whose conceptions of ancestry and ethnicity are ultimately reproduced by the industry? To answer these questions, the following sections look to the story of AncestryDNA, which has grown in the last decade into the foremost provider of DNA ancestry tests worldwide at the time of writing. In so doing, we can see how the scientific and creative processes underlying the construction of genetic "ethnicity" carry through to the workings of an international for-profit business.

The Origins of Genetic "Ethnicity"

AncestryDNA's genetic "ethnicity" test first went on sale in May 2012, but its origins date back to a project launched in 1999 by a team of Mormon scientists from Brigham Young University (BYU). Throughout the 1990s, in anticipation of the avalanche of data promised by the impending completion of the Human Genome Project (HGP), international teams of population geneticists were setting up large-scale DNA sampling projects aimed broadly at mapping the genomic variation of humans around the world. The Human Genome Diversity Project (HGDP) is a well-known example of such missions. Formally established in 1990, the project set out to gather some 10,000 DNA samples from 400 populations around the world but was eventually hamstrung by allegations of racism and bio-colonialism, raised by Indigenous groups and reinforced by the UNESCO International Bioethics Committee.[9] Where the HGDP was forced to abandon its plans other projects sprung up, proposing different sampling approaches, ethical frameworks, and research goals, but still with the aim of capturing a "diverse" sample of the world's human genetic variation.[10]

Scott Woodward, a professor of molecular biology at Utah Valley University, became the leader of one such project after being approached by Mormon billionaire James LeVoy Sorenson about the idea of "mapping the DNA of Norway." Genealogy is a central theological concern for members of the Church of Jesus Christ of Latter-day Saints (LDS), whose "temple work" involves tracing one's ancestors in order to offer them the chance of salvation, and Sorenson was particularly interested in finding out how DNA could help uncover these genealogical connections within Norway, where some of his own ancestors originated. However, unconvinced of the scientific or social value of a Norwegian genome project (particularly since a similar effort was already underway in neighboring Iceland),[11] Woodward persuaded Sorenson to invest in building a global database comprising 100,000 DNA "lineages" meant to represent a genetic coverage of "the entire world."[12]

Sampling began in summer 1999, and the resulting database was hosted initially by BYU (where Woodward held a professorship in microbiology and molecular biology) and later by the Sorenson Molecular Genealogy Foundation (SMGF), a nonprofit research institution established in Salt Lake City in 2003, with Woodward as principal investigator.[13] Scientifically, the SMGF was focused toward developing the field of molecular genealogy, defined as "the application of DNA analysis techniques and statistical population genetics to the task of reconstructing unknown genealogies from the genetic and genealogical information of living individuals."[14] Additionally, the Sorenson database was made accessible to public users through various for-profit DNA-testing services and subsequently through the website GeneTree, where individuals could create a free profile enabling them to upload their genetic data, order (for a fee) a Sorenson DNA test, search the database, build family trees, and interact with other members online.[15]

As Woodward explained to me in an interview in 2017, one of the first hurdles facing the scientists was to decide on a sampling strategy—an issue that would be key for determining the kind of diversity the group was aiming to capture. One possibility was a grid approach: mapping the world out in ten-kilometer squares and sampling one person within every square. Yet, as Woodward pointed out, this posed a conundrum: *Who* would be sampled within each square?[16] Another idea was to use language groups as a guide, based on the hypothesis that processes of genetic and linguistic differentiation have, to an extent, mirrored one another historically.[17] Ultimately, the approach taken by Woodward and his team was pragmatic, focusing partly on linguistic variation but also on broader conceptions of diversity. As is often the case with scientific sampling projects, the group—headed by Woodward's student, Ugo Perego—began by looking for donors where they were.[18] The first 10,000 DNA samples were gathered locally by recruiting BYU students in Provo, Utah, and volunteers in nearby Salt Lake City. Next, the team reached out to contacts elsewhere in the United States, seeking to diversify their dataset by including Jewish and African American sample-donors. Finally, they began to arrange sampling trips outside the United States, drawing frequently on the personal connections of members of the scientific team—including those cultivated during the missions abroad undertaken by most young Mormons after graduating from high school—to secure visas and governmental permissions. By 2010, the SMGF had reached its goal of 100,000 DNA samples, collected from 172 countries around the world.

Since the database was intended for family history research, one key criterion was to target donors who knew their genealogy to a depth of four or five generations, in order to be able to attribute particular DNA markers to populations who lived 150 years or more in the past. According to Woodward, "The real question that we were asking was, could we take a DNA sample from a person who is living today and couple that with genealogical information about who that person was, who their parents were, their grandparents and their great-grandparents . . . and then parse that living DNA sample out into those different populations in the past and essentially reconstruct the genetic signature of a population of a hundred years ago, a hundred and fifty, two hundred years ago, five hundred years ago?" In some places, where this depth of genealogical information was unavailable, the team aimed for villages whose histories seemed to indicate little demographic movement in the past hundred or 200 years. In Woodward's terms, "We like genealogies because we find that people move around, people are a mix of lots of different groups. But if we didn't have that then we went with place of collection, and we only collected if we had reasonable expectations that that person's family was not a transplant from somewhere else in the recent past. And we noted that in our database, too."[19]

Beyond its scientific aims, the SMGF had a broader humanitarian mission. A statement on the project's website affirmed that the database was designed "to foster a greater sense of identity combined with a sense of belonging among all people by showing how closely we are connected as members of a single human family."[20] Central to this mission was the idea that the Sorenson database could serve as a resource for those around the world who did not know their family origins by constructing "a worldwide family tree that will link people together based on the genetic information inherited from common ancestors."[21] While the LDS Church declined to endorse the work of the SMGF, this notion of a global family tree resonates strongly with Mormon doctrine, which teaches that all family lineages lead back to Adam and Eve (see figure 3.1).[22] For geneticists like Woodward, meanwhile, the root of humankind's biological interrelatedness is embodied by the figure of "mitochondrial Eve"—the nickname given by scientists to the most recent common ancestor of all living humans and the originator of the oldest mtDNA lineage found among contemporary populations. The database was thus designed with the idea of reconstructing deep and recent ancestry, and both Sorenson and Woodward felt that the act of making visible these connections could have a powerful symbolism, helping unite disparate and divided groups by revealing their genetic kinship to one another. As Woodward explained to me, "What if we could in fact take two people from anywhere in the world . . . and be able to show them—not just tell them that, hey, you're related to each other, you know, you're cousins, or tenth generation or something like that—but could actually show them the DNA sequence that they shared from a common ancestor—would it make a difference in their lives? Would they treat each other differently, would they look at each other differently? . . . We tried the experiment a number of times with very positive results."[23]

This humanitarian agenda, however, was cut short when Sorenson passed away in 2010. Up to this point, the SMGF's patron had channeled close to $50 million into the project, and the costs of research and maintaining the database continued to be high. As a result, two years later the Sorenson

FIGURE 3.1 "World's largest genealogy chart," displayed at RootsTech genealogy convention, Salt Lake City, February 2017. Photo by Sarah Abel.

family negotiated the acquisition of the SMGF database by Ancestry.com of Utah, one of the world's leading genealogical record providers that at the time was seeking to expand its DNA services. As one of the world's largest collections of correlated genetic and genealogical "lineages," the Sorenson database was to become a unique asset for the development of the company's new genetic "ethnicity" test.

AncestryDNA

By 2012, the gold standard in DNA ancestry techniques was no longer the uniparental lineage-testing or continental admixture analyses discussed in chapter 2. Rapidly falling prices among cutting-edge genotyping technologies made it feasible for companies to analyze single nucleotide polymorphisms (SNPs) at not just a handful but at hundreds of thousands of positions across the genome and link them to increasingly fine-scale patterns of variation among human populations. An eye-catching example of this technique was published in *Nature* in 2008 by John Novembre and colleagues (members of the Population Reference Sample project, POPRES)[24] in a letter entitled "Genes mirror geography within Europe." The study gathered genotype data from 1,386 individuals in thirty-six European countries and analyzed 500,000 SNPs across each person's genome. Using principal components analysis (PCA), the results were plotted as a two-dimensional graph that statistically summarized the relative genetic distance among sample-donors. When tilted slightly and placed alongside a similarly color-coded geopolitical map of Europe, the points (each representing one sample-donor) appeared to be distributed in a way that mirrored the geographic arrangement of their countries of origin. The authors concluded that "despite low average levels of genetic differentiation among Europeans, we find a close correspondence between genetic and geographic distances; indeed, a geographical map of Europe arises naturally as an efficient two-dimensional summary of genetic variation in Europeans." Besides holding significance for mapping the genetic bases of diseases, the authors predicted that the technique heralded important prospects for the field of genetic ancestry testing, allowing an individual's geographic origins to be inferred "with surprising accuracy—often to within a few hundred kilometers."[25]

Along with the acquisition of the SMGF database, this statistical technique formed the key to the new ancestry-testing approach being developed by AncestryDNA—as well as several of its competitors. Jake Byrnes, who worked as senior manager and later director of population genetics at AncestryDNA until 2019, was among a cohort of scientists hired in 2011 to develop the new autosomal product. On a daily basis, Byrnes worked closely with computer scientists and statisticians on the research and development side of the company, devoting his efforts to two main tasks: exploring the mass genomic data produced by the company, and developing and prototyping the algorithms needed to deliver individual sets of results to customers. These activities also brought him into contact with nonscientists—chiefly, members of the development and marketing teams, who are responsible for translating the genetic data into a user-friendly online product and tool.

The first step in constructing the test, Byrnes explained to me during our interview in 2014, was to define a "candidate" reference panel.[26] At the time, the AncestryDNA candidate reference database comprised some 1,500 samples taken from the SMGF collection (a small subset of the full 100,000 samples), as well as 800 samples from the publicly available HGDP-CEPH panel, and over 1,800 samples donated by AncestryDNA customers with known pedigrees.[27] Since the test is not static but constantly under development, the contents of the reference panel change over time to accommodate new "genetic regions" being added to the product. Whenever this happens, Byrnes explained, the team "[goes] to [the SMGF] collection and [pulls] out samples that fit the bill."[28] Samples with accompanying pedigree information are prioritized, particularly those of individuals whose four grandparents were born in the same place or country and who may be considered "representative" of the target population. As far as possible, the number of samples taken from different countries across a given region are balanced, to avoid skewing the analysis toward one country or another.

Next, the reference samples are genotyped and the data "cleaned," a process that involves identifying and removing samples that could affect the performance of the reference panel. Typically, this includes DNA from individuals who are closely related, whose allele frequencies may not capture the full genetic variation represented by a given population, or whose genetic ancestry appears to contradict the accompanying pedigree information (e.g., individuals with recent ancestral mixture), appearing as outliers on a PCA plot. The "clean" data are then once again mapped onto a PCA plot. The graphs typically show a degree of overlap between the samples, and the geneticists experiment with delineating discrete "populations" based on the clusters generated by the PCA plot. In Byrnes's words: "We start asking questions like, where can we draw a little hash mark in the sand and say we think these are two genetically distinct signals that we can accurately report?" For the West African panel, for instance, the team settled on six discrete populations representing individual countries or pairs of neighboring countries across the region (Senegal, Mali, Nigeria, Ivory Coast/Ghana, Benin/Togo, Cameroon/Congo).[29] There follows a series of experiments to test the effectiveness of the remaining samples in the reference panel, during which any low-performing samples are excluded from the final dataset. As Byrnes explained:

> We can do these exercises of, let's take an individual from, say, Mali — we have deep ancestry from Mali — we look at the genotyping signal, and they seem to cluster with other people from Mali, which suggests, OK, that what we see in the pedigree is true. Now, if we take some small segment of DNA from that individual's genotype sample and we mix it, so we make these synthetic admixtures and we say, OK, now what do we call that segment — we report it as Mali. So we've done a lot of testing to convince ourselves that yes, if you have these distinct ancestries we will call them correctly.[30]

The result is the Ethnicity Reference Panel: a collection of sampled "regions" around the world, each represented by a "somewhat distinct genetic profile."[31] When a customer submits their DNA in the form of a saliva sample, it in turn is genotyped; the statistical program ADMIXTURE is used to assign each SNP to a probable ancestral population from the Ethnicity Reference Panel and to estimate the overall contributions of different "ethnicities" to the individual's genomic inheritance. As Byrnes emphasized, the process of ancestry assignment between neighboring regions is highly probabilistic, relying on the analysis of slight variations in allele frequencies across numerous SNPs; there is no such thing, for instance, as a discrete "Malian" or "Senegalese" genetic marker. In his words:

> Often it's a collective signal across many, many markers . . . often what we're looking at is very small differences in frequencies of alleles across many sites. So, if you look at a particular site, the frequency of t in one population might be 25 percent, and the frequency of t in a neighboring population might be 25.2 percent, so you go, "OK, well, if I just reported that site, saying, here's a t, which population do you think it's from?" It's really hard to put a lot of money [on it], but it's the collective signal that you see across all sites.[32]

In the finished product, these "ethnicities" are depicted as "regional polygons": translucent shapes in varying colors that are superposed onto a map of the world that is left largely blank except for state borders. So far, the polygons have undergone various iterations as the scientific and marketing teams have sought to come up with graphics that convey the overlapping and probabilistic nature of the underlying genetic variation, in a way that is both scientifically accurate and visually appealing to customers. As Byrnes explained:

> On the initial map [released in 2012] we traced out regions on the map based on current country borders, and they were hard stop regions, so it would be, like, France, Germany, Netherlands, and Belgium were one tiny region that was "Europe West," and right next door was "Europe East," and . . . it kind of made it look, like, lift out your passport, cross the border, put it back in your pocket, you would get a completely different prediction of genetic ancestry — which is absolutely not true, right — we have built things into these regions, but everything is a continuum, the variation is a continual process.[33]

During a major update to the product in 2013, the team decided to redesign the polygons so that when a customer clicked on a particular "ethnicity" it would display as concentric rings of color on the map, indicating—in Byrnes's words—that "we're most confident here, but you could also be from here or here." Regions from which customers were attributed very low levels of ancestry (less than 5 percent) were displayed as a hollow polygon, signifying their low levels of confidence. In addition, the team included error margins in the bar charts conveying clients' "ethnicity" proportions, in an effort to communicate the probabilistic nature of the estimates.

As far as Byrnes could recall, the choice of the term "ethnicity" as a label for the genetic clusters produced by AncestryDNA was "[a decision that] was made not even really recognizing it was a decision. I think we rolled the product and that's what we called it initially and, for better or for worse, that's the term that we've used . . . and that's what the product is called." Here, the concept of ethnicity corresponds to a summary of genetic similarities found within a defined population and geographic region, coming to represent the essence of both that place and its "ancestral" people. Despite the claim by Novembre and colleagues that this correlation between people, land, and genes "naturally arises," genetic "ethnicities" are in fact highly purified categories. As we have seen, not just anyone's DNA can be included within this representation, but only those samples that contribute a clear "signal," adding to the (relative) discreteness of the genetic cluster. Moreover, many of the labels included in AncestryDNA's Ethnicity Reference Panel are not emic categories (in other words, what most local people from these regions would consider an ethnic group); for the most part, they correspond to nation-states or broad geographic regions, some of which comprise ethnically diverse populations. Yet, as Byrnes suggests, the idiom of genetic "ethnicity" is somehow intuitive, conveying the imagined kinship at the heart of collective identities articulated around a shared territory, history, and political constitution. In some cases, Byrnes pointed out to me, a single genetic cluster may encompass individuals living within a same region with strongly polarized ethnic identities, underlining the fact that groups "that have had centuries of fighting and anger really won't be that genetically distinct."[34]

Nonetheless, the concept of ethnicity always invokes difference: the presence of an "in-group" and an "out-group." While customers typically find that their results include a range of genetic "ethnicities," they will inevitably be excluded from some categories on the basis of how portions of their genome are assigned to different populations. Analyzed in this way, the concept of genetic "ethnicity" is revealed to be both relational and relative, recalling the observation made by Amade M'charek that "race does not materialize in the body, but rather in relations established between a variety of entities, including bodies."[35] In this case, the relation is set up between "rooted" populations (groups who know their ancestry and can demonstrate a long-standing link to a particular territory) and "unrooted" populations— those whose ancestry is (more) "mixed" and whose ancestors have undergone recent migrations. A further imagined relation links together "genes," "land," and "people" (echoing conventional notions of ethnicity that evoke a natural link between blood, soil, and origin)[36] so that the presence of a given combination of haplotypes within an individual's genome is coded as a connection to a particular "homeland" and extended kinship community. Producers and users of DNA ancestry tests often speak of genetic "ethnicity" or ancestry as a form of tangible heritage, congealed in the body, as something to *have* or *not have*, in greater or smaller proportions (I return to this theme in chapter 4). At the same time, owing to the test's design, genetic "ethnicity" is something that is expected to change over time—ideally becoming more detailed and refined, capable of portraying an individual's ancestral makeup with ever-greater accuracy. Hence, rather than capturing a natural liaison between genes, people, and soil, genetic "ethnicity" can aptly be thought of as a product: something that is *made* and which can be adjusted and perfected in response to the demands of particular consumers.

Feedback Loops

When building their genetic "ethnicity" product, AncestryDNA's scientists made pragmatic choices about which populations it should represent. While aiming for a test with worldwide coverage, they also sought to satisfy the interests of the company's existing customer base (chiefly, Euro-Americans and Europeans) as well as future target demographics (e.g., African Americans) by providing high levels of resolution for these groups' likely ancestral regions. The geographic distribution of the twenty "ethnic regions" boasted by the first version of the product in 2012 seems indicative of this logic of supply and demand: Europe was represented by seven "ethnic regions" and Africa by five (with a large area between Libya and Ethiopia unaccounted for), whereas a single region each was used to represent "East Asian," "Native North American," and "Native South American" populations.[37]

The release of AncestryDNA's new genetic test aroused excitement and interest among the online genetic-genealogy community—an informal, international network of seasoned and professional genealogists dedicated to sharing tips and information, often through the medium of blogs, about incorporating DNA data into family history research. Some genetic-genealogy bloggers post regular updates on the development and release of commercial DNA ancestry tools within the DTC testing industry. They offer unofficial advice for other genealogists looking to take a DNA test, and in some cases they take on roles as spokespeople for the community, by lobbying companies to make changes and improvements to their products. Some of these individuals were quick to post reviews about the new product and soon highlighted apparent faults in the test's "ethnicity" estimation tool, such as unexpectedly high levels of "Scandinavian" or "Finnish" ancestry or completely absent "French" ancestry.[38]

Some genetic genealogists made efforts to rationalize these "faults"—for instance, by signaling the disparity between the temporal scope of the DNA analysis (potentially relating to hundreds or thousands of years in the past) and most genealogists' own research. Blaine Bettinger, who writes at the blog "The Genetic Genealogist," offered this advice to test-takers:

> Remember that "Everyone Has Two Family Trees—A Genealogical Tree and a Genetic Tree." Your Genealogical Tree is the tree containing ALL of your ancestors. However, only a *tiny subset* of these individuals actually (randomly) contributed DNA to the genome that you walk around with today. These ancestors are the only individuals in your Genetic Tree. It has been estimated, for example, that at 10 generations, only about 10–12% of ancestors in your Genealogical Tree are actually in your Genetic Tree! Accordingly, even if a decent percentage of your ancestors at 10 generations originated in the British Isles, there is a possibility that your DNA—and thus your Genetic Ethnicity Prediction—could include very little or absolutely no British Isles ancestry, simply because of the rules of genetics.[39]

Other bloggers continued to voice their frustration, urging AncestryDNA to reconsider the accuracy of its algorithms, whose results were so out of line with their own genealogical research. Roberta Estes ("DNAeXplained") wrote the following in relation to a problem—the overestimation or misidentification of Scandinavian "ethnicity" proportions—that had been identified by numerous test-takers:

> The problem is that [AncestryDNA's] admixture percentages are simply WRONG. Period. Not a "tiny error," not "needs tweaking," utterly entirely wrong. Throw it out and start over wrong. There are

no secret Scandinavians hiding in the bushes, or in everyone's family tree, and the fact that they are embracing their error and trying to turn a dime by telling people that they DO have a huge amount of mythical Scandinavian blood and they just need to use Ancestry's tools to search longer and harder is not only infuriating, it's unethical and self-serving.[40]

In January 2013, Ancestry's official blog site published a message from Ken Chahine, senior vice president of AncestryDNA, stating:

Before AncestryDNA, ethnic origins were largely a breakdown of continental ethnicities. Most of us, however, don't need a genetic test to determine whether we are European, African, or Asian. So, we challenged ourselves to push the boundaries of the science and attempt a more granular ethnic breakdown, especially within Europe. . . . The good news is that the genetic ethnicity prediction is working, albeit with some challenges. Central Europeans present the most significant difficulty, especially the French, Germans, and Dutch. With few geographic barriers and extensive human population movement, their genetic signatures are very similar and difficult to distinguish. The British Isles and Scandinavia are more genetically distinct, but their signatures partially overlap with each other, as well as with parts of Central Europe. All of this makes it difficult to assign predicted ethnicities. So, let's say your German ancestry doesn't seem to be showing up in your DNA ethnicity results or it seems like you're getting a bit too much Scandinavian, know that the ethnicity prediction can be updated over time as we make advancements in the area.[41]

Chahine's comments gave the impression of a steady march toward the evolution of genetic categories that would predict, with increasing precision, the "true" ancestry of test-takers. His post began by setting up a commonsense link between the "obvious" distinctions among continental groups and the ease with which these populations could be distinguished genetically. In contrast, telling people from neighboring countries apart on a genetic level was portrayed as a difficult task, due to the geographic and historical factors that make these groups more genetically intertwined. Pursuing this goal, he claimed, may even require "push[ing] the boundaries of science." The acknowledgment of this scientific challenge was nonetheless juxtaposed with the expectation that, since "French," "German," and "Dutch" are culturally recognizable categories, they ought to be distinguishable on a genetic level, too. It seems the tendency to assume that social identities have a genetic counterpart is often irresistible, even among geneticists.[42]

Despite Chahine's insistence that the genetic test was "working," the complaints prompted AncestryDNA's scientific team to return to the drawing board in an effort to improve the product's "ethnicity" estimates. The outcome of this process was the release of a major update in September 2013, in which the total number of "ethnic regions" was expanded from twenty to twenty-six and the number of European "ethnicities" from six to eight. The new categories seemed to demonstrate the progress made by the Ancestry-DNA team in distinguishing between the "difficult" European "ethnic" groups evoked by Chahine. Whereas most of the original European "ethnicities" had been expressed as relatively broad areas, meant to encompass clusters of neighboring countries (e.g., "Central European," "Eastern European," "Finnish/Volga-Ural," "British Isles"), the new analysis included various categories corresponding to just one or two nation-states (e.g., "Finland/Northwest Russia," "Iberian Peninsula," "Great Britain," "Ireland"), conveying a sense of the test's increased biogeographical precision. The overall effect is one of a feedback loop, where the test's robustness is judged according to its ability to match the conceptions of ancestry defined by its users.

At the same time, as Byrnes explained to me, for some customers the test's credibility also relied on it being capable of offering new clues and not simply confirming their prior expectations. He recalled one member posting a comment on AncestryDNA's online message-board, stating her suspicions that the company was not actually testing customers' DNA but rather "looking at people's trees and just making a pie chart," since her own "ethnicity" results matched her pedigree so precisely. Byrnes told me: "We were high-fiving, saying 'this is awesome,' we'd picked up this pretty small contributor of ancestry in her genetic makeup. But from her perspective, without any information, she said 'I think it's all hocus pocus.'"[43]

Another major update to the product in 2013 was the introduction of six new West African "ethnic regions," an addition that was intended to appeal to African American customers by offering an unparalleled level of geographic precision for the region in comparison to other autosomal test providers. Yet, whereas Euro-American users of the test have been able to verify its accuracy at reporting their ancestral origins—and even to lobby for the test's algorithm to be tweaked in order to better reflect their ideal genealogical time frame—the lack of similarly detailed pedigrees reaching back before slavery makes it difficult for African American genealogists to do the same. Despite the rigorous laboratory tests described in the previous section, Byrnes acknowledged that it was hard to know for sure how well the test was assigning the ancestry of African American customers. In his words, "One thing that's really interesting that we have noticed is that the vast number of our customers with significant West African ancestry tend to get assigned to multiple . . . regions of West Africa—in fact, often they get ancestry for almost all of [the six regions]. To some people from the outside this might look like, 'Hey, maybe Ancestry's tests aren't working very well, it can't really distinguish the regions.' So that's one possible explanation, right—the other is that all of those ancestries arrived on the coast of North America and have subsequently been mixed in multiple generations."

While AncestryDNA's West African admixture analysis has proved popular among some test-takers, the responses from African American genetic genealogists have been ambivalent. Shannon Christmas—an urban planner who took up genetic genealogy as a second career and now presents regular talks and webinars on the topic—was skeptical about the genealogical value of the "ethnicity" estimates. Christmas told me that when he first tested with AncestryDNA his results reported 85 percent West African and 15 percent British ancestry. After the 2013 update, it attributed him 83 percent West African ancestry, portioned out across practically every country in the region. While this result coincided with Christmas's expectations, based on his knowledge of the slave trade and the history of mixtures among African groups following their arrival in the Americas, he stressed that the current science was insufficient to discern reliably between different parts of West Africa or Europe. Hence, AncestryDNA's claims to accuracy were, in his view, "a fantasy."[44] Similarly, Nicka Smith, a professional photographer, speaker, and documentarian who hosts a YouTube channel called BlackProGen LIVE on "people of color genealogy and family history," has advised her followers to take genetic "ethnicity" results with a pinch of salt. In her words:

> You are subject to the company's database. Unfortunately, genetics
> is pretty European dominant or Euro-centric, so when it comes to
> people like me who have a number of different ethnicities . . . our
> representation is actually not very large in these databases. With
> that said, you have to make sure that you don't take the percentages
> that they give you to heart, or that they're the law. It may be
> skewed, it may not be right, it may change—it really all depends
> on how companies define certain ethnic groups, so as new datasets

become available you just have to kind of keep in mind that the results in terms of the percentages may not be absolutely accurate.[45]

Generally, the African American genetic genealogists I interviewed were less interested in their admixture results than in other tools offered by autosomal DNA test providers that could help them further their genealogical research.[46] These include relative-matching tools, which generate links between participating clients based on the number and length of DNA tracts shared across their genome (a technique known in the industry as "identity by descent," IBD), and chromosome "browsers" or "painters"—programs that allow genealogists to compare the locations on their chromosomes where they share DNA with genetic relatives, which can help confirm from which ancestor a DNA match is inherited (AncestryDNA does not currently offer a chromosome browser, a fact that is particularly galling to some genetic genealogists, who explained to me that they have been requesting this feature for several years). Moreover, some genealogists raised concerns that the tendency of companies to focus their advertising almost uniquely on genetic "ethnicity" matching as the prime feature of their DNA products could discourage "neophyte" roots-seekers from cultivating other key aspects of family history research—for instance, collecting oral histories and engaging in archival research. In a blog post entitled "25 Do's and Don'ts of DNA," Melvin Collier ("Roots Revealed") writes:

> I realize that many people are only interested in those doggone admixture results, and don't give a rat's ass about family connections, ancestors' names, etc. That's fine. If this is you, please know that you are irritating many serious researchers, especially those who are high DNA matches to you. Your DNA match may be the key to solving a longtime family mystery. You are truly doing yourself a disservice, because many of us serious researchers are quite willing to tell you more about your family history and why you are sharing a good amount of DNA. It's *your* loss. Please, believe that![47]

Unattainable Objectivities

What can be said of the objectivity of DNA ancestry tests? In her discussion of the concept of objectivity in the classification of wines as conforming to particular terroirs, Geneviève Teil argues that the terroir is not an objective value, but rather an object constantly in the making, whose truth is, probably, ultimately unattainable. In her words: "Terroir and its taste are not predefined 'things,' 'data' already there, ready to be perceived by the different tasters' sensory apparatus. Each wine, as well as its judgment, is nothing but the plural, diverse, and relatively unpredictable result of a production process."[48] In contrast to the scientists in Teil's study, who "suspect that [the notion of terroir] is in fact a self-referential construction without any 'objective' referent,"[49] many DNA ancestry companies seem committed to the quest of defining genetic "ethnicity" as an ever more stable and precise object, even while the scientists who work on these techniques acknowledge that predicting "ethnic" inheritance is not—and likely will never be—an exact science.

Customers' evaluations of the credibility of the tests depend largely on their ability to cross-reference the results with other forms of evidence. Sometimes this takes the form of personal genealogical research; where this is lacking, however, customers rely on the testimonies of other "expert" users such as genetic genealogists or "native" informants who have taken a DNA test and can comment on how well it reflected their known ancestry and origins.[50] A range of explanations are also provided by companies to account for any unexpected results. For instance, you may not have inherited as much DNA as expected from a particular ancestor; or the genetic "signatures" of neighboring populations are very similar, so a "true" result might show up in another category; or "ethnicity" estimation is a work in progress. . . . [51] In this way, genetic "ethnicity" products seem to thrive by inhabiting the gap between what is known and what can(not) be proven.[52] The promise of future updates plays into this uncertainty and can even add to the attraction of the tests by constantly feeding the interest of customers.

For DNA test-takers, the pursuit of objectivity is also complicated by the range of products on offer from different companies, each boasting their own reference panel, SNP chip,[53] modes of categorization, and methodology. Technologically, the market is uneven. While most large DNA ancestry-testing companies use high-resolution genotyping approaches, they sell alongside companies that are still using low-grade ancestry informative markers (AIMs) and uniparental tests for "ethnicity" estimates. Even when testing among the more technologically advanced companies, customers may still receive quite a range of ancestry results, as I discovered after having my own DNA tested with several different services. As a White, British-born woman, with three grandparents born in Britain and one in Poland (and no other known ancestors from other locations), I expected my results to show a mixture of North-Western and Eastern European ancestry, with

Sarah Abel

Dashboard

Ancestry

Relatives

Wellbeing

Store

Profiles

Account

Help

Sign out

Collapse

● Great Britain and Ireland	81.2%
◦ South Central England	22.5% >
◦ East Anglia	14% >
◦ Northern Ireland and Southwest Scotland	11.1% >
◦ Cornwall	7.5% >
◦ Central England	4.4% >
◦ Northumbria	4.3% >
◦ South Yorkshire	3.9% >
◦ South England	3.7% >
◦ Southeast England	2.5% >
◦ Devon	2.3% >
◦ South Wales	2% >
◦ South Wales Border	1.6% >
◦ Ireland	1.5% >
● Europe (East)	11.9%
◦ Mordovia	11.9% >
● Europe (North and West)	5.3%
◦ Northeast Germanic	5.3% >
Near East	1.5%
● Levant	1.5%

© mapbox

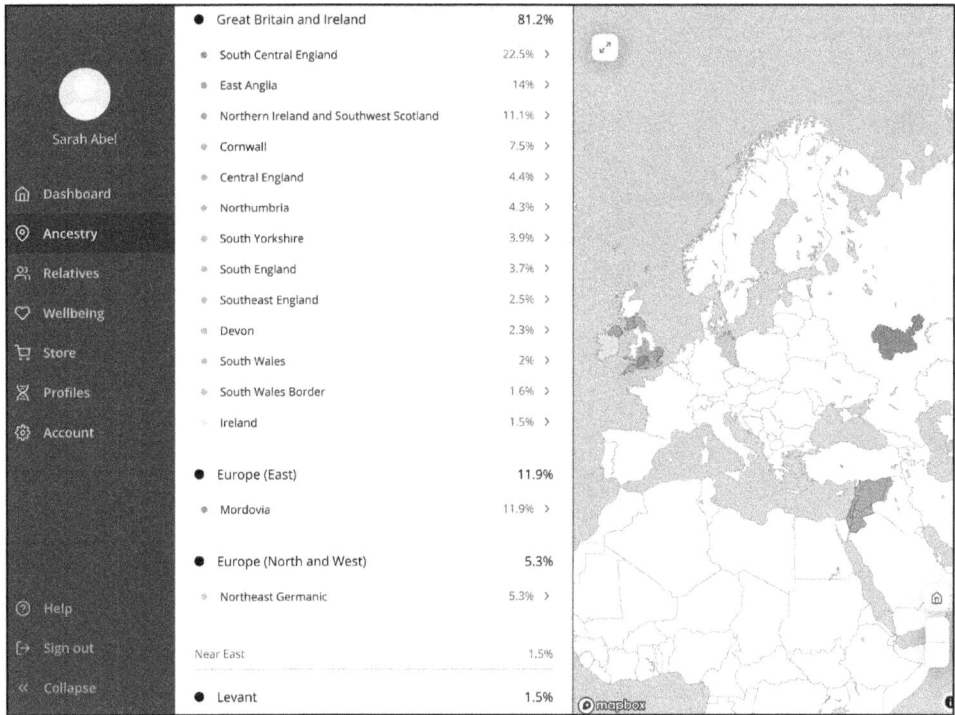

FIGURE 3.2 Author's DNA ancestry results by LivingDNA, December 2020. my.LivingDNA.com.

the strongest signal in the British Isles. Most (but not all) of the companies agreed in assigning me "100 percent European ancestry," the majority in North-Western and Eastern regions.[54] When it came to specific places of origin, however, the results were much more varied. For instance, in 2019 my "British Isles" ancestry (a region that is generally well represented in the reference databases of U.S.-based ancestry-testing companies) was estimated, respectively, at 77 percent (LivingDNA), 64 percent (AncestryDNA), 27 percent (23andMe), and zero percent (FamilyTreeDNA). A year later, in 2020, following routine updates by several of these companies, the figures stood at 81 percent (LivingDNA), 76 percent (AncestryDNA), 27 percent (23andMe), and 81 percent (FamilyTreeDNA) (see figures 3.2 to 3.5).

The colorful maps and charts produced by DNA ancestry companies are examples of what Bruno Latour has described as "immutable mobiles": scientific inscriptions that can be copied faithfully and exactly, and then transmitted and disseminated to audiences all over the world without any loss in

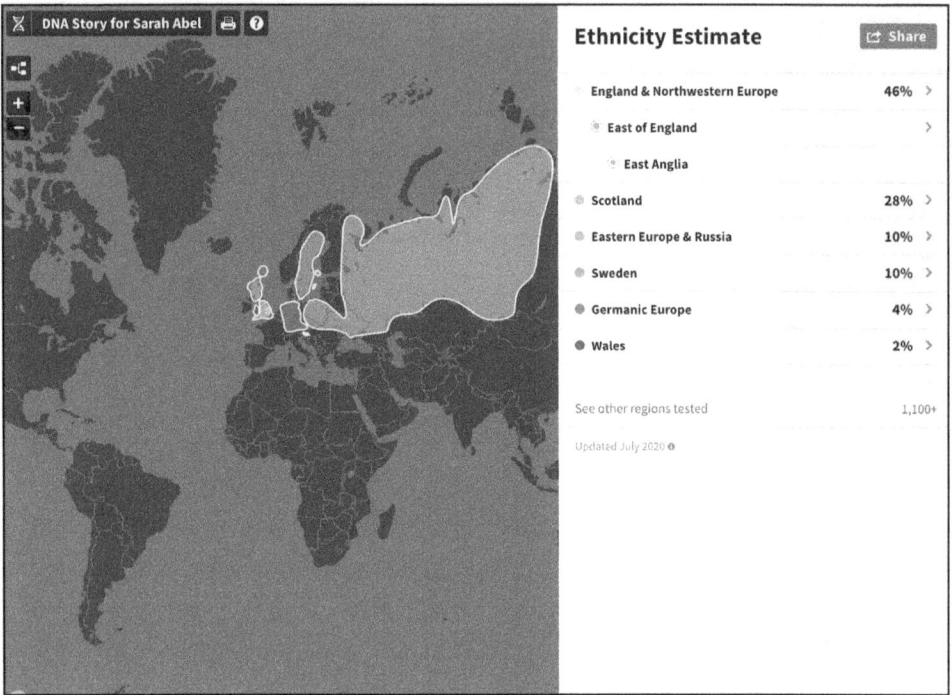

Ethnicity Estimate

England & Northwestern Europe	46% >
East of England	>
East Anglia	
Scotland	28% >
Eastern Europe & Russia	10% >
Sweden	10% >
Germanic Europe	4% >
Wales	2% >
See other regions tested	1,100+
Updated July 2020	

FIGURE 3.3 Author's DNA ancestry results by AncestryDNA, December 2020. Ancestry.com.

quality or meaning. These visual devices attest to the "two-way connection" the analysis constructs between the test-taker and reference populations via the matching traces in their DNA.[55] Personalized genetic reports are designed to be reproduced with ease across digital platforms. A "share" button on AncestryDNA's "DNA story" portal generates three alternative visual summaries of the client's estimated "ethnicity regions," with an option to save the image or share it directly to Twitter. These strategies, which suggest a desire to display a scientific "proof" of identity, fixing the evidence through replicable inscriptions, seem at odds with the mutability of results produced among and within companies. As suggested by John and Jean Comaroff, there remains a tension between a perception of ethnic identity as something innate, essential, immutable, versus something to be chosen, performed, and interchanged.[56] A similar effect arises from the commercial alliances arranged by DNA ancestry-testing companies to encourage customers to "buy into" their results and extend their "ethnic experience." In the past, AncestryDNA and 23andMe have both partnered with travel com-

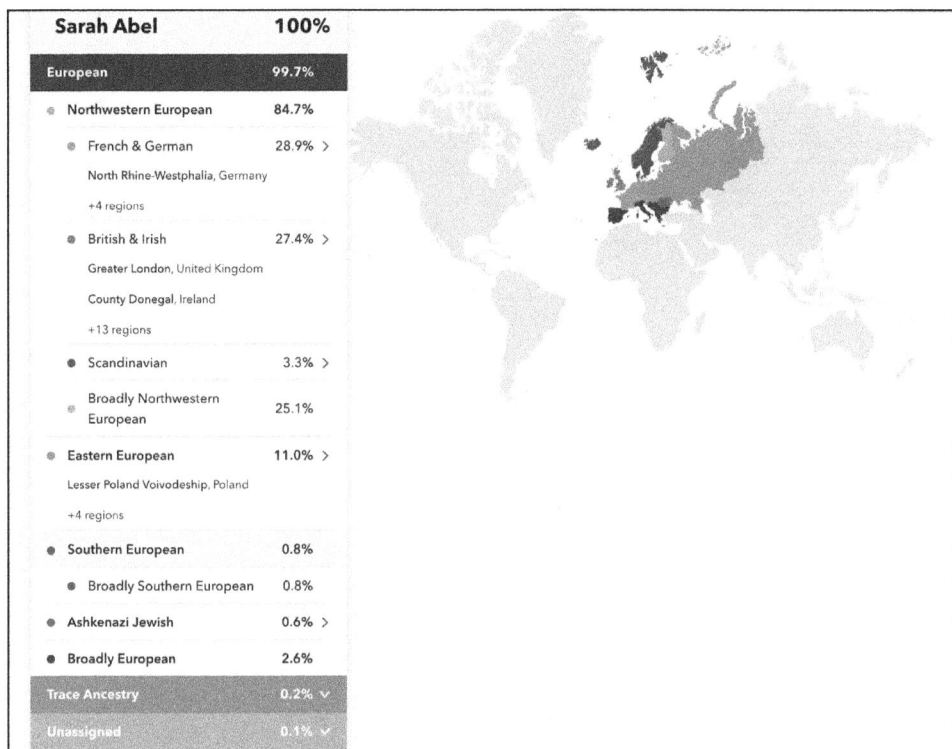

Sarah Abel	100%
European	**99.7%**
○ Northwestern European	84.7%
● French & German	28.9% >
North Rhine-Westphalia, Germany	
+4 regions	
● British & Irish	27.4% >
Greater London, United Kingdom	
County Donegal, Ireland	
+13 regions	
● Scandinavian	3.3% >
○ Broadly Northwestern European	25.1%
○ Eastern European	11.0% >
Lesser Poland Voivodeship, Poland	
+4 regions	
○ Southern European	0.8%
● Broadly Southern European	0.8%
○ Ashkenazi Jewish	0.6% >
● Broadly European	2.6%
Trace Ancestry	**0.2% ⌄**
Unassigned	**0.1% ⌄**

FIGURE 3.4 Author's DNA ancestry results by 23andMe, December 2020. 23andMe.com.

panies like Momondo (whose viral video campaign was described in the opening pages of this book) and Airbnb, offering clients the chance to win a holiday to one or more of the countries listed in their DNA results, consolidating their sense of connection through the increasingly popular genre of the "roots tour." Other commercial collaborations invite test-takers to cultivate affiliations to particular cultural and national identities from the comfort of their own home by downloading a bespoke "DNA" music playlist (Spotify) or supporting their new "home countries" in international events like the Eurovision song contest or the FIFA World Cup. In chapters 4 and 5, I consider this phenomenon further from the perspective of DNA test-takers, examining the instances when social boundaries and ethical considerations impinge on and limit test-takers' adoption of genetic categories, pitting shared DNA against lived experience as the main criterion for claiming particular racial or ethnic identities.

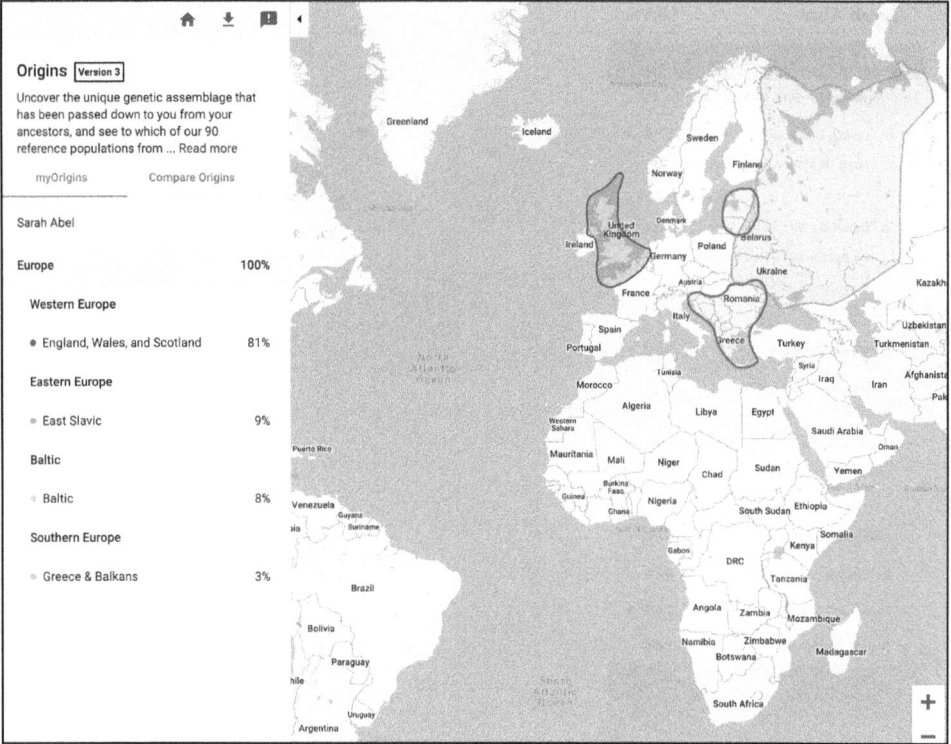

FIGURE 3.5 Author's DNA ancestry results by FamilyTreeDNA, December 2020. FamilyTreeDNA.com.

Flattened Histories

Meanwhile, the new generation of autosomal genetic "ethnicity" products has not escaped all of the methodological and epistemological problems associated with earlier DNA ancestry-testing models, such as those discussed in chapter 2. A persistent question is how to appropriately historicize these data, which capture genomic admixture from anywhere between a hundred to a thousand years in the past. This potentially deep chronological scale is not reflected in the labels that are given to genetic "ethnicity" clusters, which usually refer to contemporary states and groups. Following a presentation of AncestryDNA's new West African panel at a 2013 conference on genomics and the history of the African diaspora, an audience member pointed out that the six regions evoked by the test corresponded to geopolitical borders that were mostly established *after* the abolition of the transatlantic trade, indicating that they could not be treated as true ancestral categories for African American test-takers seeking their origins prior to slavery. She stated, "I'm a little disturbed by, you know, going 'oh, and you're from the Cameroon.' What does that mean? There wasn't a Cameroon."[57]

Furthermore, the databases of AncestryDNA, 23andMe, MyHeritage, FamilyTreeDNA, and other comparable autosomal test providers remain far from "representative" of African genetic diversity. These companies' reference panels and member databases are still disproportionately Eurocentric (a bias that mirrors the production of genomic datasets globally).[58] Many of them also tend to be U.S.-centric. For example, the original decision of U.S.-based autosomal test providers like AncestryDNA and 23andMe to focus their databases on West African reference populations broadly reflects the dynamics of the transatlantic slave trade toward the United States; however, they may be less representative of historical African migrations to other parts of the Americas and the Caribbean. The Brazilian trade routes, for instance, also encompassed parts of Central and East Africa, like Angola and Mozambique, and as a result admixture estimates provided to Afro-Brazilian customers may be less likely to reflect the true range of their African ancestry.

Companies continue to improve their coverage of regions outside of Europe, with the aim of producing "better value" for test-takers of different ancestral backgrounds. In early 2020, for instance, the British company LivingDNA unveiled what it claimed to be "the most advanced test for people with African ancestry," boasting "up to five times the detail of any other DNA test." The analysis draws on publicly available datasets produced by independent research studies into African population structures and calculates customers' admixture results in reference to seventy-two "distinct" African groups. Unlike competing autosomal companies, the LivingDNA test labels these genetic clusters after culturally defined ethnic groups: "Tikar," "Mende," "Fula," "Mankinka," and so on.[59] This innovation may be welcomed by some African American roots-seekers, whose fundamental aim is to recover a connection to named African ethnic groups with a distinct cultural heritage. On the other hand, for genealogists who are interested in tracing the origins of *particular* ancestors at *specific* points in history, this approach may still be considered unhelpful. It is one thing to know you share ancestry with a given *contemporary* group but another to understand when this connection originated, and through which ancestor.

A fundamental issue with autosomal "ethnicity" reports is that they convey information in an essentially *ahistorical* manner. It is clear that many U.S. test-takers are interested in recovering their "Old World" origins: the locations and communities in which their ancestors were living directly before their arrival in the Americas, at given points over the past 100 to 500 years. Yet, expressing these matches through the idiom of genetic "ethnicity" gives the erroneous impression that the rest of the world's populations remained essentially static and unchanged throughout this tumultuous period in global history—as if they were exempt from the impacts of centuries of colonialism, slave trades, mass migrations, and war. As Lundy Braun and Evelynn Hammonds have signaled, the fixing of cultural boundaries among African "tribal" groups was one of the goals of European colonial projects in the region—an effect that has since been naturalized by successive scientific mapping projects since the 1950s, including recent DNA sampling efforts that rely on ethnographic maps to decide which groups to approach for inclusion in their databases.[60] Genetic "ethnicity" reports arguably play into this simplistic, colonial-era perspective of African populations as discrete and invariable cultural and genetic units. What's more, representing genetic ancestry in this way reinforces the perception that these "Old World" identities are the main (or even the only) prize worth excavating from our ancestral histories—a notion that fetishizes the moment of separation from an ostensibly "pristine" precolonial origin and deflects attention from more recent family histories rooted in American societies.[61]

According to biological anthropologist and sociologist Shay-Akil McLean, this tendency to focus on historically "stable," "isolated," and genetically "unmixed" groups is widespread in genetics and has the effect of obscuring the way that "conquest, genocidal, and settler-colonial processes" have shaped the genetic structures of contemporary populations. McLean proposes that an alternative theoretical approach, centered on the notion of "eventful temporality," can help give historical depth and context to these genetic structures, framing them not as static "ethnic" essences but as the result of "dynamic, contingent, and chanceful relationships among conditions, actors, events, and human practice."[62] In recent years, AncestryDNA has developed a new ancestry-testing feature called Genetic Communities that bears some similarities to McLean's "eventful temporality" approach. The tool is designed to detect genetic similarities among test-takers relating to historical gene flows thought to have occurred since their ancestors' arrival in the Americas; the idea is that such patterns could indicate a common ancestry inherited from a group brought together by historical migrations or settlement events. Once detected, these putative genetic connections are given additional context by drawing on test-takers' genetic "ethnicity" profiles, as well as geographic, chronological, and onomastic information uploaded to their family trees (for instance, by searching for recurring places and surnames among ancestors' genealogical profiles, relating to a specific historical period).[63] At the time of this writing, AncestryDNA has established ninety-four "genetic communities" to which customers of African American and Afro-Caribbean descent may be linked (the feature does not currently cater to other African-descendant American populations), within a time frame spanning the 1700s to the 1950s. Customers who are matched to a particular community receive a likelihood rating, which expresses the confidence of the match, and additional details explaining the community's sociohistorical origins. For example, "Alabama, Georgia & South Carolina African Americans. Members with this community may have ancestors that were enslaved and working on rice plantations in South Carolina and Georgia. When cotton fields came to the area in the late 1700s, many enslaved African Americans were brought to work those fields. Following the Civil War, the Great Depression, and World War II, many South Carolinians followed rail lines up North to New York and Philadelphia. This group was one of many communities that were part of the Great Migration—which was the movement of millions of African Americans during the 1900s from the South to cities in the North and West."[64] While many of these communities still tend to be expressed in ethnic terms (e.g., "Alabama, Georgia & South Carolina African Americans," "Munster Irish," "French Canadians"), the feature nonetheless represents an effort to provide test-takers with clues about the sociohistorical and demographic events that may have marked their families, as well as the routes taken by their ancestors *since* their arrival in the Americas.

Global Biological Citizens?

I want to end this chapter by returning to the paradigm of biological citizenship proposed by Nikolas Rose and Carlos Novas.[65] Earlier, I suggested that DNA ancestry-testing could be considered a kind of "technology of the self," oriented, like DTC services in the biomedical field, toward practices of self-improvement and recovery. In this case, rather than addressing a physiological condition, ancestry tests are aimed at helping individuals retrieve ethnic and geographic connections lost through processes of migration, separation, and colonialism—thus helping heal traumas that have resonated down through the generations. Individuals who have taken these tests are sometimes moved to describe themselves as "citizens of the world," based on evidence of the multiple populations worldwide with whom they share an intimate genetic link. While the benefits for test-takers seem great, they are less clear for the groups whose DNA facilitates these connections.

Critics have noted how some DNA ancestry-testing companies call on customers' sense of altruism, asking them to "gift" their genomic data to medical research, then converting it into a form of free labor (or rather, labor that the client has partially paid for).[66] Although the exchange has a reciprocal element, it is sharply uneven. Customers receive insights into their personal ancestry and medical predispositions, while the company is able to monetize their data by sharing mass datasets with pharmaceutical businesses for tens of millions of dollars.[67] Individuals and groups who contribute DNA for reference panels are typically promised even less. When the scientists of the SMGF began collecting for their database, they offered $10 each to students in Provo, Utah, in exchange for a blood sample and were surprised at the enthusiastic responses they received. During their sampling trips outside of the United States, Woodward explained to me that the team told their donors quite honestly not to expect anything in return for the gift of their genetic and genealogical information. Their aim was to build an online database that would eventually allow access to people all over the world, turning these lineages into a kind of world heritage; however, nothing concrete was guaranteed.[68] Although for several years the SMGF collection *was* made publicly available through a dedicated web portal, the site was shut down in 2015 after it came to light that the database had been used for evidence in a cold-case murder investigation.[69] Currently, it can only be accessed partially and indirectly through AncestryDNA's genetic "ethnicity" test.

In recent years, Indigenous scientists and activists in the United States and Canada have redoubled their critiques of the genetic ancestry-testing companies that levy "Native American" DNA (often obtained without full community consent) in ways that can legitimize and even condone claims on their identities by non-Indigenous people. Such claims are not only politically costly, they can also contribute to racializing such groups, portraying membership as strictly a matter of "blood" rather than the outcome of a conjunction of formal, legal, historical, and cultural factors.[70] Groups that are already included in the reference databases of DNA ancestry-testing companies have little leeway to resist being co-opted into the two-way connection these technologies set up; consumers, meanwhile, wield comparatively more collective power to demand the addition of new samples to improve the estimates for a particular "ethnic region." Since customers are disproportionately centered in the Global North (in particular, North America and Europe), this arrangement echoes uncomfortably what Jenny Reardon and Kim TallBear have identified as "the old and familiar position of [Europeans] making a moral claim on the natural resources of indigenous peoples."[71] Notwithstanding their good intentions, the desires of scientists and ancestry companies to collect the DNA and genealogies of Indigenous groups as a form of "world heritage" can be interpreted as a form of "salvage anthropology," which anticipates that such groups may soon disappear[72]—a notion that many Native and Indigenous American communities have been fighting against for centuries, amidst repeated state-sponsored efforts to dispossess groups of their ancestral lands, eradicate them through wars, or "acculturate" Native children by removing them from their families. Despite such groups' opposition to these products, the "biological citizenship" fostered by DNA ancestry-testing companies is not founded on national legal or political frameworks, but rather operates in the fuzzy, deregulated economic space of the international market. As the above examples suggest, this is a space in which "not all have equal citizenship."[73]

There are, additionally, crossovers into the realm of political citizenship, where the expansion of the DNA ancestry industry overlaps with the spread of surveillance networks, raising the potential for ethical and privacy violations. In recent years, accounts have emerged of DTC genetic ancestry-testing databases being used by law enforcement officials in attempts to solve cold cases. DNA profiles are uploaded to the platforms and the automatically generated genetic and genealogical matches among existing customers can provide additional clues for identifying a suspect or missing person.[74] While some companies have taken a public stand against such practices, on the basis that they are conducted without members' consent and constitute an infringement of their privacy, in practice it is hard for businesses to identify or prevent such undercover uses of their databases. Others have agreed to process samples from agencies like the FBI as if they were regular customers, requiring a court order for law enforcement agencies to acquire further information.[75] Similarly concerning are reports of border agencies using DNA ancestry tests to determine the nationality of detained migrants who lack necessary documentation of their identity. Such cases—which are likely to disproportionately affect migrants from the Global South—risk treating DNA as a silent witness whose evidence may be used against the individual's nationality claims, to speed up deportation procedures.[76] Beneath the celebration of family and ethnic heritage, of openness and diversity that is feted by these companies, there remains a potential for human rights infringements and racializing tendencies that cuts both ways, affecting consumers *and* contributors of genetic ancestry.

4 Marked Bodies

· ·

Commercial DNA tests are frequently presented to the public as technologies that can, and even *should*, challenge our lay conceptions of race, ethnicity, and national identity. They are pitched as having the potential to open up possibilities for individuals to recuperate long-lost kinship connections, identify simultaneously with multiple ancestries and imagined communities, or embrace altogether new forms of self-identification. At the same time, critics have raised concerns that the spread of personalized DNA ancestry technologies may lead to a "geneticization" of race, reinforcing beliefs that racial identities are "hardwired" rather than socially and historically constructed and/or leading individuals to alter their modes of identification in line with their DNA ancestry results.[1]

To date, empirical studies of DNA ancestry-testing practices in the United States have observed that test-takers are not simply replacing their existing ethnoracial identities with their received genetic ancestry information. Instead, test-takers tend to engage in modes of "affiliative self-fashioning," selectively adopting new forms of identification from the "genetic options" provided in their DNA report.[2] These observations connect to a broader literature that has underlined the role of choice in the definition of personal identities in the United States, since biological-essentialist conceptions of race have become less widespread.[3] Contrary to claims that DNA testing will logically lead to a popular resurgence of these perspectives, Nadia Abu El-Haj has argued that the values of agency and choice are hardwired into the DNA ancestry industry. The widespread availability of these services means that one can now choose (or not) to receive genetic information about one's ancestry, also which company to test with, which analysis to invest in (autosomal, mtDNA, Y-DNA, or a combination of all three), and whether to retest later with another business.[4] These selective behaviors have even been observed among White nationalists who take DNA tests to try and prove their racial "purity," a phenomenon that seems to challenge the idea that ancestry testing can act as an antidote to existing biological-essentialist racist ideologies.[5]

There have been fewer such studies in Brazil, given the relative paucity of commercial DNA ancestry-testing services in the country until very recently.[6] The existing research has tended to focus on the extent to which DNA ancestry reports match or contradict Brazilian concepts of racial difference, which are traditionally linked to visible phenotypic markers ("color," *cor*). In 2009, a study into Brazilian high school students' reactions to their personalized admixture results found that although DNA reports often contradicted test-takers' "color" identities, this rarely led to changes in forms of identification. On the contrary, many participants declared the results irrelevant to their personal identities—although some made speculative comments about the potential relevance of DNA ancestry results for gaining access to university quotas.[7] These findings seem to support the idea that Brazilian conceptions of race are still guided primarily by "color" rather than ancestry (as in the United States).[8] However, another Brazilian study, conducted among the families of Bahian individuals diagnosed as genetic carriers for sickle cell anemia, signaled that interviewees' perceptions of their racial identity drew on elements of *both* "color" and ancestry, which were interpreted in the light of existing myths of national identity as well as emergent discourses about Blackness and affirmative action initiatives.[9] Similar findings have arisen from studies among Colombian and Mexican DNA test-takers, where interviewees drew on a range of factors including "color," family and regional histories, national origin myths, and theories from the social and biological sciences to interpret their personal DNA ancestry estimates and to make sense of the broader ontological linkages between race and genomic ancestry.[10]

By comparing the experiences of Brazilian and U.S. individuals who underwent autosomal analyses, receiving a mixture of continental or (in the case of U.S. test-takers) "ethnic" ancestry results, this chapter attempts to discern how exactly DNA ancestry data feed into everyday practices of racial affiliation. My analysis draws on a cohort of interviews gathered from fifty participants of the CANDELA project in Brazil and forty-one DNA test-takers in the United States (my methodology and interview scripts are detailed in the appendix).[11]

One way to approach this comparison would be to highlight how these data are "read" differently in the light of the divergent national racial narratives (for instance, *mestiçagem* in the case of Brazil, and the "one-drop rule" in the United States). Yet, in recent years, scholars have signaled a growing convergence in institutional and lay conceptions of race between the two countries, bringing further complexities to this apparent dichotomy.[12] Since the 1970s, the U.S. government has recognized five ethnoracial categories in official forms and statistics (American Indian/Alaskan

Native; Asian/Pacific Islander; Black/African; Hispanic/Latino; White/European/Middle Eastern), ostensibly doing away with the binary order of the color line. In the 1990s, lobbying from multiracial activists spurred further shifts. Since 2000, U.S. citizens may now identify with one or more racial categories in census and other federal documents—although research suggests that still only a relatively small number actually choose this option.[13] Although official U.S. definitions of race still tend to be predominantly linked to ancestry, scholars have suggested patterns of racial stratification in the United States (propelled by de facto impacts of structural racism) are increasingly marked by gradations of skin color, similar to the "pigmentocratic" social structures observed in Brazil and other Latin American societies.[14] Thus, the phrase "person of color" has gained currency to signal how structural disadvantages and everyday racism can affect individuals of varying ancestral origins who, based on their phenotype, are racialized as "non-White."

Official Brazilian racial classifications continue to revolve around traditional "color" categories (branco/a, pardo/a, preto/a, amarelo/a) rather than ancestry, with the category indígena added in the early 1990s.[15] During the same period, Black movement activists lobbied for the introduction of the racial term negro/a into official statistics, in the aim of merging the "colors" pardo/a and preto/a under a broad "Afro-descendant" or "Black" category.[16] While the label negro/a has been adopted more readily by younger generations and members of the middle classes, many Brazilians still associate the term with negative connotations, preferring intermediate "color" labels on official forms, like moreno/a and pardo/a, which can refer to a range of phenotypes, from "light-skinned with dark hair" to "dark-skinned."[17] Recent research indicates that formal identification with the category pardo/a has increased since the 1990s—a possible consequence of the category being mobilized for the administration of race-based university quotas—and some scholars argue that the policies have had the effect of sharpening the demarcation between branco/a and pardo/a, introducing a tacit color line between "White" and "non-White."[18] Ethnographic research, meanwhile, has suggested that in everyday parlance, some Brazilians use a biracial schema alongside "color" designations as a way of signaling broad structural inequalities between Whites and people "of color" or "of the Black race."[19] At the same time, the idea of Brazilian national identity as essentially mestiço (mixed-race) remains strong among all sectors of the population.

Based on these events and conceptual shifts, the following is a series of hypotheses about how test-takers might interpret their admixture results.

First, evidence of mixed genomic inheritance might destabilize binary claims to Black or White racial identities (this could apply in both the United States and Brazil), lending greater legitimacy to "mixed" or "multiracial" categories. Alternatively, without disrupting existing racial binaries, the data could lead test-takers to reorient their racial identification. For instance, following the "one-drop rule," White U.S. test-takers might claim a Black identity after discovering minor levels of African genomic inheritance. In Brazil, where "racial" mixture is already held to be the norm, the results might be used pragmatically to "darken" or "lighten" the test-takers' claimed identities. An emphasis on Whitening would be coherent with the country's historical ideologies of *branqueamento*; on the other hand, the recent introduction of university quotas and prominence of Black movement discourses might incentivize Brazilians to claim a "darker" (*pardo/a* or *negro/a*) identity based on their DNA results.

Instead of imagining racial ideologies as discrete worldviews that uniformly permeate societies, Wendy Roth has argued that people tend to acquire multiple racial schemas over the course of their lifetimes, with some becoming more "salient and available than others, which leads individuals to activate them more easily and frequently."[20] During my interviews I observed that DNA reports tended to act like a mirror or prism for concepts of race and ethnicity,[21] opening them up to scrutiny and allowing test-takers to interpret their results in the light of various schemas. Taking account of these multiple and overlapping schemas allows me to detect not only divergences but resemblances among the experiences of Brazilian and U.S. test-takers who self-identify in equivalent racial terms. My analysis is therefore organized, in the first instance, around the question of how individuals' racial positionalities and adherence to particular racial discourses mediate their interpretations of their DNA results. Drawing inspiration from the existing literature, I emphasize how these data are evaluated in relation to other markers and dimensions of test-takers' ethnoracial identities (e.g., physical appearance, family lore, experiences of racism and racialization, feelings of cultural affiliation) and incorporated selectively into individuals' identity narratives. This approach allows me to delve deeper into the perceived relationship between appearance and ancestry (a theme that has been predominantly explored in Brazilian studies but less so in the United States) and the role of choice in the incorporation of genetic identities (a key theme in U.S. studies, which has been given less prominence in research into Brazilian ancestry-testing practices). How do test-takers reconcile their DNA ancestry data with other dimensions of their racial experience and identity when they do not coincide? To what extent are individuals (and indeed, *which* individuals?) free to choose their racial affiliations, based wholly or partially on their genomic ancestry data?

One limitation of interview-based studies of DNA ancestry-testing practices is that they tend to rely on abstract, hypothetical questions about how the new genetic knowledge has affected personal perceptions of race, ethnicity, identity, and so on. However, such processes of interpretation are never a sole undertaking, and self-perceptions of identity often conflict with how we are categorized by others. Where possible, I therefore draw attention to instances and contexts in which test-takers recalled feeling challenged or conflicted about their adoption of "genetic identities," whether by friends and family members or by the imposition of institutional categories—for instance, in census documents and university entrance or civil service exams, which require individuals to present a single and coherent racial identity. To what extent, and in which contexts, are genetic data seen to be more or less socially salient than other markers of racial identification?

Finally, it should be noted that while I used very similar scripts for my interviews in both countries, the personal genomic data received by Brazilian and U.S. participants varied substantially. The CANDELA volunteers all received their results in the form of a static document, which expressed their ancestry proportions in relation to just three continental groups, whereas many of the U.S. test-takers had their ancestry broken down into dozens of genetic "ethnicities," producing a wider range of possibilities for self-identification. The latter were also frequently given access to online services such as DNA "relative-matching" databases, which gave users additional tools for testing the validity of their genetic ancestry by gathering family history knowledge from users with whom they shared portions of DNA. The plethora of Facebook groups, Instagram threads, and blogs dedicated to the sharing of DNA results contributed to the perception among U.S. test-takers of ancestry testing as a dynamic, ongoing social experience. In comparison, while the CANDELA volunteers also took opportunities to discuss and compare their genetic results with other test-takers—whether in person (at the "sampling" days) or online in the dedicated Facebook group set up by the project's scientists—the sense of the social relevance of these results was much more restricted. I mention this to underline that it is not only the *content* of DNA ancestry reports but also the possibility of sharing, comparing, and publicly discussing results that informs these data's social significance and legitimacy as a basis for identity construction.

Blackness Out of Mixture

I begin by analyzing how participants of the CANDELA project in Brazil interpreted their results in relation to discourses about Blackness. Before taking their DNA test, many of the interviewees signaled that they saw genetics as potentially significant for informing their sense of racial identity. In the pretest questionnaires they filled out for CANDELA, most people ranked "knowing about my ancestors" and "knowing more about my roots" as the primary reasons for their interest in DNA testing, followed closely by "knowing more about my identity." In the questionnaire, participants were asked to estimate their genomic ancestry proportions (divided into African, European, and Indigenous American categories) and explain the basis for their predictions. Only ten of the fifty individuals I interviewed mentioned "family stories" or "genealogy" as the basis for these estimates, whereas thirty referred to their own "color" or "appearance," or those of their relatives. After receiving their DNA report, two-thirds of the interviewees stated that the results differed from their expectations regarding their ancestry (this proportion was lower among a sample of 320 individuals who responded to the postresults questionnaire sent by the CANDELA scientists: 51 percent said their results were "as expected"; 45 percent "different from expected"; and 5 percent "very different from expected"). Nonetheless, only seven interviewees said that the DNA ancestry-testing process had affected the way they thought about their identity, and just two declared that their results had led them to change the way they identified racially (one from *negra* to *parda*, and another from *parda* to *negra*).

Alondra Nelson has used the phrase "genealogical disorientation" to describe the often negative affective reactions she observed among African American DNA test-takers who found that their genetic identity did not coincide with prior beliefs about their origins or identity.[22] In contrast, while a large proportion of the CANDELA volunteers said they were surprised by their DNA results, this rarely triggered the sort of identity crisis described by Nelson. Instead, many of the Brazilian test-takers pointed to the variation of "colors" and racialized traits found in their own family trees as visible clues of this underlying genetic mixture, as well as to the "old sayings" that testified to Brazil's history of "racial" mixture. As one interviewee stated, "Everyone says that our country is *the* country of racial mixture . . . and that was only confirmed by the [DNA] results." Another volunteer referred to Brazil's "racial" mixture as "madness" (*uma loucura*), a phenomenon that naturally resisted attempts at systematization and order.

Ariana,[23] a student at the Universidade Estadual do Sudoeste da Bahia (UESB) in northeastern Brazil, who self-identified as *negra*, was one of the volunteers I interviewed who *did* experience a form of genealogical disorientation after her result showed a much higher proportion of European ancestry than she expected: 70 percent, rather than her predicted zero to 20 percent. When she shared the report with her family and friends, many of them "didn't believe the result. It was really unexpected for everyone and lots of them said it was false and the test was way off. Others got all 'critical,' saying I was *negra* with blue blood and other comments that I thought were funny, because even I fought with my result. . . . At the time [when I received the report] I thought it wasn't accurate, but then I calmed down and read all the material that came with the result, and I think it probably is accurate." When asked about whether the result had affected her sense of identity, Ariana stated that she "hadn't really thought about that." She continued to see herself as *negra*, which she defined as "someone with mid-tone or Black [*negra*] skin, who has kinky or tightly curled hair, a not very thin nose, among other characteristics, but someone who *can* be a successful person and who is growing all the time."

Sâmela, a student at the UESB, was also taken aback by her percentage of European ancestry (55 percent, rather than her predicted zero to 20 percent). She arrived at our interview wearing a bracelet in the colors of the Pan-African flag and explained that she saw her Black identity as a political statement, a recognition that Black Brazilians "still have to fight [for equality]." She said she found her result "surprising," and that it had provoked conversations at home about how it was "possible for me to have a lineage that was more White than Indian." However, she stated, "I don't think the genetic test influences what I think—whether I think I'm more Black or more White. But it made me reflect on that; knowing your genetic lineage is important. I'm glad I took the test." Whereas Ariana saw her Blackness as self-evident, based on certain phenotypic traits, Sâmela espoused one of the ideals of Brazil's Black movements when she claimed that being Black in Brazil has less to do with objective measures of ancestry or "color"; rather, it is a *choice* to recognize and embrace one's African and Indigenous origins and traits and, by the same token, to refuse the country's historical ideology of Whitening.[24] In this light, deciding not to mobilize a DNA ancestry result that could be perceived as contradicting one's chosen identity can be a way of exercising a Black political consciousness.

In other cases, though, the DNA results were perceived as helping solidify a claimed Black identity. Eduína, a student at the UESB, decided to take part in the CANDELA project because she thought it would help her identify an unusual surname that ran in her family. She knew that her family was "very mixed," and because of her tightly curled hair (*cabelo caracolado*), she thought she would have "a Black majority." In Eduína's words: "I was right, and I thought, 'oh, certainty,' I got certainty with the test." During our interview, Eduína spoke proudly and enthusiastically about how the test results (which attributed her 67 percent African ancestry) had helped her—and members of her family—to understand the truth about their racial identity:

> For me, [being *negra*] is recognition; now, I can have a better recognition. I can say, 'Look, I'm *negra*, my origin is . . . the most . . . I have origins from all three races, but the majority is Black,' and so on. . . . So it's better. I think it improved for me. I identified more [with it], I accepted [*assumi*] my origin. Before that, I felt embarrassed to say that I was *negra*. People here make comments about it, and so on. But nowadays I don't listen, I feel good, I feel happy, and that's that. . . . And also, with my family it got better as well . . . even with my own mother, who is the same color as me— she didn't call herself *negra*, she thought she wasn't *negra*. Then I said to her, "Mom, it's like this," and I explained, and . . . her level of knowledge improved as well.

In her narrative, Eduína identified the experience of receiving the DNA results as a trigger in her own process of assuming a Black racial consciousness. Previously, she stated, she had always identified as *parda*—a label that suggests "racial" mixture, but which can be used in Brazil to refer to people of diverse origins (African, Indigenous American, Middle Eastern, among others).[25] According to Eduína, the DNA test helped her understand the Black movements' criticisms of intermediate categories, which they describe as a means of rejecting Blackness: "There are lots of people who claim that *pardo* isn't a color; so before I thought that was, you know, ignorant. Now, with the knowledge of the project, I identified with the Black race because I have that origin and *parda* is like, it's as if you wanted to camouflage reality, I think."

From Eduína's perspective, her majority African admixture results provided "objective" confirmation of her Black identity. At the same time, her comments indicate the influence of Black movement discourses in naturalizing the idea that dark-skinned Brazilians should actively embrace a Black racial identity at all times—an idea that goes against traditional sociological conceptions of Brazilian "color" identities as fluid and relational.[26] These narratives meant that individuals who identified with the movement were less likely to feel their identity was destabilized by "contradictory" genomic results. Another Brazilian test-taker, Nivaldo, described how his "strong Afro-Brazilian consciousness" had led him to think of himself as "almost 100 percent African," prior to taking a DNA test. Nivaldo had lived in the United States for several years and remembered being surprised to find that he was not automatically perceived there as Black. He told me: "Since identity is contextual and relational, sometimes you have to take into account how people see you as well. So [in the United States], I imagine they might accept me as Latino in some contexts, but in my conception I'm Afro-Brazilian or Black."

When I asked Eduína what she thought could be the societal importance of DNA ancestry testing, she brought up the topic of affirmative action, stating:

> Actually, for us it's good, because when we do a university entrance exam or some type of public services test, there are times when they ask—there's a socioeconomic questionnaire—and they want to know what color we identify as, whether it's *preto, branco*—if it's *negro, branco, pardo*. I usually used to put *parda* because I didn't know, and now I can say that I am of Black origin. And so it's good for us to clarify that, because this whole *pardo* business doesn't really exist. You're either *negro*, or *branco*, or *índio* in my opinion, that's what I think. And that's why this research is important.

Eduína was one of five interviewees who affirmed that DNA testing would be a good measure for determining who should benefit from the quotas. Three of the other volunteers who held this view were openly opposed to the quotas—for example, Darlene, a UESB genetics student who identified as *branca*, declared, "If you claim you're *negro*, go and take one of those tests and show it. Everyone is *negro* in that case!" The only other Black Brazilian in the cohort to support the use of DNA ancestry testing for quotas was someone who, like Eduína, perceived her Black racial identity to be unambiguously supported by the DNA results.

Appearances That Deceive

For other volunteers, the question was not so clear-cut. Ludmila, a biologist working at the UESB, who identified as *mestiça* and was attributed 77 percent European genomic ancestry, wrote: "These tests would really 'screw' with our conceptions of race. I, for example, could apply for a place through the quotas for selective processes, based on my appearance. But if I was asked for this test, I would lose that right. The question would be: what defines our race, genotypic or phenotypic characteristics? At this point, I really don't know." Mariana, a medical genetics student at the Universidade Federal do Rio Grande do Sul (UFRGS) in southern Brazil, who identified as *mulata*, was similarly conflicted by the outcome of her results. She took part in the project initially because, in her words, "I've always been curious to know what ethnicity I'd fit into, because I have never managed to define myself." Mariana's father, she explained, was Argentinian, "descended from Spanish and Indigenous people"—but the side of her family she had grown up with and to which she felt closest was her mother's: "the Blacker part of the family." In the pretest questionnaire, Mariana predicted she would have 60 to 80 percent African genomic ancestry, an estimate that was not borne out in her results, which attributed her just 16 percent African ancestry. She told me:

> The test result came out in the same week that I registered for a public service examination, but it was an exam that asked what my ethnicity was. It was the first time that I had been given that question in the context of an exam, and not in the context of a research study, from the government, etc. And I had the option "Afro-descendant" and "not Afro-descendant." I said, "Well, I'm Afro-descendant." And then below that it said that if I lied in relation to that question, I could be imprisoned, that it was a legal document, and I was like "Wow, if the person that collects this exam paper looks at me and says I'm not *negra*, are they going to think I'm trying it on?" And I sat for a moment thinking, "I'll wait until the CANDELA project result comes out, because then I'll have a genetic counterproof," but then it didn't come out in the genetic test, and I was like "oh no!" . . . After that, I ended up speaking to a few people, and I said, "It's a concept that's much more complex, I don't think anyone's going to. . . ." But you feel bad, you feel bad about thinking, "Gosh, I call myself Afro-descendant, [but] if I wanted to prove it, I'd have to use a different means, like family history."

Notions of race seem to congeal around the question of quotas. The public service exam mentioned by Mariana required entrants to declare their "race" as a coherent, stable identity; yet in her own case, Mariana found there was a marked divergence between her "color" and genomic ancestry, neither of which matched up with a third dimension of her identity: her feeling of affiliation to Afro-Brazilian culture, rooted in her upbringing. Mariana's hesitation over how she should self-declare in the public service exam also speaks to a broader confusion about who affirmative action initiatives are *supposed* to benefit. According to David Lehmann, there is disagreement about whether the policies' main objective is to reduce overall socioeconomic inequality (in which case ideal beneficiaries would be those whose potential for social mobility is likely to be doubly impacted by their "color" *and* class status) or to increase social recognition of Black Brazilians and incorporate them into the elite (in which case "color" would be the main criterion).[27] Another possible interpretation is that if quotas are meant as a form of historical reparation for slavery, then its beneficiaries should be those who identify as "Afro-descendants" (meaning that ancestry might be a salient factor, in addition to "color"). Even if "color" is taken as the key variable, there are further complications. Perceptions of "color" are subjective and context-dependent. For instance, a person who is considered *branco/a* in Bahia (the Brazilian region with the greatest historical influence of African populations) may be perceived as unambiguously *negro/a* in the south of Brazil. Physical appearances are also subject to manipulation: hair can be straightened or curled, skin can be lightened and darkened. Even when Brazilians perceive unambiguous "Black" traits in their own phenotypes, their awareness of the contingency of "color" identities contributes to feelings of uncertainty about whether they are Black *enough* to apply for quotas. Furthermore, studies show that while a majority of Brazilians of all "colors" agree that there is "substantial racism" in their society, relatively few believe they have been directly affected by racial discrimination, even among those who identify as *preto/a* (the darkest "color" category). Hence, the veiled aspect of racism in Brazil may further complicate individuals' ideas about whether they count among the ideal beneficiaries of affirmative action.[28]

The assumption that DNA tests can offer clear solutions to the question of who should benefit from affirmative action stems from an erroneous idea that race is a primarily biological phenomenon, entirely separate from class or context.[29] In Mariana's view, her unexpectedly low level of African genomic ancestry offered paltry support to her claim to be Afro-Brazilian. Nonetheless, there have been other reports of light-skinned and White Brazilians attempting to use DNA tests to justify their university quota applications, provoking renewed concerns that the initiatives' effectiveness may be undermined by "race fraud."[30] Since my fieldwork in 2013, these accusations have led to the institutionalization of candidate "verification commissions" by various federal universities, following the petitions of Black movement activists and, more recently, the publication of government directives on the allocation of racially targeted quotas for federal public service positions.[31] Similar to the controversial approach adopted by the Universidade de Brasília (among others) in the 2000s, these commissions use interviews, and in some cases photographs and videos provided by candidates, to confirm the latter's racial identification, based primarily on phenotypic criteria.[32] As Antonio Sérgio Alfredo Guimarães has noted, these measures indicate an increased, strategic emphasis on skin color as a "racial" marker, which runs counter to the Black movement's historic efforts to construct a collective identity based on broader, more subjective notions of "Afro" culture and heritage.[33]

Meanwhile, the perceived disjunctions between self-described "color" and genomic ancestry led some of the CANDELA participants to interrogate the way certain phenotypic traits are habitually racialized in Brazilian society, questioning their reliability as markers of ancestry. Camille, a medical student at the UESB, who described herself as *morena*, was surprised by the high level of European ancestry she was attributed (71 percent). She explained:

> My friends thought I would have a lot of White ancestry, a bit more
> White than Black. I thought it was going to be half-and-half, right
> down the middle; my mother is *negra*, my father is *branco*, it'll be
> like 52 [percent] and 48 [percent], more or less. But the test came
> out with more White [ancestry], and it was funny because some of
> my colleagues took the test and some of them who are a lot Whiter
> than me came out with a higher Black percentage. Everyone was
> joking, like, "oh my god, you had more White blood all along," that
> sort of thing. People think that the outside coincides with the inside,
> with our genetics, but our phenotype doesn't always coincide with
> our genotype. I found it surprising because I thought I would have
> just a little bit more Black ancestry.

It is worth underlining the unconscious way in which Camille converted genetic terminology (e.g., European ancestry) into racial terms ("White blood"), a common verbal slip among both Brazilian and U.S. interviewees. As Camille herself pointed out, this slippage underscores the idea that the racial traits manifested in a person's "color" correspond proportionally to an underlying genetic essence. For instance, the more "Black" phenotypic traits a person has, the more "Black blood" or African genomic ancestry they will have. Even then, calculating ancestry was tricky. Based on their evaluations of her appearance, Camille's friends thought her more White than

Black, whereas Camille believed herself to be "half-and-half"—a calculation based not only on her own appearance, but also on her appraisal of her parents' "color" and her estimate of the racial inheritance she had received from each of them.

Camille put forward a theory to explain the disjunction between her family's beliefs about their ancestral origins and her DNA results. She described her confusion at not being attributed any Indigenous American genomic ancestry, despite the fact that her maternal great-grandmother was reputed to have been *indígena*, because she was "*morena* with straight hair." To square these facts, Camille attempted to reclassify the genetic origins of her ancestor's physical traits. Straight hair combined with "*pele morena*" (mid-tone skin) are usually considered "Indigenous" characteristics, but in this case, Camille suggested, her great-grandmother's straight hair must have been a "White" trait that combined with her mid-tone skin (a "Black" trait) to give the deceptive impression of Indigenous ancestry. Throughout the interviews, the physical traits typically signaled by the volunteers as markers of their family origins were those ascribed to an Indigenous or Black ancestry (high cheekbones, kinky hair, a wide nose); Whiteness was therefore given a "recessive" genetic status, often being perceived as the *absence* of these telltale "racial" markers. The idea of Blackness as a biological "stain," most commonly associated with the U.S. "one-drop rule," is also conveyed through certain Brazilian expressions like *ter a barriga suja* (to have a dirty womb), which is sometimes said of women in Bahia who bear a child of darker skin than her parents.[34] Camille's theory of genetic inheritance challenges these implicit hierarchies, enabling "White" traits (e.g., straight hair) to be rendered visible alongside "Black" ones (e.g., skin color). She concluded, "I believe the truth is deceptive because we always think that people who have kinky hair [*cabelo crespo*] are of Black ancestry, but probably our mixture [*a mestiçagem*] makes it so that White people pass down their straight hair and Black people [pass down] their color."

The idea that "appearances deceive" while DNA markers told the truth about race was evoked by several of the CANDELA volunteers, as well as participants in a 2009 study of Brazilian DNA test-takers.[35] Others tried to reconcile this disjunction between the exterior and the interior of their bodies by imagining particular circumstances in which each would gain or lessen in relevance. For instance, Mariana explained that her training as a genetics graduate made her aware of how her genotype could influence her susceptibility to certain genetic conditions. In her words:

I thought I was more like my mom's side, and when I saw a larger quantity of White markers, I thought, "perhaps I'm underestimating my dad's side," so I think what changed is how I'm going to deal with those illnesses as I grow older. So I've got a greater predisposition to respond [to illnesses] like White people than like Black people. . . . So I think I sort of forgot, I was influenced by my phenotype; since I'm so similar to my mom, I thought I would have more predispositions from my mom's side. Race really doesn't make much sense, but that's what I thought naturally. So I think it's more in that sense, of no longer seeing myself as being as Black as before and realizing that my White side needs looking after, in terms of sunscreen, various things— gosh, I always thought I was *negra*, so I didn't need to bother with that kind of thing.

Mariana's affirmation that she "now" needed to protect herself against illnesses affecting White people denoted another type of racial logic: the idea that certain conditions are associated with particular "racial" ancestries. Attempts by civil rights campaigners to draw political attention to the impact of structural and institutional racism on the health outcomes of racialized minorities have in some cases reinforced popular beliefs that certain diseases (e.g., sickle cell anemia) are racial in origin.[36] This idea has been rejected by prominent medical geneticists, who stress that both "color" and continental genetic ancestry classifications are likely to be inadequate markers for the inheritance of complex genetic conditions among Brazilians.[37] Nonetheless, what I found particularly interesting about Mariana's remark was what it illustrated about the way her upbringing had influenced her racial self-identification, as well as her ideas about her *bodily* "racial" inheritance. Mariana indicated that her perceptions of racial identity and "color" were informed mainly by her mother's family, who raised her. Nonetheless, the revelation of her genomic inheritance (evenly split between her mother's and father's side of the family) suddenly brought her "White" ancestry— which she previously regarded as invisible as far as her body was concerned— into view as a phenotype requiring specific attention and care. It seemed telling that the first "White condition" that came to mind for Mariana was related to skin color, the "racial" marker par excellence in Brazil. In connecting the dots between genotype and phenotype, her dark skin acquired a "White" characteristic: the need for sunscreen. For Mariana, the DNA ancestry test caused new reflections about how certain physical traits were passed down within their families and what this meant for how she considered her identity to be "made up" of different "racial" influences.[38]

Debating Multiraciality

In contrast to the Brazilian cohort, the U.S. test-takers I interviewed rarely mentioned "identity" as a reason for taking a DNA ancestry test. Rather, they said they did it to "find out their origins or ethnicities," "discover their ancestral breakdown," "further their genealogy," or simply "out of curiosity." Nonetheless, while only fifteen out of forty-one interviewees stated that their DNA ancestry results were different, or somewhat different, from their expectations (a slightly lower proportion than the Brazilian test-takers), sixteen individuals overall stated that their experience with DNA testing had made them think differently about their identity. Roughly half of these sixteen individuals referred specifically to "ethnic" results that had contradicted their expectations (but not necessarily challenged their sense of racial identity), while the other half stated that the test had given them a new appreciation of how racially mixed they were, suggesting that the DNA-testing experience had brought to light facets of their ancestral origins that were previously obscured by their racial identities.

Although "racial" mixture has occurred throughout U.S. history, it is only in recent decades that multiraciality has begun to take root as a discrete identity category, and today the term remains contested, as we shall explore further below. One of the hypotheses I outlined at the beginning of this chapter was the idea that admixture testing could lend greater salience or legitimacy to mixed-race identities. The experience of Lezlie,[39] a writer and actor who grew up in Texas, appeared to fit this theory. I contacted Lezlie through her Instagram profile, where she had uploaded a screenshot of her 23andMe results. We corresponded by email about her experience, and she also sent me links to several video blogs (vlogs) and blog posts that she had created on the topic. Her reason for wanting to take a genetic test, Lezlie told me, was "to get some confirmation and possibly closure with my life-long questions, 'What am I?' I always knew I was mixed but I have been asked all of my life by strangers what I am." From around the age of six, Lezlie quizzed her grandparents frequently on their family origins. Based on the stories they told her, she knew that each of her parents came from racially and ethnically mixed backgrounds—with African- and European-descendant ancestors on both sides of the family, and possibly some Jewish and Native American ancestry—although both her parents identify as Black. Because of her pale skin and tightly curled dark hair, throughout her childhood Lezlie received many questions and remarks from friends, schoolmates, and strangers regarding her ethnic and racial background. People frequently asked about her family origins, and some even seemed to want to debate her ancestry—for instance, pressing her on whether she had Asian heritage.

Despite being born to two Black parents, Lezlie felt that her experience was that of a biracial child: someone who did not fit comfortably in either "Black" or "White" racial categories. Numerous times, Lezlie's White classmates failed to recognize her Black ancestry. For instance, on one occasion she was invited to attend a sleepover, hosted by a popular blonde girl from a wealthy Mormon family. During the party, the young host informed her guests that her parents had forbidden her from inviting any Black girls. When Lezlie informed the girl that she herself was Black, the latter replied: "Well, you know what I mean, you aren't really Black, Lezlie." After the sleepover, the girl stopped hanging around with her. Meanwhile, Lezlie remembered countless demonstrations of what she perceived as hatred and jealousy from her female Black classmates, which she found particularly painful because of her profound desire to be accepted as a Black girl. One of her strongest memories is of a girl calling her a "yellow bitch" and trying to cut Lezlie's hair off in the school hallway. In her words, "I did nothing to this girl previously aside from try to be friendly."

In search of answers, Lezlie took an interest in her family history; she claims that she "always" wanted to know her "genetic breakdown." When she was in her late twenties, she saw that personalized genetic testing products were becoming available to the public, although it was a few more years until she "bought into the idea that it was scientific and real." In 2014, after a good deal of searching online, Lezlie decided to test with 23andMe, which was highly rated on various user blogs, and a few months later, she took a second test with AncestryDNA. Upon receiving her results, Lezlie told me that she "wasn't too surprised and was relieved." Both companies attributed her similar admixture results: 58 percent African, 40 percent European, and 2 percent Asian ancestry from 23andMe; and 57 percent, 42 percent, and 1 percent, respectively, from AncestryDNA. Lezlie saw the admixture results as a validation of her affirmed identity as "a mixed woman." In her words, "I never felt that I could say that because I am not the result of one parent being one ethnicity and one being the other. They are both mixed. Even within my family, people choose to self-identify in various ways.

Many will just say they are Black despite their clearly mixed appearance. But because my experience my entire life has been one of an ambiguous woman, or at least of a mixed woman, I always wanted to claim every part of me. Now I feel that I can."

Lezlie perceived a convergence between her DNA results and her experience of being racialized as mixed-race, which gave her the confidence to adopt this identity in certain social situations, against the prevailing logic of the one-drop rule. Similar arguments have been used by supporters of multiracial movements to argue for the discontinuation of concepts of hypodescent for defining Blackness in the United States, which some describe as a necessary step for dismantling the old systems of racial domination.[40] Multiracial modes of identification are presented, in contrast, as more socially inclusive and genetically accurate than binary schemas. Nevertheless, when I asked Lezlie how she self-identified since taking the tests, she told me: "I still go back and forth between saying 'African American' or 'African and European.' It usually depends on how I am asked. For instance, the other day I had to fill out a form and it said 'pick one.' I wanted to pick 'other' at first, but I chose 'African American.'" As we saw with Mariana's hesitation over the public service exam paper, for individuals whose racial appearance does not coincide strongly with their ancestry or sense of cultural affiliation, responding to single-option questions about race on official forms means second-guessing which dimension of their identity is deemed most significant by the state. Likewise, Krista, a photographer from Colorado, who identified as "of mixed heritage and ancestry," told me that while growing up she had always hated responding to these single-option questions, yet she could not shake the feeling that self-defining as biracial or multiracial did not really count as an identity. Krista's experience of growing up with her "Caucasian" mother and knowing very little of her father except that he was a "very light-skinned Black man" led her to feel that identity was "not as cut-and-dried as you might think . . . you never know when there's another race or heritage that's been in your bloodline."

On the other hand, other U.S. test-takers who—at least on the surface— shared similar backgrounds and phenotypes to Lezlie did not necessarily regard multiraciality as a desirable option. Jarreau, a political science graduate who had grown up in Baltimore, received autosomal and uniparental DNA results from 23andMe in 2011 after a friend alerted him that the company was offering free kits to African Americans in an effort to diversify its database. Later, in search of greater detail about his African ethnic origins, he took further mtDNA and Y-DNA tests from African Ancestry. In an email questionnaire, he explained that he was descended from two African American grandparents on one side of his family and a Black grandfather and White Italian grandmother on the other. Jarreau contrasted his own self-identification as "Black, as African American, as an African child of the diaspora, as a Black American" with the dominant identity narratives in the other side of his family, who "claim to be of good Italian stock and downplay their Black American father . . . even though no one outside of themselves consider them Italian." Jarreau considered his perspective to be validated by his admixture results, which showed he was "less than 14 percent Italian," rather than the one-fourth one might expect for someone with an Italian grandparent. He stated: "I've never gone by mixed-race. My dad is mixed and even he just claims being Black. . . . I've had my issues with my light skin color before, where I was either too White or smart or well-read to be fully accepted by Black kids, or too Black and rap loving to be accepted by White kids. But that never deterred me from knowing exactly who I am. I'm a Black man in America, with the blood of Mbunda, Fula, Mende, and Mandinka peoples. Love it or leave it." Jarreau's discourse echoes that of Black activists in Brazil, who identify the espousal of mixed-race identities with historical tendencies toward racial Whitening and the erasure of African roots. Jarreau made this connection himself when he argued that DNA ancestry testing was most likely to benefit "Black people and mestizo Latinos . . . seeing how they can paint a clearer picture of origin and how much a person is Indigenous or African rather than European."

Multiraciality was appealing to some younger Black DNA test-takers who did not perceive themselves as racially ambiguous. Régine, a social media recruiter and performer from New York, became interested in taking a DNA test after taking a genealogy class in an African Studies course, in which her teacher showed a clip from one of Henry Louis Gates Jr.'s documentaries on genetic ancestry testing. In her words, "I said wow, I want to know where in Africa I come from. And I was a little curious about where in Europe I could be from, too." Prior to taking the test, Régine had been aware of several stories about her family's African origins. Her mother's family, who were from South Carolina, claimed to be of Nigerian origin ("specifically the Igbo race"); her maternal grandmother, on the other hand, was known to have been half Irish, with "lighter skin and wavy hair." Régine's father was from Jamaica; his family was rumored to be partly descended from an Asian ancestor, although no one knew exactly where this person was from, or how many generations ago they had lived. Régine's DNA results attributed her "95 percent African, 2 percent Irish, 1 percent Italian/

Greece, [and] less than 1 percent West Caucasus" ancestry. She posted a screenshot of her results on Instagram, with the caption: "I knew it!!!!!!!!! Nigerian, Togo, Cameroon, Irish and since I am an African studies major there are a lot more to these countries. A lot of Arabic hence when I saw I am Part West Asia (Iran & Iraq), makes a lot of sense!!!! #african #arabic #european #middleeast #iraq #fulani #angola #mixed #multiracial #blackgirl #heritage #dna #ancestrydna."

I understood Régine's use of the hashtags "mixed" and "multiracial" as an attempt to publicly acknowledge and embrace the small percentages of non-African ancestry in her report alongside her Black identity. In our interview, she told me the test had made her question her racial identity, and the general expectation in the United States that individuals "are one thing" and not a mixture of various ancestral influences. This idea, she claimed, was not generally questioned within her own family, who for the most part seemed to pride themselves on being "fully Black with Nigerian heritage" and not being mixed with anything else (with the exception of her grand-mother's Irish ancestry). Régine told me that she wanted to use the term "multiracial" more often, as a means of celebrating the diversity in her genetic makeup, but that she had been criticized by Black friends and relatives who accused her of "wanting to be White." While she rejected this accusation, Régine was struck by the injustice of being forced into a single racial category. She mused: "Why can't we be American first, and then our race second? . . . Can you accept others even if they make up only a small percentage of what you are? After all, you're still a part of that heritage; someone fell in love to make you."

Régine's disagreement with her family and friends resonates with the nationwide debates that gripped Brazil during the first decade of the 2000s, in which two antiracist paradigms were placed in opposition: one promoting mixture and racial fluidity, and the other collective action around a binary racial model, as antidotes to racial inequalities and prejudice. In the United States, the notion of Blackness as a historically constructed collective identity has been naturalized by the "one-drop rule" and today is much stabler than in Brazil. Yet, while some interviewees in 2014 mentioned the popularity of Black music and the reelection of President Barack Obama as signs of receding racial divisions in the country, some older African American interviewees raised concerns about the idea that Black culture was being homogenized and assimilated as simply "American culture," and that Blackness as an identity was becoming less and less meaningful among younger generations. In a similar vein, campaigns to introduce a "multiracial" category to the 2000 U.S. census were largely opposed by Black intellectuals and activists who—recognizing that many African Americans are of mixed ancestries and could technically fit into this category—argued the change could have an adverse effect on the political visibility of African Americans by decreasing the number of people who identified officially as Black.[41]

Do multiracial and Black identities have to be mutually exclusive? Sociologist Dorothy Roberts recalls having similar thoughts to Régine as "a little girl growing up in a liberal community in the 1960s":

> I used to cherish the fantasy that the intimate hybridity of my own biracial, multiethnic family constituted a blow against the racial order. But that was before I formed my own moral allegiance to black people based on a sense of my common struggle against racial oppression. Looking back, I can see that my childhood fantasy was not only unenlightened but privileged by my middle-class existence, largely disconnected from the majority of black residents in other parts of the city who may have lived out their entire lives without ever experiencing even one moment when race did not matter or any chance of gaining some benefit from "mixed ancestry."[42]

Roberts's statement underlines how focusing on deconstructing beliefs of ancestral purity as the linchpin of antiracist action can create blind spots about how structural conditions (e.g., class inequalities) contribute to the reproduction and intensification of socially engineered racial distinctions, which in turn reinforce societal beliefs that these differences are "natural" and "innate." As Roberts identifies, the solution to these problems requires not *only* ideological shifts but *also* (and principally) political and economic action. As an expression of personal commitment, Roberts draws a moral distinction between *knowing* about one's mixed ancestry and making it the focus of one's *public* identity.

The strategic cultivation of Black identities among biracial children (who could feasibly have access to different "ethnic options") has been framed elsewhere by France Winddance Twine as a form of "racial literacy": a set of "practices that resist racial hierarchies that privilege whites and people of multiracial heritage over blacks in a context in which the boundaries between blackness and whiteness are permeable."[43] Many of the Black U.S. and Brazilian test-takers I interviewed demonstrated their own racial literacy by pragmatically affirming the salience of their existing racial identities over their DNA ancestry portraits, based on their understanding of how racism continues to operate in these societies. As Jessica, a U.S. college student, put it: "I self-identify as African American. I identify as such because genetically I am predominantly African American, not to mention that, when people see me, they automatically assume I am African American. Just because I have European blood in me does not mean that people won't see me a certain way, that's just how it is. That's the bad part about self-identification; just because you see yourself that way doesn't mean the world will."

Nonetheless, some Black and mixed-race interviewees indicated that they saw their DNA ancestry reports as a way of opening up certain "ethnic options" *within* Blackness, at a moment when cosmopolitanism and multiethnicity are increasingly valued.[44] Hasan, a financial executive who had taken several DNA tests to try and deepen the scope of his genealogical research, told me that he also wanted his children to "have a sense of where they came from outside of slavery." In addition to gaining information about their African ethnic origins, he felt that the admixture tests offered them "a larger view of the world and their place in it—they are citizens of the world, to borrow the quote. My wife's parents are from Jamaica and Cuba, and their recent ancestry includes Chinese, Native American, England, and African in high percentages. So the world is really them." Others found that the diverse categories in their admixture reports were good for striking up new friendships or strengthening cultural affinities. For instance, one test-taker reported that after discussing his newfound "Jewish" genetic ancestry at his workplace, a Jewish colleague had invited him for dinner with his family, and they had since become firm friends. Similarly, a Mexican American test-taker who found she had a small percentage of "Middle Eastern" DNA said that on hearing the news, her Middle Eastern friends "were just so excited and they right away said 'welcome, sister!'" For others, these new identities came into focus on specific occasions—for instance, during international sporting events or in relation to current affairs. Jarreau stated, "It definitely makes me watch soccer differently. When I watch the Africa Cup of Nations now, I feel like I can watch with an interest of my people rather than just picking a country because of a shirt color or star player. It makes it more emotional and tangible." He hoped in the future to be able to strengthen this attachment by visiting the countries depicted in his ancestry report, to "sit with people from the respective tribes and be able to share in the culture I lost."

In chapter 5, I return to the issue of genetics and the politics of belonging, to explore the experiences of individuals who have sought actively to adopt an African ethnic identity, based on their DNA reports. For now, I go on to explore how test-takers interpreted their genomic data in relation to discourses about Whiteness, and how these practices may be further affecting racial boundaries and politics in both countries.

Toward Critical Modes of Whiteness?

In most of the accounts described above, defining one's racial identity was described as a process that required balancing personal preferences and "invisible" types of knowledge (e.g., family history knowledge, DNA data) with an awareness of how one is perceived phenotypically by others. In contrast, Whiteness is often perceived, by those who fit into this category, as a racially "unmarked" identity that entails being unaffected by experiences of racism and discrimination—something that can open up greater possibilities for expressing one's *personal* identity beyond the framework of race. Among the individuals I interviewed who described themselves as White, none expressed any overt emotional attachment to their racial identity. Unanimously, the Brazilian test-takers told me that being *branco/a* was "just a matter of skin color"; some further commented that it meant "not receiving the same burden of prejudice as *negros* and *índios*." In the United States, the answers were varied. Some test-takers stated that Whiteness was a question of physical appearance, whereas others seemed at a loss to explain what it meant. Still others preferred to define themselves using an ethnic descriptor (e.g., "American of British/Irish/Italian descent"). Many of the individuals I interviewed, nonetheless, expressed a desire to discover some proportion of non-European genomic ancestry. This was actively expected by test-takers in Bahia, who said that Africanity was part of their regional identity.[45] The younger U.S. test-takers, in particular, tended to be disappointed when they received a "100 percent European" result: they remarked that their ancestry was "boring," or joked self-deprecatingly that they were "*so* White."

These reactions may seem surprising when compared with traditional U.S. definitions of Whiteness as the absolute *absence* of non-European ancestry. In Brazil, however, the "color" category *branco/a* has not historically been conceptualized as exclusive of "racial" mixture; rather, phenotypic Whiteness could be the product of generations of tactical mating, coupled with cultural and bodily manipulations intended to hide any visible traces of "non-White" ancestry. The question of who counts as White varies from region to region and according to social context, so that "one can be white in one realm but 'not quite' in another."[46] Whereas racial Whitening has historically been at the center of Brazil's national project, more recently the introduction of affirmative action policies and increasing prominence of public debates about racism may have lessened the appeal of Whiteness, leading some Brazilians to strategically "darken" their "color" and racial designations.[47] Moreover, Cheryl Harris has argued that Whiteness was constructed historically and legally as a form of property, which, in American societies characterized by settler-colonialism and slavery, licensed or prohibited individuals' access to specific rights and privileges.[48] Following a similar logic, scholars have argued that in the United States, DNA testing provides a way for some White Americans to legitimize claims on the identities of non-White peoples "without having to experience the social consequences of visible, embodied nonwhiteness."[49]

The widespread desire for "Native American" DNA among non-Indigenous test-takers has been widely remarked on in the scholarly literature, and this was also a marked trend among the Brazilian and U.S. test-takers I interviewed.[50] Kim TallBear dates this desire for "Indian blood" to the emergence of nineteenth-century U.S. political projects aimed at eradicating the "Indian" presence, seen as an obstacle to national progress, and Eduardo Viveiros de Castro has made similar comments regarding claims on Indigenous identities in Brazil.[51] For many White (as well as Black) Americans, "having" Native ancestry is often seen as an embellishment to one's personal identity: a way of legitimizing a claimed "spiritual" connection to the land and natural environment, for instance.[52] The Brazilians I interviewed likewise conjured up romantic stories of ancestors who were reputed to have been "an índio/a from the forest." Ironically, this fondness and even glorification of "ancestral" Indians is rarely matched by public attitudes toward *living* Indigenous populations in either country.[53]

In contrast, I found that African genomic ancestry was viewed with ambivalence by White U.S. and Brazilian test-takers, and was not always readily incorporated into their identities, for various reasons. Ryan, a parkour athlete from Colorado, took a DNA test to verify the results of his family's genealogy research. Based on the report, he surmised that they were "mostly right" about their heritage, commenting that "the one big surprise was that I am 3 percent West African." A 2015 study conducted by 23andMe—the company that processed Ryan's test—estimated that "a substantial fraction, at least 1.4 [percent], of self-reported European Americans in the United States carry at least 2 [percent] African ancestry," a phenomenon the authors attributed to the history of light-skinned Black Americans "passing" into the White population.[54] A generation or two ago, the revelation that an ancestor had racially "passed" could be a cause for deep shame and psychological conflict within White families.[55] Even today, discovering small percentages of African ancestry or shared DNA with African American test-takers can raise uncomfortable questions about one's ancestral connections to slavery, which many White Americans would prefer to ignore.[56] In comparison, Ryan's response appeared nonchalant: "We all kind of laughed about [it] because we had no idea." Yet, there is a possible ambiguity to his answer. Laughing at a result might signify that it is "no big deal"; alternatively, it could be a way of signaling disbelief, by laughing something *off*. Ryan did not elaborate further on this, but he stated that overall the results had not changed how he thought about himself, since "I always considered myself somewhat of a mutt, but that was always normal to me and my friends/family growing up."

Kate, an archeologist from Maine, had more to say after she was attributed just over 1 percent African ancestry and a "Native American/East Asian" mtDNA haplogroup by her DNA test. In her family, she stated, "As far as the African ancestry . . . nobody was particularly surprised, particularly if it came from the paternal line, because my dad's family was Irish and in Maine there were a significant number of Irish and Black pairings, historically. So, they were excited, though. It got my dad interested in taking a test, and my brother, from my results." Nonetheless, Kate said that the result had not affected her personal identity:

> I always kind of knew that—based on my phenotypical features,
> that there had to be some sort of slight mixing of some other races,
> because I have hooded eyes, and that's typically along the Asian and,
> you know, Native American phenotypical features, so I guess it really
> hasn't changed how I think about who I am, though; I mean, I don't
> identify as someone—it's not a large percentage of my DNA and I
> don't identify as someone who is mixed racially because I'm still
> predominantly White, it's less than 5 percent of my identity. And it's
> not something that I have ever lived with or identified with, and
> neither has anyone in my family.

Kate's conception of her Whiteness did not coincide with the traditional racial logic of ancestral "purity"; on the contrary, she claimed that she had always read her physical features as indicating some subsumed "racial" mixture. While this appeared to be borne out by the DNA test, Kate was unable to find further information about where in the family tree her non-European ancestry might have originated. She explained: "Either there's no evidence for it because there's no recording of those types of things; it's from the fact where it wasn't written down, or I don't know. So I have tried, but I haven't had any results with that, unfortunately." It is possible that the value placed historically on racial "purity" for White families led this knowledge to be lost to memory generations ago. Despite her keen interest, this made it difficult for Kate to identify personally with an ancestry which—as she put it— neither she nor her relatives had ever "lived with."

Kate's account denoted a concern for authenticity in affirming a racial identity—something she saw as bestowed ideally by embodied experience or, at the very least, the unbroken intergenerational transmission of this racial knowledge. A year after our interview, the U.S. press was ablaze with the story of Rachel Dolezal, a regional leader for the National Association for the Advancement of Colored People (NAACP), who was publicly accused of "passing for Black." The accusation was sparked by a letter from Dolezal's parents to a national press agency, in which they asserted that their daughter was of German and Czech ancestry, and that for more than a decade she had been masquerading as a Black woman. The letter included a photograph of Dolezal as a teenager, with straight blonde hair, blue eyes, and a pale, freckly complexion. In the subsequent media-storm, it was revealed that Dolezal, a graduate of Howard University (a historically Black institution), had worked to gradually transform her physical appearance by darkening her skin and adopting a variety of "Afro" hairstyles. In an interview on *The Today Show*, Dolezal claimed that she was transracial, affirming that as early as five years old she was "drawing self-portraits with the brown crayon instead of the peach crayon."[57] She also pointed out that she had been married to a Black man, with whom she had two children, and that she was a member of a circle of close African American friends who accepted her as Black and whom she regarded in return as adoptive relatives.

The story provoked a public outcry, with Black commentators likening Dolezal's deliberate physical transformation to "blackface" and condemning her for "cultural appropriation." As Jamelle Bouie wrote for the online magazine *Slate*: "[She] is adopting the culture without carrying the burdens."[58] Dolezal was stripped of her position at the NAACP, and her affirmed transracial identity was largely met with scorn and disbelief.[59] At first glance, Dolezal's case suggests that Black *biological* ancestry is still perceived as crucial to being "legitimately" Black in the United States. Yet Bouie's assertion underlines the important dimension of Blackness as lived experience: it brings with it "burdens" that cannot—or, from a moral position, *should not*—be acquired from a position of Whiteness. From this perspective, Blackness may be thought of as a "blood-infused but more-than-biological" identity;[60] it is ancestry *plus* the inherited and embodied knowledge of what it has meant to live as Black through key events in U.S. history (e.g., slavery, Jim Crow segregation, the civil rights movement).

It is worth highlighting that the primacy of lived experience over genetic data is not recognized by all White U.S. test-takers. Natasha Golbeck and Wendy Roth studied the discourses of White Americans who took a DNA test to try and verify family stories about their ancestral Native American origins. For these individuals, being attributed "Native American" DNA was seen as a way to legitimate their identity claim and distance themselves from "Wannabes"—those who had heard rumors of a distant Native American ancestor but had "little to offer by way of proof."[61] There have also been reports of DNA tests being used by White Americans to gain access to affirmative action programs.[62] In a recent case, a Seattle businessman who took a DNA test and found he had 4 percent African DNA filed to sue the Office of Minority and Women's Business Enterprises (OMWBE) after it declined to provide him a Disadvantaged Business Enterprise certificate, on the basis that he did not meet their criteria of belonging to a minority group.[63] Like in Brazil, such cases—while relatively uncommon—have sparked fears that DNA ancestry testing may be used to dismantle affirmative action policies by making the fair administration of these initiatives appear unviable. In contrast, a critical stance for White test-takers could mean recognizing and learning about one's "non-White" ancestry *without* choosing to leverage this knowledge to serve self-interested identity claims, which could have damaging repercussions for disadvantaged groups.

When I mentioned the topic of DNA ancestry testing to people I met during my fieldwork in Brazil, many felt sure that these technologies would only be of interest to Brazilians as a way to prove *how European* their ancestry was. In contrast, while the topic of Whitening was raised by numerous CANDELA volunteers, it was usually in negative terms, as a mentality linked to prejudice and racism. Leonora, a student at the UESB who described herself as *parda*, told me: "I think people generally forget the Indigenous or African part [of their ancestry]. When they say 'My ancestry is from . . .' they'll talk about their European ancestry. That's common, really . . . because people, however dark their skin is, they only see, only want to see the European side, which is like, it's the one that's most—that doesn't have prejudice. . . . Among my own colleagues, people wanted to know how much European [ancestry] they had; they didn't even care about the Indigenous or African part . . . they were even surprised when the result wasn't what they expected, when it gave more Indigenous or African [ancestry] than they expected."

Leonora's observation contrasted with CANDELA's overall findings— namely, that volunteers from across the five Latin American countries under study tended to overestimate their proportion of African genomic ancestry and underestimate their European ancestry.[64] It also differed from the data I collected from interviewees and from the respondents to the CANDELA posttest questionnaire, who generally expressed disappointment that their African and Indigenous ancestries were lower than expected. It is possible that this is an effect of a sampling bias: those who feared to learn they had more African and Indigenous ancestry than expected may have simply declined to take part in the CANDELA study. Even within this cohort, those who agreed to be interviewed by me could have been the ones who were a priori more interested in their non-European ancestries.

Yet I did find some subtle clues that supported Leonora's claim. For instance, five interviewees expressed spontaneously that they wanted to know more about their European countries of origin, whereas only one individual said that she wanted to find out which African country she was from (none inquired about their Indigenous ethnic origins). There was also one case among the interviewees of an individual who *did* "Whiten" her racial designation after learning her DNA results. Jânia, a student at the UESB, described herself as *negra* on the initial CANDELA questionnaire and predicted she would have 40 to 60 percent African ancestry and 20 to 40 percent European ancestry. In an email exchange, she told me she did not know much about her family's origins, except that "my dad's family is all Black. We're always joking that my dad's part [of the family] was all African. All from Africa." After finding out that the DNA result attributed her 53 percent European and 29 percent African ancestry, Jânia told me, "I saw it and I got all happy. I told everyone, 'I'm *branca*, I'm *branca*!'" Since receiving the results, she said that she no longer described herself as *negra* on official forms, but *parda*, "because I discovered that I'm not as *negra* as all that!" When asked what it meant to be *negra* or *parda* in Brazil, Jânia wrote: "*Negro*, I think everyone goes by skin color: the darker you are, the more people consider themselves *negro*. If you're lighter you'll consider yourself *pardo*, but almost no one considers themselves *branco*. Because everyone has mixture [*a miscigenação*]." While her skin color was, of course, not affected by the CANDELA results, Jânia described her ancestry revelation as having moved her racially along a sliding scale further away from Blackness and closer toward Whiteness.

Another commonly held belief among the CANDELA volunteers was that Brazilians (in particular those with lighter skin) would benefit from finding out how much African and Indigenous ancestry they had, as a means of challenging their idealization of Whiteness (this assertion was also made by Jarreau in the previous section). In fact, among the individuals I interviewed who identified as *branco/a*, most said that the results reflected their expectations about their ancestry (i.e., majority European with smaller percentages of African and Indigenous ancestry)—a trend that contradicted the public claims by geneticists like Sérgio Pena about the absolute dissociation between "color" and genomic ancestry in Brazilians.[65] These interviewees also said that their DNA results did not alter the way they identified racially, since skin color was "what counts in Brazil." Yet some were keen to underline that their self-identification as White did not signify a rejection of their non-European ancestries. Ricardo, a drama student at the UESB, described himself as White "in parts," explaining:

> The fact that I consider myself *branco* is really based on my
> appearance, on what's outside, on the skin color that people see, on
> the skin color that I have. I'm not *that* White. I don't consider myself
> that White. And now . . . the [DNA] results came to prove that
> I can't say that I'm White. I have portions, I have descendants [*sic*]
> of White people, I'm not . . . I have Indigenous, African descendants.
> So, from the result, I now can't say—I already knew before I got the
> result . . . that I wouldn't be able to say I was 100 percent *branco*.

For Ricardo, acknowledging that he was "White but not *that* White" seemed to constitute a moral stance aimed at rejecting Brazil's historical idealization of Whiteness. His positionality could be interpreted as reflecting a broad form of Black consciousness. As Alexandre Emboaba da Costa has argued:

> [It] is inclusive rather than exclusive, something blacks and whites
> can share as a means toward respect, understanding, and social
> transformation through a mutual struggle for equality and
> decolonization. . . . It [is] also about different forms of self-
> reflexivity, e.g. questioning one's position of power (for whites),
> affirming one's heritage and skin color as positive (for blacks), and
> reflecting on what histories and experiences differentiate as well as
> bind people together (for all Brazilians).[66]

Conversely, Liv Sovik has contended that such assertions can also be used as a way to *avoid* acknowledging the personal advantages afforded by phenotypic Whiteness in Brazil, as well as broader discussions about how the ongoing prestige of Whiteness plays into the maintenance of racial hierarchies. She cites the popular adage that "no one [in Brazil] is White,"[67] which conveys the belief that "real" (i.e., "racially pure") Whites inhabit other places like the United States and Europe, or the colonies of second- and third-generation Northern European immigrants in southern Brazil.[68] By extension, "real" forms of racism (for instance, the desire for racial separatism) are also held to be found elsewhere—a claim that prevents a deeper understanding of how equally pernicious and lethal forms of racism can thrive in contexts of "racial" mixture. Similar to the United States, a critical stance for White Brazilians could therefore entail developing a sense of racial literacy by understanding how their "color" (combined with other factors such as class, gender, sexual orientation, etc.) may afford them social advantages or otherwise remove obstacles to social mobility that are likely to be encountered by darker-skinned peers, in spite of their common ancestral heritage.

What of test-takers who count themselves within this category of "unmixed" Whiteness? One Italian-descendant volunteer from Flores da Cunha, a municipality in Rio Grande do Sul, emailed the CANDELA scientists to describe her amusement at hearing her father (whose family originated in northern Italy) produce multiple hypotheses to explain her 15 percent African ancestry: "In his theory, that percentage most likely came from my mother's family, since one of her ancestral lineages originated in Sicily and, because of that, it was probably those individuals who mixed with Africans, before they immigrated to Brazil. . . . He brought the matter to a close by saying that the research team had no way of knowing with absolute certainty that these genetic variations are exclusively African. And so, by discrediting the study, he resolved his racial dilemma."

To the test-taker, it seemed clear that her father was bending over backward to avoid a fact that clashed with his own racial prejudice. Yet, one of the hypotheses he proposed to explain away the unexpected result was actually supported, indirectly, by one of the CANDELA scientists, a Euro-descendant Brazilian who was also attributed 11 percent African ancestry by her DNA test. Since she knew her genealogy in detail, she explained to me that the result was most likely a statistical error, owing to the fact that the European reference populations used for the test were meant to simulate Spanish and Portuguese ancestry, which she saw as "very far from the ancestry of Rio Grande do Sul, which is predominantly Italians, from the north of Italy; Poles, Czechs. . . . We knew that for the rest of the Americas, the rest of Brazil, the European result would work 100 percent, but our [ancestry] could produce a deviation. Since the standard deviation is 11 percent, I wasn't worried [about my result]."

For those who are critical of such ideologies, these small percentages of non-European ancestry may seem a convenient way of debunking myths of White racial "purity." But would things look different if the tests were re-done using an alternative methodology—for instance, one that reduced the error margins in assigning continental ancestries—and more volunteers *were* attributed "100 percent European" ancestry? Aaron Panofsky and Joan Donovan have shown, for instance, that error margins are often invoked by White nationalists to explain away non-European genetic ancestries, while the fact that some test-takers *are* attributed "100 percent European" results continues to fuel beliefs in the existence and attainability of racial purity.[69] In these cases the reputed "truthfulness" of DNA ancestry data becomes contingent and malleable: it is accepted when the results uphold a desired identity, and contested when they do not.

The issue of error margins also holds relevance for individuals who hope to use their DNA tests to recuperate evidence of long-lost ancestral mixtures. Almost unanimously, the geneticists I interviewed advised that test-takers should not put too much stock in the small percentages found in their DNA ancestry reports. Conversely, figures like Henry Louis Gates Jr. have proposed that White Americans should take seriously the small proportions of African ancestry in their DNA reports, which he believes can be evidence of Black ancestors who "passed" for White.[70] As I indicated through Kate's account, some test-takers clearly do treat these percentages as real; however, because of the very nature of these concealed histories, it can be difficult, if not impossible, to distinguish between genuine ancestral traces and statistical errors without—and even sometimes with—additional in-depth genealogical research.

Invisible versus Visible Markers of "Race"

The small sample size of DNA test-takers interviewed for this chapter makes it hard to generalize about how representative their accounts are of the broader social impacts of DNA testing on practices of racial and ethnic identification. There were other limitations to my analysis. Most of the Brazilian test-takers were students in their early twenties with a relatively high level of formal education, and the U.S. cohort, while encompassing a broader age range, was also skewed toward middle-class individuals with a high level of formal education. Arguably, though, the financial cost of commercial DNA testing, and the somewhat specialized knowledge required to interpret the results offered by some companies, means that these groups are likely to be fairly representative of the "typical" demographic of U.S. DNA test-takers. In Brazil, at the time of my fieldwork DNA ancestry tests were neither broadly known about nor widely available to the public beyond scientific initiatives like CANDELA. However, in the last few years two São Paulo–based companies have begun selling direct-to-consumer autosomal admixture tests to Brazilian clients, while African Ancestry and the Israeli company MyHeritage have also begun shipping tests to the country.[71] It remains to be seen how these technologies will be taken up by the Brazilian public and what impacts they might have on modes of self-identification, genealogical practices, the administration of racially targeted quotas, among other issues.

Despite these limitations, I was able to identify some trends in relation to my initial hypotheses. First, consistent with existing studies, I found only weak signs of DNA testing contributing to a geneticization of modes of racial identification. On the contrary, among both cohorts there was a widespread acknowledgment of the idea that ethnic and racial identities are essentially multiple, contextually defined, and constituted through acts of self-affirmation and classification by others. Genomic data were therefore seen as an additional layer of knowledge that could be incorporated (or not) in relation to other dimensions of racial identity (e.g., physical appearance, family background, cultural affiliation). Several Brazilian test-takers who perceived their results as misaligned with their phenotype suggested that genomic ancestry categories (rather than "color") expressed their "real race"; however, others argued the opposite. Although some asserted that DNA testing could be an objective way of defining eligibility for race-based quotas, when applied to individual cases, disjunctions between DNA results and affirmed identities often reinforced a sense of the ambiguity and subjectiveness of racial identity. The perception that DNA ancestry testing could say something about the "race" of different individuals may have been strengthened among the CANDELA volunteers by the categories with which they were presented, which strongly resembled traditional "racial" categories. In contrast, U.S. test-takers received a much wider variety of "ethnic" designations in their results, which did not always map easily onto their existing racial schemas. Indeed, numerous U.S. test-takers stated that the

DNA results made them appreciate "how *much* of a construct notions of race really are."

Another hypothesis I explored was whether evidence of continental genomic mixture might destabilize binary claims to Black or White identities, lending greater legitimacy to "mixed" or "multiracial" categories. In Brazil, I found that while adherence to Black movement discourses often primed individuals to expect a higher level of African ancestry than they were actually attributed, the internalization of these narratives also worked as a buffer against genealogical disorientation. These test-takers tended to repudiate mixed categories, asserting that "color" and personal identity politics were more important than DNA ancestry for orienting their racial identities. Among Brazilians identifying as *branco/a* or *pardo/a*, perceived mismatches between their ancestry expectations and genomic results were often seen as a "natural" effect of *mestiçagem*. Many reflected on the unreliability of appearance as an indicator of ancestry, but the results rarely led interviewees to change their self-declared "color," whether to Whiten or "darken" their identity (although some claimed to have noticed Whitening trends among other test-takers). This finding runs counter to traditional assertions about the fluidity and instability of Brazilian identity categories. Although it could simply be a product of the artificial setting of the interview, this tendency could also be linked to the influence of debates about university quotas, which have impressed on young Brazilians the need to develop a more coherent, stable racial identity.

Meanwhile, among African American test-takers, the issue of multiraciality was contentious. Some test-takers (in particular younger people) preferred to embrace mixed-race identities because they felt they better described their genomic ancestry and/or phenotype or because their personal experiences did not fit into monoracial categories. Others did not reject their mixed heritage, but they continued to identify as Black on the basis of their experiences of racialization, sense of cultural affiliation and family history, and identity politics. Although many U.S. test-takers (as well as Brazilian volunteers) argued that knowledge of ancestral "racial" mixture could help erode racist ideologies, a small number of African American test-takers suggested that discourses of mixture could play into practices of cultural Whitening. Although other studies have found evidence of White Americans changing racial labels on the basis of their DNA results, the test-takers I interviewed did not use their genomic ancestry as a basis for affirming Black identities (although both Black and White test-takers used their DNA results to make claims on Native American ancestry). Indeed, overall, most Brazilian and U.S. test-takers perceived that it was not these *invisible* ancestral mixtures but rather their *visible* appearance that was more important in shaping their lived experiences of racialization—a perspective that supports theories of a convergence on "color" as the most salient marker of racialization across the Americas. The furor caused by Rachel Dolezal "passing" for Black in the United States, and the denunciations of "race fraud" in the administration of affirmative action in Brazil, could have the effect of cultivating racial literacy more widely and strengthening critical stances against forms of "racial" appropriation.

Overall, the experiences explored here belie the idea that DNA ancestry tests are mainly attractive to members of the public as a way of unsettling existing modes of racial identification. In both countries, I noticed that test-takers tended to be less fascinated by their major ancestry proportions than by the smallest percentages represented in their reports. These categories were tantalizing either because they diverged from traditional family history narratives (possibly symbolizing an origin that was forcibly suppressed from collective memory) or because they chimed with half-remembered and never fully substantiated tales of an "exotic" ancestor. This, I think, is a major part of the appeal of DNA ancestry testing. It is the idea that our bodies "remember" our ancestral origins, even in the wake of processes of enforced cultural erasure, and that genetic techniques can act as a way of externalizing these traces. Following this idea, in the next chapter I shift my focus from race to ethnicity to examine the potential of DNA ancestry as a tool for recuperating "lost" ancestries: in this case, the identities of African ancestors displaced by slavery and the Middle Passage.

5 Essential Origins

. . . .

Ethnicity is sometimes envisaged as the antithesis of race. Whereas race is seen as the process by which communal connections and personal identities were broken in the context of slavery, ethnicity tends to be understood as denoting cultural specificity, intergenerational ties, and the inheritance of tradition. As Peter Wade has pointed out, however, the distinction between race and ethnicity is less clear-cut than it seems.[1] In the aftermath of the Second World War, scientists recommended the term "ethnic groups" as a substitute for the divisive concept of "races" when referring to culturally or linguistically defined groups.[2] While the term certainly evokes ideas of *cultural* distinctiveness, in many circumstances it also connotes beliefs in a common ancestry—often expressed, in Western societies, through the idiom of "blood."[3]

As we saw in chapters 2 and 3, in the context of DNA testing this mythical essence congeals in the form of "ancestry informative" genetic markers. Sampled reference populations stand in for entire "ethnic groups," and their shared genomic inheritance is mapped onto particular geographic regions, producing a naturalized connection between DNA markers, people, and soil. These processes have been criticized for geneticizing identities that are above all culturally and politically defined. Treating DNA markers as a means to recuperate preslavery identities, it is argued, ignores the demographic and political changes that have occurred throughout, and since, the period of the transatlantic trade, artificially fixing these categories in an idealized past.[4] For some observers, to rely on genetic ties to cultivate deep personal bonds to African societies is to miscomprehend the sociopolitical nature of such attachments. In Dorothy Roberts's words: "African American [DNA test-takers] are paying for a false sense of connection to a contemporary ethnic group in Africa, a connection that could be established through other, more authentic means."[5]

In her ethnographic study of the "social lives" of the DNA tests provided by African Ancestry, Alondra Nelson nevertheless notes that the consumers of these products are neither uncritical nor reductivist in how they interpret their genetic results in relation to their personal identities.[6] On the contrary, they demonstrate a keen concern for the social and scientific authenticity of these data. Nelson describes the case of one genealogist who, after finding that her DNA results contradicted oral histories about her family's origins, remarked: "We still don't technically know who we are." What used to feel certain was now cast into doubt. In Nelson's terms, "In her search for family, she has lost the familiar."[7] Even in cases where individuals fully accept their DNA results as proof of their ethnic origins, they make a distinction between the kinship links they make on the basis of this acquired knowledge and those that preexisted the genetic test—for instance, using tautological phrases like "DNA cousins" and "genetic kin." In Nelson's analysis, "The circulation of these phrases seems to suggest that the associations supplied through genetic genealogy are qualified and, therefore, must be rhetorically set apart from 'natural' kinship; or, in other words, that the results of genetic genealogy are categorical but imprecise."[8]

By delving further into how test-takers deal with their concerns regarding the historical and social authenticity of genetic identities, I illustrate the attempts of genetic roots-seekers to convert supposedly unknowable and unverifiable questions (i.e., the geographic and ethnic origins of their ancestors prior to slavery) into social and historical facts. Unlike Roberts, I do not take ethnic identities to be exclusively sociopolitical in nature; following John and Jean Comaroff, they can be "two things at once: the object of choice and self-construction, typically through the act of consumption, *and* the manifest product of biology, genetics, human essence."[9] Based on this premise, I focus instead on the choices and actions undertaken by DNA test-takers to verify and "activate" their genetic ties by social means, in order to convert this "unnatural" knowledge into something familiar and familial.[10] I also explore what happens when genomic data are perceived to contradict beliefs about personal identity and family history: What authority is given to DNA in relation to other forms of genealogical and embodied knowledge, as well as to considerations of personal choice and preference regarding ethnic and kinship affiliations? Moreover, how do quests for genetic roots, and the kinship claims they generate, dovetail with broader political and economic dynamics surrounding the memorialization of the transatlantic slave trade in West Africa?

The Genealogical Imperative

Genealogy has long roots in the United States, first originating in the era of the British colony. The nineteenth century marked the establishment of the first antiquarian societies whose members strove to standardize genealogical methods in an effort to weed out counterfeit pedigrees and elevate their passion to the status of science. This period also saw the founding of the first Black genealogical societies, established by groups of well-to-do African Americans for whom the study of illustrious family lineages was similarly a sign of personal pride and respectability, oriented toward the commemoration of ancestors who were considered pioneers (for instance, for having gained their own freedom and that of their family members) or who had won particular recognition and standing within their community. Since the 1950s, the field of family history has undergone a process of democratization, marked by the opening of local genealogical societies, the publication of genealogy magazines and manuals, and increasing public access to genealogical archives made available by libraries and Family History Centers founded by the Church of Jesus Christ of Latter-day Saints.[11]

Genealogical research can have many purposes and signify different things for different people. As Catherine Nash observes, genealogy today is "a practice that is both self-centered and collective, both individualized and relational. It is fueled by a desire to know oneself through a family past and the appeal of making connections—of finding relatives, joining up family trees."[12] Many practitioners enjoy the thrill of detective work, painstakingly collecting clues and tracking down long-lost relatives in order to piece together their family history. By the same token, genealogy "is also a practice of making relations."[13] It often involves reclaiming ties with living relatives who, for their part, may be more or less keen to be "rekinned." As well as a form of intellectual labor, Fenella Cannell has suggested, genealogy can be a form of emotional work, a way of caring for the dead and "exploring what the dead and the living owe each other in the contemporary world."[14]

The value of family history is abundantly apparent to African American genealogists, for whom recovering one's family lines means triumphing over systematic historical attempts to divest their ancestors of their ethnic identities and kinship networks and render them mere "property." Those who embark on this work are confronted with numerous historiographical challenges, including (1) the destruction of records kept by Black beneficial societies during the nineteenth century; (2) the enforced illiteracy of the majority of enslaved people, meaning that most left no written accounts of their own lives; (3) the frequent covert sexual relations between White slaveholders and enslaved women, which hindered the reliable identification of paternal lineages; (4) the replacement of African names on arrival in North America and habitual renaming of enslaved individuals as they were passed from one slaveholder to another; and (5) the sometimes unpredictable adoption of new surnames by the formerly enslaved on emancipation.[15]

Since the 1970s, numerous guides and manuals have been produced to help African Americans tackle these unique obstacles.[16] Today, a wealth of resources are available through web forums and blogs, courses and conferences, and there are communities of genealogists sharing online an avid interest in developing new techniques to shed light on the past—DNA testing being one such avenue.[17] Genealogists are particularly interested in DNA relative-matching techniques, which broadly involve searching for shared genomic segments in the DNA of two or more individuals, as a means of testing particular genealogical connections. This can be done manually, by comparing uniparental "lineages" (e.g., Y-DNA or mtDNA haplotypes) between potential genetic relatives; alternatively, numerous companies now offer relative-matching as a feature of their autosomal products. They use algorithms to detect identical sequences among the DNA of all participating customers, and the number and length of matching genomic segments are used to calculate the degree of genealogical relatedness between each pair of individuals—from paternal or sibling matches to sixth cousins.

The emergence of the first DNA ancestry-testing companies in the early 2000s was hailed with enthusiasm by some genealogists, who saw these technologies as a means to confirm existing research and break through genealogical "brick walls"—parts of the family tree for which no oral histories or documentation exists.[18] Yet it also raised concerns among those who believed that attitudes of "genetic exceptionalism" (the idea that DNA is inherently more powerful than other types of data) may cause family historians to treat this new information uncritically, raising its epistemic value above that of other historical sources. Among some African American genealogists, the success of African Ancestry's "ethnic lineage" tests, for instance, was viewed with ambivalence. While many welcomed the opportunity to emulate Alex Haley's feat by gaining concrete evidence of their African origins, others feared that these technologies could lead African Americans to neglect other forms of ancestral knowledge and disregard the potentially rich histories that could be gathered about their families' U.S. roots. In a 2009 interview Tony Burroughs, author of *Black Roots: A Beginner's Guide to Tracing the African American Family Tree*, gave the following advice to any Black genealogists considering taking one of these tests: "Genealogy is tracing your ancestry backward into time, one generation at a time, showing linkages between each generation. When you take a DNA test and that DNA test tells you something, that's not genealogy. Those results can sometimes be used within your genealogy research to sometimes prove certain things or sometimes disprove certain things."[19]

Burroughs's statement conveys a concern for scientific rigor and authenticity in the genealogical process, which was shared by the African American genealogists I interviewed during my fieldwork. When asked whether they would consider taking an "ethnic lineage" test, several responded that they "didn't feel ready for that," indicating that they had not yet reached far enough back in their family trees to be able to trace their roots to Africa. The methodology mentioned by Burroughs is standard among family historians. Gradually building up a family tree, one generation at a time, provides a solid and trustworthy route into the past; there can be no skipping steps. As much as a matter of intellectual pride, this is seen as a question of honoring one's ancestors and building a solid tradition that can be transmitted to future generations. Melvin J. Collier, author of *Mississippi to Africa: A Journey of Discovery*, advocates for the careful use of DNA data to complement and strengthen traditional genealogical methods, both for locating kin in the United States and for verifying the ethnic origins of African ancestors; in his words, together genealogy research and DNA technology can make "an indelible marriage."[20] In his book, Collier narrates his use of several African Ancestry uniparental tests to trace the origins of African-descendant individuals in his family tree. Where possible, he cross-references the DNA results with onomastic analyses of his ancestors' personal names, and with family lore about particular rituals or cultural traditions preserved in that part of the family, which may attest to a particular ethnic or regional origin.[21] Based on these experiences, and contrary to the long-held belief that it is "virtually impossible" for African Americans to trace their origins beyond slavery, Collier remains positive that "definitive links to specific West African cultures can still be made."[22]

In Brazil, the idea that little or nothing can now be learned about the origins of most enslaved individuals remains a common assumption. In part, this is the result of specific historiographical problems. First is the fact that a large proportion of nineteenth-century fiscal and customs documents relating to slave ownership were burned two years after the abolition of slavery—a purposeful act of destruction aimed at forestalling claims for indemnification from former slaveholders against the government for the loss of their human "property." While many other archives relating to slavery still survive (for instance, church records of baptisms and marriages and judicial archives relating to criminal processes and wills), for decades the infamous *queima do arquivo* (burning of the archive) was regarded by Brazilian historians and sociologists as an insuperable obstacle to reconstructing the Brazilian population's African ethnic origins.[23] Second is the issue that very few firsthand accounts of slavery were recorded in Brazil prior to abolition, while the first institutional attempts to collect oral histories from descendants of the enslaved took place nearly a century after abolition, in the 1980s.[24] Nonetheless, as Ana Lucia Araujo has signaled, this does not mean that such memories do not exist; rather, "they were restricted to the private spaces and . . . they were not recognized and valued."[25] This observation is supported by ethnographic data. For instance, while conducting a study among working-class Afro-Brazilian families in the state of Rio de Janeiro in the 1990s, France Winddance Twine observed that her informants used various strategies to retrospectively Whiten their family lineages—for instance, avoiding naming Black ancestors when recounting oral histories and showing only light-skinned relatives and acquaintances in the family portraits that decorated their living rooms (photos of ancestors with telltale "African" features tended to be kept safely out of view in boxes and closets). Twine also found that numerous individuals whom she identified as *mulato/a, moreno/a,* or *negro/a* had been registered by their parents as *branco/a* on their birth certificates—a strategy that allowed African-descendant Brazilians to disappear from the nation's official statistics.[26]

Similarly, in an interview conducted in 2004, Frei David dos Santos (one of the nine celebrities to take part in BBC Brasil's *Raízes Afro-Brasileiras* special, described in chapter 1) illustrated how processes of selective remembrance and omission informed his own racial identity while growing up. Frei David describes the moment he came to recognize his own Black ancestry as a young man training in a Franciscan monastery run by a German monk. One day, the Franciscan Brothers carried out an activity to encourage the Black novices to commemorate their enslaved ancestors, inviting them to eat at a table in the canteen together and receive a special homage to their ancestors:

> And since I never imagined myself to be *negro*, I always saw myself
> as someone who was "a little sunburnt from the beach" . . . I didn't
> accept my Blackness. And so, because of that, there fell this
> awkward atmosphere. To be honest, I didn't even feel targeted by
> the call to sit on that middle table. I sat down at the side tables with
> the other *brancos*. And when the activity began someone shouted:
> "Oops, there's an empty seat. Someone's missing. It's David." So half

a dozen Germans came and grabbed me by the arms and legs and placed me in the seat, in the middle of the table. I said: "Wait a minute. You're offending me in public. You're defaming me, you're calling me *negro* in front of everyone. That's assault. I don't accept that." And as soon as they let go of me in the middle of that table I swiped my hand out at the jug of water, knocked over two glasses, broke some things and left, I went to my room to pack my bags and leave.[27]

Before Frei David could leave, the Franciscan in charge asked to speak to him. He asked Frei David to bring him a photo of his mother and father. Frei David first showed him a picture of his mother, whom he described as "*branca*," and then one of his father, at which the Brother exclaimed: "Your father is *negro*!" The Brother went on to tell Frei David that he had been suffering from "an extremely dangerous, contagious illness . . . called the 'ideology of Whitening.'" He pointed out that he, a German monk, read in his language and studied his culture every week, to feed his sense of connection to his people. He asked Frei David if he did the same thing, to which he replied, "No sir. I never read a book about Black people." Frei David continues: "And that began to awaken in me a strange thing: 'goodness me, my father is a Black guy [*negão*], he never spoke about Black people to me.' And I began to think it over, to think back in the past: 'my father practically erased . . . his family, his siblings, his parents.' I mean, we all grew up without knowing his family. And he brought us as close as possible to my mother's family: *brancos*. . . . And so there I began to understand how it grew in us, in me and my siblings, the consciousness of the rejection of the racial issue."[28]

I met with Frei David in August 2013, at the headquarters of EDUCAFRO, the network of university preparatory courses for "Blacks and people in need" that he founded and directs in São Paulo. On the day we met, Frei David was accompanied by Flávio Carlos Nogueira, a volunteer who contributed regularly as a teacher and mentor in classes at the center on the topic of Black identity and self-esteem. During our conversation, Nogueira pointed out that Frei David frequently made a point of asking EDUCAFRO volunteers and attendees about their family background—something he said was unusual in Brazil:

You listen to anyone, even to me, and [you'll hear that] we don't question ourselves, in the way that Frei [David] has always questioned me, about our origins. What happens a lot here in Brazil is that we don't know our ancestry—which is completely different from over there in Europe, where people study that from the cradle, from their homes. Here in Brazil we don't study it, because most of our families are disorganized [*desestruturadas*]. The state helps to keep us disorganized, and what happens? The whole of society takes your roots away from you. Why? Because you're not interested.[29]

Nogueira's mention of "disorganized" families relates to reports of the increasing incidence of "nontraditional" family arrangements in recent years, including the prevalence of single-parent units, which are often linked to poor and dark-skinned Brazilian communities.[30] In his own case, Nogueira explained:

My father and my mother separated. I was three years old. I went to live with my father, and I didn't see my mother for twenty years. After Frei David questioned me about it, when I was twenty I went looking for my grandfather, because I had a memory about my grandfather being *negro*. . . . And he called my mother because he had her contact details, and I met my mother when I was twenty years old. There are lots of Brazilians like me . . . the majority—let's say 80 percent or more of children in the periphery are the children of single mothers. They don't even know who their fathers are. Others don't even know their mothers, like I didn't.[31]

For Nogueira and Frei David, this "disorganization" of poor families can be linked directly to the state's historical policy of Whitening, designed to "discriminate against Blacks and completely lower their morale and self-esteem" by forcing them to negate their African origins. A similar idea was put to me by Marcos Lopes de Souza, a member of the Órgão de Educação e Relações Étnicas (Office of Education and Ethnic Relations, ODEERE), a teaching and research network for continuing education based at the Universidade Estadual do Sudoeste da Bahia (UESB) in Jequié. Souza, a biology professor, related the problem of intergenerational memory within Afro-descendant families to systemic attempts to dismantle Black kinship structures under slavery:

That exercise of asking your grandfathers, your grandmothers—that's something that, in the case of Afro-Brazilian culture, was denied, because here you were really separated from those groups. The purpose was to separate those families so that there wouldn't be rebellions, or rather, to stop people from organizing. So that's why it's important for you to go through that process—get to know your ancestry, because people might think, well, Afro-Brazilians don't want to know their origins. No, they want to know. It's just that the enslavement process was so perverse that it separated families, so that you don't know who—where you came from. You knew it was Africa, but you didn't really know whereabouts or who your kin were.[32]

In recent decades, increasing efforts have been made to recover Afro-Brazilian histories and heritage as a means of repairing the psychological damage wrought by the legacies of slavery and the Whitening ideology, and of (re)constructing Afro-Brazilian subjectivities and identities. One scholarly approach has been to gather oral histories, particularly from *quilombos* (predominantly rural communities descended from runaway slaves), some of whom retain knowledge of their ancestors' origins in Africa.[33] Afro-Brazilian religions are also regarded as rich sources of African cultural heritage: Candomblé *terreiros*, in particular, have long positioned themselves as sites of resistance against the erasure of African culture and memory in Brazil. Since the 1960s, Candomblé has gained social prestige as a space for initiates of all racial and ethnic backgrounds to "become 'African'" by receiving elements of the cultural heritage preserved by the *terreiros'* spiritual communities.[34] Rather than focusing on divining initiates' genealogical origins (a practice pursued, for example, by devotees of the Akan movement in the United States),[35] the African ethnicity conferred in these rituals is understood to be a *cultural* identity, bearing no necessary relation to the person's family roots.

In 2003, moreover, a new law (Lei 10.639/2003) made the teaching of Afro-Brazilian and African culture and history compulsory in Brazilian schools—an initiative meant to revise the traditional portrayal of Brazilian culture as singular, homogeneous, and *mestiço* by valorizing the history, culture, and identities of people of African descent and their contributions to today's multicultural society. Initially, the program was criticized by academics who feared this multicultural teaching approach might essentialize Black and "Afro" identities and serve to aggravate current racial tensions, producing too much of a clean opposition between descendants of the enslaved and descendants of slaveholders in Brazilian society. As historians Martha Abreu and Hebe Mattos summarized: "How to break with a notion of a *mestiço* Brazil without reifying equally homogeneous, closed or semiclosed cultural groups within a multicultural paradigm that is quite widespread according to the North American experience, but certainly artificial in relation to Brazilian realities? How to stimulate intercultural conviviality and tolerance without thinking about mixtures and exchanges, especially cultural ones, even if we now think of them in the plural?"[36]

Those tasked with implementing the new law also faced practical and political obstacles. Alexandre Emboaba da Costa describes how the legislation has been unevenly implemented at state and municipal levels due to a lack of funding, time, and resources (among other things) that could enable teachers and administrative staff to undergo training and prepare adequate materials for teaching the new curriculum. There is also pervasive resistance to teaching "racial thematic[s]" at schools, as well as a scarcity of university degree programs specializing in African and Black Brazilian topics, which affects the quality of teaching most educators can provide.[37] Nonetheless, some Black organizations and cultural centers have been active in providing educators with pedagogical resources to fill in these lacunae. The emphasis here is less on individual ancestries (although many cultural and educational organizations do encourage their students to delve into personal and local Black histories) than on the concept of *ancestralidade* (ancestrality), defined as "a historical engagement with identity by way of an ancestral past and . . . the meanings and practices through which one cultivates, maintains, and realizes these links and a sense of self in new contexts and present circumstances." For Costa, the strength of this approach is that it is concerned less with historical authenticity than with contemporary invention. In his words:

> For black Brazilians, the idea of "knowing what we are" and "what we want to be" through *ancestralidade* does not simply involve reconstruction of the past to recover "tradition" or an essential identity. Rather, *ancestralidade* involves reconstruction of the past on one's own terms, taking a relation to history through one's own experience, and maintaining African and Afro-descendant ways of being, values, integrity, and knowledge. . . . Rather than an identity politics where the struggle to secure an identity drives action and often succumbs to essentialism, reification, and fundamentalism, the past as project involves a future-oriented vision that contests the multilayered effects of coloniality.[38]

The diverse trajectories taken by African Americans and Afro-Brazilians to try and reconstruct memories and traces of their African origins have created different standards for what can be thought of as "authentic" ancestral identities and how they can be retrieved. The genealogical tradition of the United States sets a high bar for epistemic validity since it requires genetic or documentary proof of unbroken "bloodlines" and ancestral kinship. Recent efforts to (re)construct African and Afro-Brazilian identities, on the other hand, have largely revolved around culturalist conceptions of identity and ancestry, since "racial" mixture is seen as an obstacle to grounding Afro-Brazilianity *predominantly* in notions of genetic continuity or racial exclusivity. Meanwhile, as we saw in chapter 1, affirmations of ethnic identity are regarded very differently in each country. Whereas the "ethnic hyphen" is integral to U.S. identity, in Brazil it is more likely to be seen as a rejection of one's *brasilidade*.

This does not mean, though, that Black Brazilians are uninterested in using genetics to trace their individual African origins. Indeed, in 2014 when a production team from the Brazilian studio Cine Group set out to make a five-part television documentary based on this premise, they encountered a great deal of enthusiasm. By exploring the experiences of participants of the resulting documentary, *Brasil: DNA África*, alongside those of African American roots-seekers, I suggest the extent to which these different epistemic traditions may influence the validity and salience that test-takers attribute to their genetic "ethnic" identities.

Strange Familiarities

Brasil: DNA África was filmed as a five-part documentary series, with each episode focusing on one of Brazil's main slave-importing states: Bahia, Pernambuco, Maranhão, Rio de Janeiro, and Minas Gerais. The production team offered African Ancestry mtDNA tests to 150 Afro-Brazilians, including celebrities, community and religious leaders, and members of *quilombos*, among others. The first half of every episode included overviews of the region's Afro-Brazilian history and culture and interviews with the DNA test-takers; the second half followed one individual traveling to an African country to meet members of their DNA-matched ethnic group. According to one of the show's directors, the genetic test was intended as a form of "narrative device"; the volunteers were free to make up their own minds about the value and significance of the information it yielded. Overall, the aim was to create a documentary that offered a positive and celebratory vision of Brazil's African heritage, which could also be used by educators to stimulate discussions about the country's history of slavery.[39]

I met Juliana Luna, one of the show's participants, in June 2015. The filming for the documentary had already concluded, and Luna (as she is known in Brazil) was one of five individuals who had been selected to travel to Africa to meet her "genetic kin." A designer, entrepreneur, and influencer from Rio de Janeiro, Luna is known in Brazil for her social engagement on issues of antiracism and women's rights, as well as for her African head-wrap designs. As she explained to me, she first learned to use headwraps while staying with a Nigerian family of Yoruba origin in the United States. At the time she was in an abusive relationship, and the contact with the family, the headwrap, an African culture helped her find the strength to get out of the situation. Since then, the headwrap had become the symbol of her business venture, Project Tribe, a creative platform to inspire women to seek for a deeper meaning through their ancestral identity.[40]

Luna was approached by the Cine Group film crew in early 2015 and agreed to participate in the project. In an early scene, she is asked what she expects from her DNA results. She replies, "I didn't want to create any expectations, to be honest . . . because what was, will be. I *am*, you know, I'm here, I exist, and it's not up to the DNA test to determine who I am, for better or for worse." When the mtDNA report came back two months later, it indicated that she shared ancestry with Yoruba and Fulani peoples in Nigeria. The moment was captured on film, and Luna is visibly moved. When she is asked by someone off-screen if she would like to travel to Nigeria, her lips tremble and she wipes away tears before replying, "Of course I want to go! How could I not?"[41]

Luna traveled to Nigeria in May 2015. The producers had arranged a schedule, and although it "didn't really go to plan," she was able to meet various prominent Nigerian artists, including musician Femi Kuti, playwright Wole Soyinka, and textile designer Nike Okundaye. The latter made a strong impression on Luna. Okundaye greeted her with the words "Welcome back home, my daughter," and later presented her with one of her own neckbands, telling her, "I want you to have a piece of my spirit wherever you go." These words "made me feel at home," Luna said. Okundaye sent Luna to meet the ruler of Osogbo, the capital of Osun state, telling her that she needed a Yoruba name and an *orixá* to become a functioning member of Nigerian society. The meeting between Luna and Oba Aderemi Adedapo was captured by the documentary crew. The oba welcomes her with a declaration: "We are happy to welcome you back here, because your genes have been here for millions of years. They have only been there for less than 500 years. So you can see the connection and you are welcome back home." Speaking in Yoruba, he initiates a naming ritual, telling Luna that in her first incarnation she was a princess, and it is these royal roots that have allowed her to return to her homeland. He confers on her a Yoruba name, Osun Yemisi, meaning "Osun has honored me," in reference to the water goddess who "called her back across the water." As soon as she left the *oba*'s house, a heavy rain fell. Luna remembered feeling it was sign from Osun and "almost like, in a Christian sense, a baptism."

The final destination on the trip was the Slave Port at Badagry, close to the border with Benin. Standing on the beach opposite where the slave ships used to dock, Luna told me that she cried when she realized her surname (De Moura) was a slave name, signifying that her ancestors were owned by the Portuguese De Moura family. She thought about all the people who are "still living the legacies of slavery in Brazil" and recalled hurtful experiences of her own, such as going into a restaurant and being asked if she worked there or, more recently, being taken for a foreigner in her own country because of the African designs she wears. Returning to Africa was "powerful," Luna said, and on arriving back in Brazil she felt that "everything had changed."

For Luna, there seemed little room for doubt over the truth of her Yoruba identity. In fact, Luna's DNA results listed two different ethnic matches (Yoruba and Fulani), yet at no point in the documentary was there a suggestion of exploring the Fulani link. The connection with the headwraps—which had become highly significant for Luna as a symbol of her personal development and the core of her enterprise—was compelling, and she recalled that many of her friends had taken it as a sign that she was "chosen for this." Chosen by whom? Roots-seekers of varying backgrounds express the feeling that they are being guided to recuperate lost origins and ancestral knowledge. Fenella Cannell observes that apparent coincidences, or the accidental finding of key information, are often described by genealogists as "serendipity," whose function is "to gift to you the ability to continue to connect to your 'dead family.'"[42] Luna's experience of having lived with a Nigerian-American family (again, by choice or by accident?) who taught her to use headwraps could be regarded as a sign of predestiny. Conversely, it could be the personal affinity Luna felt for the headwraps that led her (and the documentary team) to choose to solidify this particular ethnic link, rather than pursuing her connection to the Fulani (or neither of the two).

Asserting an ethnic identity, of course, is not merely a question of self-definition; it also depends on being recognized by an ethnic community. Whereas Luna was told that a Yoruba name and link to an *orixá* were the two things needed for her to become part of Nigerian society, other roots-seekers featured in the documentary were told differently. Zulu Araújo, a

Black movement leader from Salvador who was president of the Fundação Cultural Palmares[43] from 2007 to 2010 and also acted as a research consultant for the series, was genetically matched to the Tikar of Cameroon. The result was a surprise for him. Having grown up in Bahia with the influence of Candomblé, Araújo assumed he was of Yoruba or Angolan origin. During a visit with Chief Ibrahim Gah II in the town of Bankim, Cameroon, Araújo asked what it meant to be a member of the "Tikar family." The chief replied, "You will have to be familiar with our territory. Then, we'll introduce you to the men of the tribe, find a wife for you to marry and a plot of land for you to build your home."[44] His response made it clear that the DNA connection was only the first step to becoming Tikar, and that much weightier social commitments were needed to solidify Araújo's status as "kin." In the final scenes of the episode, Araújo reflected that the trip had reinforced his sense that he was *not* African, but Brazilian. Nonetheless, he later reiterated the importance of the experience as a form of reparation for Afro-Brazilians, affirming: "I was always aware that one of the greatest crimes against the Black population was not torture, nor violence: it was taking away the possibility of knowing our origins. We are the only populational group in Brazil that doesn't know where they come from."[45]

Luna was one of many roots-seekers I met who felt that their DNA ancestry results had confirmed an ethnic affinity at which they had already arrived, whether through imposition, choice, or serendipity. I met Ofosuwa in February 2014 during my fieldwork in the United States. A researcher of African history who also worked as the manager of an African dance company, Ofosuwa had taken two different DNA ancestry tests a few years back. Her interest in African culture, she told me, originated in her childhood in New York City, where she grew up during the 1960s. In her words, "There was a lot of racism and things going on . . . it made me feel like an outsider, so as a little girl I would often lie on my bed and imagine being back in Africa, because that's where I felt like, I must have belonged there, if I didn't belong here. So as I grew up . . . I just grew more and more interested in African culture, so I changed my name to Ofosuwa, and as I progressed along, I felt like I was doing things instinctively that were African. I wanted to know if that was true."

Ofosuwa's perception that she was "doing things instinctively that were African" was reinforced by the reactions of African-born people she had met in the United States and West Africa. For instance, she recalled attending a concert in the early 2000s in the United States, where the dancers kept bringing her up on the stage to dance: "I was telling [my two sons who were with me], 'Yeah, they must know that I'm a dancer, they keep pulling me on the stage to dance'—but later, my ex-husband told me that they thought that I was Fulani, from the Gambia." Soon after, Ofosuwa traveled to the Gambia to study dance. At the time, she told me, she kept an eye out for other people who resembled her physically, "and I didn't find that. I found some Fulani who in terms of complexion were the copper brown or the honey brown as they call me, but more people were very dark complexion, and even some Fulani that I met were very dark complexion, so I was like 'wow, I don't look like anybody here.'" Nonetheless, locals continued to assume that Ofosuwa and her family were Fulani, and to point out curious coincidences in her choices and actions. For example, on one occasion when she was invited to have a henna design painted onto her hands and feet, friends and acquaintances observed that she had chosen "specifically a Fulani design."

On returning to the United States in 2005, Ofosuwa decided to take a genetic ancestry test to find out whether there was any deeper foundation to these coincidences. Initially, she took an mtDNA test with FamilyTreeDNA, which provided her with a technical description of the haplotype and the marker's broad biogeographical origin (mainly found in African populations). "Beyond that," Ofosuwa told me, "there were no real details; it wasn't really tied to an ethnic group or even really a region, so it wasn't really satisfying." A few years later, she heard about African Ancestry and decided to take a second test in the hope that the company would provide her with an affiliation to a specific ethnic group. This time, Ofosuwa recalled, the result came back "100 percent Fulani" from northern Nigeria, "and I said, 'wow, this is really something.' The Fulani part, it didn't blow me away, but I was very intrigued because I said 'wow, this is what they have been saying when I was in the Gambia the whole time,' so in the way I was kind of surprised but wasn't, because they had already been saying that."

Despite feeling pleased that the observations of numerous West African friends and acquaintances had been borne out by the test, two specific aspects of the African Ancestry results gave Ofosuwa pause for thought. One was the regional estimate. In her words, "I was more partial to the Senegambia region, which is the region I do my research in, so I said, you know, well, I already felt I had this African connection, which is what led me to get the DNA [test], so wow, that I would be totally wrong [about] this. . . ." The second element was the "100 percent"—a figure frequently included in African Ancestry's uniparental results as a "sequence similarity score" but which Ofosuwa interpreted as an admixture proportion, reflecting her maternal ancestors' lack of exogamy with other ethnic groups:

I said: "How is that possible?" We've been there, obviously intermarrying—you know, there's Native Americans, I thought that there'd be some European ancestry in there—how could it be 100 percent? Then I started thinking about my family who traced their lineage back to the woman that got off the slave ship in Newport News, Virginia. And I started doing research and I found that most of the slaves stayed generally in the area where they were dropped off; the slave owners purchased slaves from the ships . . . [and] they kept them in that main area, for the most part. So I said, "Obviously, they must have intermarried with like people, people with like culture, so other Fulanis," and then I did read also that . . . slaves did look for like cultures, like ethnic groups, because they were in this strange land and, you know, under this oppressive system of slavery, so of course they're looking for the most familiar thing they can find. So quite often two married each other, quite often Fulanis married Fulanis, Mandinkas married Mandinkas, and obviously we kept doing that.

Nevertheless, Ofosuwa felt compelled to confirm the accuracy of her genetic result. In 2012, she took the Genographic Project's Geno 2.0 test, which included an admixture analysis. Although the mtDNA results did not offer a more precise estimate of her haplogroup origins, Ofosuwa's autosomal results attributed her a large percentage of "sub-Saharan African" ancestry, with smaller proportions of "South African" and "North African," but no "European" or "Native American" ancestry. Despite her incredulity at the result—which contradicted not only general historical accounts of the racial and ethnic mixing that took place under slavery in the United States, but also her own family lore, which included references to Native American ancestors on her maternal side—this time, Ofosuwa took the result to be definitive. In retrospect, the genetic evidence that she was not only Fulani but also "100 percent African" seemed to confirm the numerous observations made by African friends and relatives, as well as certain mannerisms and customs that she had noticed among her own U.S. family members. For instance, Ofosuwa remembered showing a package of Gambian lye soap to her mother, who instantly recognized the stuff, explaining that her grandmother had made it for years at their family home in Virginia. Although she knew of no family lore affirming her ancestors' connection to the Fulani, Ofosuwa felt that such acts spoke for themselves, describing them as "just inherent."

In addition, Ofosuwa had begun to conduct some research into a theory that she thought might account for the incongruence between her African Ancestry genetic result—which linked her most closely to a Fulani population in Northern Nigeria—and her own sense of affinity with the Senegambian region. This theory rested on the idea that Ofosuwa's ancestors might have migrated into Northern Nigeria from the Senegambian region in the late eighteenth century, in the company of the Islamic leader Usman dan Fodio. She told me, "I'm thinking, maybe—and again, this is more of a feeling, I haven't got any confirmation yet—but I'm thinking we probably did migrate from that area, and I was told that by folks in the Gambia. They said that they think that Fulas came from the Guinea region—that's what I call the greater Senegambian region."

Ofosuwa's cautious observation that her theory was based on "feeling" aptly encapsulates the tension that many test-takers experience between the desire to prove the authenticity of an affirmed ancestral identity and the sense that any historical legitimation of this identity is out of reach. During our meeting, Ofosuwa—like many other U.S. test-takers that I interviewed—affirmed her sense of affinity with her result, while simultaneously asking my opinion about its scientific value, as if searching for further confirmation of an identity that already seemed overdetermined by her own preferences and choices, not to mention the recognition of others. I was struck by the similarity between Ofosuwa's and Juliana Luna's reactions to their African Ancestry results. Both indicated that they were "surprised, but not surprised," as if the DNA test had confirmed an instinctive "feeling" about their affinities to Africa that had always seemed too good to be true. This incredulity perhaps speaks to the power of the myth that few, if any, original traits survived slavery and that all "true" Africanisms must be learned anew for members of the diaspora, inspiring a permanent quest for authenticity.

One of the strategies Ofosuwa used to test the authenticity of this identity was to search for physical likenesses between herself and Fulani people she met in the Gambia. While the idea that all genetic kin share physical resemblances is not universally held among cultures, for many roots-seekers, finding "people who look like me" is a way of gaining additional confirmation that they are on the right path toward their family origins.[46] Similarly, in Brasil: DNA África, Zulu Araújo met a Tikar queen whom he said reminded him physically of his mother, and upon arriving in Yaoundé he perceived numerous likenesses to the gestures, greetings, and physiognomies of his native Bahia.[47] On the other hand, a lack of resemblance can also be used to shed doubt on ethnic claims. For example, one African American roots-seeker

I spoke to was attributed "markers that closely aligned with the Fulani and Yoruba peoples of Nigeria." Upon sharing the results with several Nigerian acquaintances, the reactions were skeptical. One woman said she could not see any Yoruba in her and wondered where that information had come from. Another stated, "You could have Fulani in you, but you look more like Igbo to me."

In Ofosuwa's case, the likenesses perceived by her Fulani acquaintances appeared less rooted in physical appearance than in her behavior and personal tastes—characteristics she could only describe as "inherent." While researching popular theories of heredity in a northern English town, Jeanette Edwards spoke with one informant who described how he shared certain personality traits, like preferences for particular hobbies and views on certain topics, with his deceased father, whom he never met. These characteristics, he believed, must have been "biologically passed down."[48] Genetics and biology are often drafted in to explain the uncanny likenesses of different kinds that run in families. Yet they are not the only possible explanation. In his discussion of musical genealogies within the "Black Atlantic," for instance, Paul Gilroy has written of how different communicative forms, such as music, gesture, and dance, came to act as surrogates for written or spoken language amid the terror regime of the plantation.[49] These cultural cues, repertoires, and "ways of doing things" could be understood as the bases for an embodied, kinesthetic memory, comprising familiar gestures, activities, textures, rhythms, and aesthetics that continue to be passed down imperceptibly, long after verbalized memories of Africa have been suppressed.

For Ofosuwa, what the DNA test provided was the recovery of a name ("Fulani") that seemed to explain all of the "African" things that she already felt she was doing. Her identity, though, was not merely hereditary, but something that she had cultivated and worked at; it was ascribed to her by others, but also something she chose repeatedly, through her work, relationships, and artistic pursuits. By the time of our interview, Ofosuwa said that she now felt comfortable affirming her African/Fula identity in certain contexts, and that she had even come to feel this affiliation more prominently than her African American identity. During recent trips to Senegal, where she had begun to learn Wolof, her interlocutors frequently had difficulty believing that she was from the United States, typically judging her to be Nigerian (on account of her speaking English) or else South African. The ability to "pass" as African is often greatly prized among U.S. roots-seekers, as a sign that their belonging in their adoptive societies is now beyond question.[50] This "African" identity was even something Ofosuwa had passed on to her children. In her words, "My son still tells everyone, 'well, I'm Fulani'. . . . Even though his father's DNA does figure in, and I do tell him that, but he says 'no, I'm taking it from my mother, you're straight Fulani,' so I'm like, OK. . . . My youngest son . . . says, 'well, everyone thinks I'm African anyway'—and they do, most people—and he tries to tell them; they see the African name, and not only that, but his features are very striking, and he tries to tell them 'I was born and raised here,' and they don't believe him."

For her part, since our interview in 2015, Luna had been living and working in the United States, but she also continued to solidify her connection to Nigeria and Yoruba culture. She returned to Nigeria twice more and spent time studying textile art with Nike Okundaye. When we spoke again in 2020, Luna told me that during this time she had begun to focus less on the aesthetic aspects of ancestry (embodied by her headwrap art) and more on spiritual practices and philosophies of Africanity—what she referred to as "the invisible aspect of ancestry." Whereas she had always felt ambivalent about the political objectives of Brazil's Black movements, Luna signaled that her DNA ancestry experience had reinforced her sense of connection to a global diasporic community. Her new project, the Aluna Method,[51] is inspired by Yoruba philosophy and oriented toward "other people in the diaspora." It involves teaching a set of techniques for understanding ancestry and how it can equip individuals to leave a legacy of good, care, sustainment, and community. In Luna's words, "It teaches us that we're not alone, we're not separate, there are no coincidences."

Getting to the Root of It

The accounts described above suggest that test-takers' notions about the validity of their DNA ethnicity results are partly personal and partly informed by broader societal trends. Ofosuwa's efforts to verify her DNA results by retesting with several other companies reflect a common strategy among test-takers in the United States, where a high value is placed on the historical and biological authenticity of ethnicity claims. In comparison, the participants and producers of *Brasil: DNA África* seemed less aware of the possible epistemic limitations of DNA ancestry tests and more inclined to accept the results at face-value. Nevertheless, they did not assume these identities unconditionally or wholesale. For her part, Luna regarded her DNA results not as the end point of an identity quest, but rather as information that contributed to forging her sense of purpose in life.

For some African American genealogists, the appeal of DNA testing is less about adopting an African ethnic identity than it is about identifying the historical origins of a specific ancestor and connecting with long-lost African relatives—tasks for which genetic "ethnicity" matching may be seen as too broad an approach. In one of my interviews I was told of the case of a genealogist named William Holland from Atlanta, Georgia, who had successfully used DNA testing to identify living kin in West Africa. Holland's story is relayed in a series of blogs published between 2010 and 2013 by science writer Alan Boyle for NBC News. Contrary to the reputed precision of DNA as a technology of identification, Holland's case illustrates the complexities of piecing together family lineages in the absence of conventional forms of genealogical evidence (e.g., personal names, oral histories, written documentation)—particularly in contexts where the trauma of the slave trade remains buried just beneath the surface, so that digging into this past can bring up painful narratives of inherited guilt and victimhood.

The first posts detail Holland's initial trips to the Mankon region of northwest Cameroon in 2010. He had taken a Y-DNA test with the company GeneTree, a now defunct genetic testing service based in Utah, which compared his DNA with that of other users in the database, as well as with pedigrees from the Sorenson Molecular Genealogy Foundation (SMGF, discussed in chapter 3). Having discovered several matches with a community in Mankon, Holland traveled there—first alone, and later accompanied by several members of his immediate family.[52] On this second trip in November 2010, Boyle stated that Holland had been "embraced . . . so completely [by the king of Mankon] that the American was ceremonially given the name of the king's father."[53]

The meeting did not mark the end of Holland's roots search. Having subsequently discovered another "high genetic match" through his Y-DNA haplotype to a clan in Ghana, which the GeneTree scientists attributed to a common ancestor who lived some 1,000 to 1,500 years ago, he traveled to meet the Akpaglo royal family of the Ghanaian village Adidokpoe-Battor. The title of Boyle's blog post on the episode—"Atlanta family's roots get tangled up in Africa"—implied a sense of genealogical disorientation: How could Holland be matched to (at least) two clans in two different African countries? Which ones were his "real" kin? In fact, the Akpaglo elders explained, their own ancestors had roots elsewhere: they migrated southward from Sudan more than a millennium ago, eventually coming to settle in present-day Ghana, as part of the Oyo Empire. Other migratory groups had settled elsewhere in the Gold Coast—a fact Holland believed might explain his link through the same Y-DNA sequence to the group living in Mankon. Holland told Boyle that he now hoped to try and identify the original "patriarch" of his Y-DNA lineage, potentially going back thousands of years.[54]

In his account of the saga, Boyle described Holland's DNA-led discoveries as "an embarrassment of genealogical riches." For many roots-seekers, there is certainly a sense that accumulating a long family history constitutes a form of intangible heritage, a precious "asset" to be passed down to enrich future generations. The question of "how far back" a genealogist has managed to trace a particular pedigree is usually a matter of great pride—especially for members of the African diaspora, who are inevitably confronted with the "brick wall" of slavery. Being able to trace a paternal lineage back to Africa is even more challenging given the large proportion of enslaved children who were fathered by White men. Rick Kittles, the scientific director of African Ancestry, has estimated that around a third of Y-chromosome tests processed by the company are matched to European populations.[55] For their part, the Akpaglo welcomed Holland to their clan and invited him to receive three new names: Togbe (meaning "old wise man"), Korsi ("born on a Sunday"), and Degboe ("brave person who went away and returned"). In return, Holland invited members of both Ghanaian and Cameroonian groups to attend a family reunion in June 2011, hosted in Virginia near the plantation where his ancestors had been enslaved and worked for many generations. In arranging for his African American and West African relatives to meet in this context, Holland hoped to enlighten his family "about Africa and what happened in the slave trade."[56]

By the end of 2011, however, Holland's relationship with the Mankon had begun to sour. The first hitch was when Fon Angwafo III had to cancel his trip to the Virginia family reunion "because of political obligations at home." Instead, the reunion was attended by his wife, son, and nephew, as well as other representatives from Mankon.[57] In a blog post dated November of that year, Boyle noted: "A year ago, Holland thought the genetic linkages showed a strong tie to royalty in a Cameroonian region known as Mankon. But after additional genetic tests and consultations with historians in Africa . . . he has focused on [the Cameroonian region of] Oku instead. In fact, some of the people living around Mankon just might be the descendants of tribes that were involved in the slave trade."[58] According to Holland, the realization that some groups from Mankon acted as intermediaries in the slave trade propelled him to reconsider his genetic affiliation to the community. He told Boyle that after discovering this he did not speak to some of his Mankon contacts for a month. In contrast, having spoken at length with members of the Wambeng family of the Oku community, Holland began to feel a new sense of affinity for this group, even recognizing certain mannerisms and linguistic details from his U.S. family among them, which increased his conviction that they—rather than the royal family in Mankon—were his closest African relatives.

In turn, historians of the region helped Holland to piece together a story that could account for his genetic affinity to both Cameroonian groups, originating at different points in history. According to them, the Oku and Mankon were both descended from groups that migrated to the area between the seventh and tenth centuries and became unified within the Tikar kingdom in the thirteenth century. Based on the GeneTree scientists' calculation that his genetic link to the fons of Mankon had originated "about 440 years ago," Holland estimated that his shared ancestor with that group had lived around the year 1550. Oku, on the other hand, was founded a century later, in around 1650, and the present-day Wambeng family was said to be descended from the third fon, who lived at around the time that Holland estimated his own ancestor to have arrived in Virginia, in the early 1770s. Holland's hypothesis was that his ancestor was the guard of an Oku palace, who was captured during a slave raid on a province not far from Mankon and sold to European traders. He stated, "Now it makes sense that I was not directly related to the palace in Mankon. Did my people come from there? No. Did they pass through there? Yes."[59]

Traditionally, genealogy is concerned with organizing ancestors into orderly lineages that stretch straight back into the past. In Holland's saga, however, we see that time and ancestral ties are not always perceived as linear; rather, they become distorted as they pass through periods of conflict and trauma. The European trades in enslaved Africans and the prolonged social crises they provoked in African states are a prime example. Slavery created stark oppositions: communities were at war with one another; people who were once kin become strangers and foes. These events echo through time: in Holland's case, they affect perceptions of how close or distant a relationship is. Whereas the Akpaglo were regarded as family, based on an ancestral connection dating to over 1,000 years ago, the Mankon (with whom Holland shared a more recent ancestral connection) came to be seen as "not directly related" and not "my people," because of their antagonistic role in the slave trade. Subjective choices of this kind are integral to genealogical practices, which may be seen as a way to recuperate and nourish ties with ancestral kin. By the same token, some kin may be seen as closer, more worthy of care, than others—a fact that need not have anything to do with temporal or genealogical distance.[60]

The discovery led Holland to reexamine his earlier dealings with the Mankon. In retrospect, he told Boyle he had felt uneasy with his relationship to the fons of Mankon since their early meetings, and that this discomfort had intensified during the organization of the Holland family reunion in Virginia. "Something about the event felt wrong," Boyle noted.[61] Holland reported that certain members of the Mankon had strongly resisted the idea of a reunion. "That told me that 'this is not your family, because they should be happy, they should be welcoming you.'"[62] Conversely, Holland said that when he met the Oku, "You felt the sense of coming back. You felt the welcoming that you should have gotten. They were running down the hill to come and meet us. That's how it was." After lengthy discussions with the tribe's elders, Holland now believed that his own enslaved African ancestor was descended from "a widely respected member of the Oku tribe named Bailack who lived in the 1700s," several of whose sons were abducted and passed on to European slavers over the course of that century. Relating this narrative back to the genetic evidence, Boyle asked, "Do the genetics support Holland's status as Bailack's great-great-great-great-great grandson? The evidence isn't indisputable. Thirty-one of the thirty-six genetic markers on the test that Holland took match up with the results from the Cameroonian clan. Genetic genealogy is a matter of probabilities, and the more markers two people have in common, the more likely it is that they're closely related. Thirty-one out of thirty-six is not super-close, but close enough for Holland to feel as if he's on the right track."[63]

As much as a "matter of probabilities," Holland's negotiations with the Mankon and the Oku seemed to be led by affective responses to his reception among each group. Elsewhere, I have explored the role played by instinct and reciprocity during genetic family reunions in influencing whether genetic kin choose to consolidate a "family" relationship.[64] The dimension of choice is central here too, and it operates on multiple levels. For many African-descendant roots-seekers, one of the most painful and incomprehensible aspects of the transatlantic slave trade is the historical complicity of certain African states that traded with Europeans and profited from this human traffic. Since the period of slavery itself, this foundational trauma has often been portrayed as a family betrayal, as illustrated by the metaphor of "Africans selling their brothers and sisters into slavery" (an adage beloved by European and American apologists of slavery, since it alleviated their own culpability for these atrocities). From Holland's perspective, the Mankon's reticence to solidify their family bond suddenly seemed indicative of an old guilt for their ancestors' alleged part in helping subjugate their own "brethren," including Holland's enslaved ancestor. In contrast, the enthusiasm shown by the Oku was taken as indicative of their clear conscience in this respect, and their commitment to restoring ties with their U.S. kin.

The Past in the Present

The above account traces a common theme in transatlantic encounters between African-descendant roots-seekers and those identified as their African genetic kin. In their quests to be reunited with an ethnic community, roots-seekers are often confronted, paradoxically, with a persistent and troubling schism between those who stayed and those whose ancestors were sent across the ocean in chains. In these encounters, time seems to crumple as each interlocutor steps into their respective ancestors' roles of "victim" and "perpetrator." Ana Lucia Araujo has observed that this "presentist" regime of historicity is characteristic of contemporary projects to memorialize the transatlantic slave trade and American plantation slavery, in which "memory is no longer just the transmission of an account preserved by an individual or group; [it] is an instrument *allowing individuals and groups into the present*—a moment or place of rupture that produces a search for a denied, lost, or suppressed identity."[65] This opposition is dealt with in different ways by the African communities that receive roots-seekers from the diaspora. For instance, we can recall the speech given by the Yoruba chief, Oba Aderemi Adedapo, in which he told Juliana Luna that her ancestor was a "princess," and that this had given her the ability to return on behalf of her forebears. The conferral of royal epithets on African-descendant returnees is sometimes referred to, pejoratively, as a way for the latter to "jump slavery" by adopting an (often romanticized) African name and social identity. Yet, it may also be understood as a gesture of reconciliation: a status given to recognize the resilience and greatness of spirit of those who survived slavery.[66]

For Saidiya Hartman, such actions obscure the complex social dynamics at play in the internal African slave trades. Hartman argues that "contrary to popular belief, Africans did not sell their brothers and sisters into slavery. They sold strangers: those outside the web of kin and clan relationships, nonmembers of the polity, foreigners and barbarians at the outskirts of their country, and lawbreakers expelled from society."[67] Not all those who were enslaved were sent across the ocean, and many African communities remain riven by deep social divisions between the historical ruling classes and those whose ancestors were forced into servitude.[68] Hartman's analysis raises uncomfortable questions: How can one search for truth about histories of slavery in societies where these pasts are still taboo? If slavery was the fate meted out to those defined by the ruling classes as "outsiders" and "barbarians," is Africa the right place for diasporic descendants of the enslaved to look for family?

Gestures of apology, meanwhile, are becoming an increasingly common way of seeking reconciliation between West African communities and members of the diaspora. William Holland's search for his roots resulted in him requesting an official apology from the leader of the Cameroonian town of Bakou for his people's historical involvement in the capture and enslavement of the Oku, ostensibly including one of Holland's ancestors. The negotiation of the apology began in early 2013, when Holland discovered three long-lost ceremonial masks belonging to the Oku and Nso clans being sold on eBay.[69] During his visit to repatriate the masks, Holland took with him chains and shackles used during the Middle Passage to show to the groups and encourage them to make amends for their ancestral roles in the trafficking of Africans to the New World. The public apology—which was to be given by eight local leaders in front of hundreds of members of the public—apparently did not go smoothly. At the last moment the leaders "balked at signing the English-language document that Holland had prepared. Instead, they put their names to a different document that was drawn up in French, Cameroon's other official language."[70] On Holland's insistence, the fon of Bakou later signed his English version of the document, which specifically mentioned Holland and his family. This apology contained the statement: "We are sorry and issue an official apology for our involvement and the involvement of our ancestors in the horrible institution of transatlantic slavery. The United States of America, France, and the United Kingdom should issue similar formal apologies for this evil institution that broke up families and caused generational hardships that continue to the present day."

In his discussion of the memorialization of the transatlantic slave trade in Benin over the past two decades, Gaetano Ciarcia has argued that "rhetorical" gestures of apology by West African communities and nations are often mobilized pragmatically in the hopes of securing business and economic relationships with members of the diaspora.[71] For his part, Holland mentioned his ambition to take a "role in . . . U.S.-supported programs to upgrade Cameroon's water and sanitation facilities and preserve the remains of a historic slave-trade port in Bimbia," as well as his interest in "starting a tour business that would be focused on his ancestral home in Oku country"—a mission that could give an economic boost to the region.[72] While such arrangements stand to benefit West African economies, they can introduce uneven power dynamics between African-descendant and African communities and produce dilemmas for those called on to shoulder moral responsibility for their forebears' actions. Often, African leaders use the opportunity to call on powerful nations to apologize in turn, thus forcing these nations to formally assume their responsibility for the transatlantic slave trade and, by extension, address the possibility of negotiating reparations for its long-term impacts on the African diaspora and African states alike. As Gwendolyn Midlo Hall has pointed out, despite the rising trend of African communities accepting responsibility and apologizing for their role in the transatlantic slave trade, the historical responsibility for this period cannot be placed equally on the shoulders of African and European states. In her words, "Although European maritime traders had to negotiate as equals—and often as inferiors—with African traders along the Atlantic coast, in broad perspective over time, African power was undermined and fractionalized by the slave trade and the warfare, social disorganization, and population loss that it involved."[73] So far, however, explicit apologies and discussions of reparation have not been forthcoming from European or American nations.[74]

The use of genetic genealogy as a basis for requests for apology gives these interactions a personal dimension, turning them into "family affairs." While Holland's saga seems exceptional, efforts are being made to facilitate more DNA-assisted reunions among African-descendants and Africans.[75] Since 2017, for example, the African Royale DNA Project, run by the volunteer-led organization DNA Tested African Descendants, has been collecting DNA samples from "African royals, village chieftains and clan leaders" and uploading them with accompanying genealogical data to the platforms of autosomal DNA test providers, where they can generate "relative matches" for diasporic roots-seekers.[76] These DNA-matching services are likely to be of great interest to genealogists attempting to trace their lineages beyond the Middle Passage, and the rationale for focusing exclusively on members of African royalty and their extended families is likely to link DNA profiles to extensive genealogies, dating back to the time of the transatlantic slave trade. Yet this focus also introduces a significant bias: the only relatives that may be found by these methods are those included in the database, even if they are not the closest living kin. Benedicte Ohrt

Fehler has pointed out that in the United States, genealogical research and roots tourism are available only to a privileged class who have the economic resources and leisure time to pursue these activities.[77] Initiatives like these raise similar questions about the role of class and socioeconomic power in determining who in Africa is able to be identified as "family" by these means.

In recent years, numerous DNA ancestry-testing businesses have partnered with tour companies, stimulating a rise in "genetic heritage travel."[78] This trend has been embraced enthusiastically by some West African governments. For instance, the Ghanaian government designated 2019 the "Year of Return" to mark the 400th anniversary of the arrival of the first enslaved Africans in Jamestown, Virginia, and hoped to attract half a million additional visitors from the diaspora. The cases of celebrities like Isaiah Washington, Samuel L. Jackson, Tiffany Haddish, and the rapper Ludacris, who have been offered dual citizenship by African governments on the basis of their DNA test results, may give hope to other African-descendants who dream of being officially welcomed back to their claimed "homelands."[79] According to Katharina Schramm, however, these gestures are likely to be exceptional. Even in Ghana, successive governments have been extremely reticent about awarding dual citizenship to foreign nationals. The topic is politically contentious. Some argue that dual citizenship gives a privileged status to "returnees," which would allow them to abandon the country in the case of a crisis; others argue that these dual citizens are not fully Ghanaian—a claim that is strongly contested by those who have been settled in the country for many years and have chosen to lay down their own roots in Ghana.[80] As part of the 2019 Year of Return, the government reportedly granted dual citizenship to a record 126 foreign nationals; yet, the overriding focus of the campaign was on stimulating tourism to the country—in other words, welcoming "back" members of the diaspora as visitors, but not necessarily inviting them to stay.[81]

The Limits of Authenticity

By studying roots-seekers' strategies to socially activate the ethnic and kinship relationships established by DNA technologies, we add new nuances to the aura of certainty that often surrounds genetic evidence. A definitive test result rarely signifies the end of searches for personal origins and kin. Those who adopt a strictly genealogical approach may feel that a DNA test indicating "shared ancestry" with an entire ethnic group is not specific enough to meet their goals of identifying a given ancestor's origins. Meanwhile, as more African genetic and genealogical profiles are made available online, the problem may not be finding a DNA match as much as deciphering which are the "right" kin from among many possible matches. Likewise, for those less interested in piecing together their family lineage than in claiming an affinity to a particular African culture and region, genetic bonds are rarely uncritically accepted as historically or socially legitimate. Even in cases where DNA markers appear to coincide perfectly with family traditions and personal affinities to a given group or region, roots-seekers may find it hard to dispel the doubts about the "authenticity" of their claimed identity.

In a sense, these doubts are well founded. The search for authentic ethnic identities—if by "authentic" we mean "pure," "pristine," "ahistorical"—is chimerical. Commenting on a parallel discussion about the use of anthropological technologies to determine who is authentically "Indian" in Brazil, Eduardo Viveiros de Castro has said:

> No matter how complete the process of de-Indianisation that was and is being carried out by catechism, missionarism, modernisation, and citizen-ization, this has not been enough to reset history and to erase all memories, because human collectives exist crucially and eminently in the moment of their reproduction. . . . And even when they *are*, when they are reduced to their individual components, extracted from the relationships that constitute them, as occurred with the African slaves, those components reinvent a culture and a way of life—a relational world that, however restricted it may have been by the adverse conditions in which it flourished, never stopped being an expression of human life exactly like any other. There are no inauthentic cultures, because there are no authentic cultures. Likewise, there are no authentic Indians. Indians, Whites, Afro-descendants, or whoever—because authentic is not something that humans are.[82]

Offering test-takers a link to an apparently discrete ethnic community and culture gives the sense of retrieving an identity that has remained more or less unchanged since the time of American slavery. However, this approach obscures the genetic and cultural mixtures that occurred among African ethnic groups in the Americas, both during and since the time of slavery, which complicate the idea that African-descendants are the inheritors of a single, "pure" ancestral identity. It also simplifies the complexities of cultural identities in cosmopolitan, multiethnic West African nations (both today and historically) and ignores the impacts of the transatlantic trade and European colonialism in shaping African kinship and social structures.[83] The ancestors of communities inhabiting the same region or ethnic group may have played antagonistic parts in the historical slave trades— identities that can prove to be more significant to diasporic roots-seekers than the search for an ethnic community, and which may complicate efforts to rekindle diasporic kinship ties.

At the same time, I disagree with the claim that using DNA to produce connections between diasporic and African communities is inherently less legitimate than other modes of affiliation. Undoubtedly, there are many ways to forge collective identities, kinship ties, and enduring social bonds that do not rely on the sharing of DNA. Sometimes, genetics and genealogy are not effective tools for producing links to a desired ancestral community; this has notably been the case in Brazil, where Black activists have turned to broader, non-essentialist modes of "ancestrality" to forge an ongoing engagement with their claimed African heritage.[84] Even where DNA evidence does seem to provide the key to personal identities and kinship ties, like all other social bonds these connections must still be consolidated through mutual processes of affirmation and recognition, reciprocal expressions of commitment and obligation, and active personal choices. Having said that, it is important not to underestimate the symbolic and political significance represented by genetic "ethnicity" results in contexts where African identities have been subjected to systemic devaluation and erasure. As Zulu Araújo remarked: "The trip [to Cameroon] completed me as a citizen. If anyone asks me where I'm from, now I know what to respond. Only someone who is Black can understand how much that means."[85]

Epilogue

Historically Modified Organisms

· ·

When the Danish travel company Momondo, in partnership with Ancestry DNA, released the "DNA Journey" viral video in June 2016—the story that began this book—it marked a significant moment in the maturation of the DNA ancestry industry. It aligned with the beginning of a boom in sales by large U.S.-based companies like AncestryDNA and 23andMe, which had been gradually expanding their business outside the United States and into Canada, Europe, and Australia, among other regions, since 2014. In 2017 alone, leading U.S. and European DNA ancestry-testing companies processed almost triple the number of tests sold cumulatively over the previous decade. Collectively, the size of their DNA test-taker databases rose from an estimated 4.5 million at the end of 2016 to 12.2 million at the beginning of 2018 (of which 7 million profiles were held by AncestryDNA alone).[1]

Yet there was more to this moment than a business story. The Momondo campaign coincided with a political and human rights crisis, whose reverberations were beginning to be felt throughout the Atlantic world. As my native country was rocked by the results of the "Brexit" referendum, which determined by a tiny majority that the United Kingdom would leave the European Union, I was holed up in a studio apartment in Paris, busily writing the final chapters of my PhD thesis. Just a few blocks from where I lived, at a stone's throw from the Gare du Nord, hundreds of refugees from North Africa and further afield were sleeping rough in improvised camps beneath the arches of the raised Métro line. Throughout that sweltering summer they were periodically moved on by the Parisian police, only to be replaced by more families fleeing war, destitution, and environmental crisis. Many were hoping to seek asylum in the United Kingdom; the British government, for its part, was hastily pulling up the drawbridge. In November 2016, millions around the world watched in dismay as Donald Trump won the U.S. presidency by a similarly fine margin, riding a campaign based on national chauvinism, openly flavored with xenophobia, racism, and anti-Muslim sentiment. Trump's leadership was celebrated by White nationalist groups, who have made their presence and racist ideologies known nationwide through public rallies and violent acts of terror.[2] Two years later, the far right-wing populist candidate Jair Bolsonaro—who is openly nostalgic for a reprise of Brazil's twentieth-century authoritarian military regime—comfortably won the Brazilian presidency. Bolsonaro has poured scorn on the idea that Brazil still needs to address the legacies of slavery and colonialism and has actively worked to suppress the rights of Indigenous, Black, and LGBTQI+ populations. During his campaign, taking inspiration from a formulation that had already been popularized and used to great effect by Trump's administration, Bolsonaro described the existence of racism in Brazil as "fake news."[3]

Against this backdrop, the public appeal of a technology that claims to unequivocally belie notions of racial or ethnic "purity"—proving that migration and mixture, rather than xenophobia and isolationism, are the main constants of human history—is certainly understandable. Nevertheless, portraying genetic categories as more "real," more "truthful" than socially and historically constructed identities (however flawed their origin myths) is a dangerous game. For a start, it can be used to delegitimize the claims of those who attempt to highlight ongoing forms of racism and racial inequality, framing their activism as misguided or divisive. I recall, for instance, that after giving a public talk in the United Kingdom on the potential and limits of DNA ancestry to shed light on human identities, I was approached by an elderly White British man who told me, in a conspiratorial tone, that the great thing about DNA tests was that once enough people had taken them, "they'll just have to stop going on about race and racism and all that, won't they?" As we saw in chapter 1, a similar discourse has been deployed in Brazil to claim that since most Brazilians have some degree of African genetic ancestry, any attempt to forge a Black political identity based on a shared racial consciousness is fundamentally flawed. In some cases, this claim is extended further to denounce critiques of Brazilian racism and affirmations of Afro-Brazilian subjectivities alike as "unpatriotic" and "reverse racism."[4]

Treating racism as primarily an issue of public misinformation, which can be remedied by spreading the genetic facts of humanity's connectedness and overall biological similarity, ignores the structural dynamics that reproduce social inequalities between historically racialized groups.[5] These include the frequent alignment of racial and class hierarchies, which condition groups' access to inherited wealth, education, health care, and their vulnerability to police violence, racism, environmental stressors, among other things. This very problem was addressed by the interdisciplinary groups of scientists assembled by UNESCO between the 1950s and 1970s to address global problems of racism. In the 1950s, experts treated racism primarily as an ideological disease that needed to be treated with the public dissemination of science. By the late 1960s, they were forced to agree that racism and racial conflicts were not disappearing but mutating, finding new ways to "make existing differences appear inviolable."[6] Tackling racism, some argued, needed more than reeducating publics about the scientific facts of "race"; it required governmental and institutional interventions in the form of corrective policies in education, housing, employment, mass communication, and legislation to close the entrenched socioeconomic inequalities between racialized groups. Nevertheless, as UNESCO rapporteur Michael Banton observed in 1967, "The use of positive discrimination to help a backward group catch up can evoke resentment from other groups. Policies of this kind require careful management."[7] In both the United States and Brazil, narratives about the genetic inexistence of human "races" have been used to challenge the logic and viability of racially targeted affirmative action, which are sometimes mischaracterized as favoring African-descendants and other ethnoracial minorities at the expense of Whites. Sociological understandings of racism and its effects on social stratification can provide an important corrective to these perspectives. For instance, a study into Brazilians' attitudes toward affirmative action found that individuals were more likely to support these initiatives when they believed Black Brazilians faced structural and institutional "barriers of racial exclusion" and less likely to show support when they believed racism was mainly an issue of mindset—that is, of Blacks "discriminating against themselves" or becoming "accustomed to their situation."[8]

A further danger of presenting DNA ancestry tests as a salve to racial prejudices is that, in the guise of inviting members of the public to reflect on the falsehood of notions of race and nationhood, which are founded in ideas of shared "blood" and a "pure" ancestral stock, companies are simply offering an alternative palette of ethnic identities to choose from, which are similarly predicated on notions of genetic homogeneity and geographic belonging. While it is assumed that DNA ancestry technologies appeal most to groups who have suffered different kinds of ancestral trauma (forced migrations, enslavement, colonization, genocide), as I showed in chapter 3, it is clear many companies cater to large numbers of majority Euro-descendant roots-seekers.[9] In recent decades in the United States, maintaining affiliations to one or more ethnic identities has been a way for some White

Americans to keep at arm's length a racial identity that positions them uncomfortably—and, many feel, unjustly—as beneficiaries of the social inheritance of slavery, racism, and settler-colonialism.[10] Studies have found White Americans are indeed more likely than members of racial and ethnic minorities to incorporate genetic "ethnicity" categories into their personal identities, feeling they add "color" and "uniqueness" to an otherwise bland racial identity.[11] Although my own research indicates that some White test-takers maintain a distinction between their genetic ancestry and their racial designation, viewing family histories through the lens of ethnicity can nonetheless feed relativizing narratives about the past. Affirmations like "we're all mutts" and "we're all migrants," which abounded among the Instagram posts I surveyed during the research for this book, gloss over the vastly divergent conditions under which diverse groups arrived and were permitted to live, work, and put down roots in American societies.

Moreover, the assumption that genetic evidence of "ethnic" mixture can neutralize racist ideologies rooted in notions of biological "purity" has been challenged by studies that underscore the lively interest paid to these technologies by White nationalist groups. Rather than debunking racist ideologies among these communities, the rise of DNA ancestry testing appears to be propelling racial supremacists to adapt their dogma, finding ways of defining Whiteness that reconcile new genomic evidence with their long-standing political agendas of racial terror.[12] In Britain, ethnic nationalists have attempted to co-opt population genetic studies, and the supposed biological particularities they identify among "native" European populations, to argue that the latter should be accorded indigenous status and protected from the corrupting influence of "foreign" migrants.[13] Darryl Leroux has shown that the proliferation of "Native American" DNA testing services in Canada has similarly emboldened White settler-descendants to transform themselves into "indigenous" peoples, as part of an anti-Indigenous activist agenda.[14] These examples demonstrate the ability of racist ideologies to adapt and mutate in ways that *incorporate* forms of genetic logic, rather than simply being defeated by scientific reason. Challenging the spread of these dogmas requires consistent efforts among scientists, educators, the media, and DNA ancestry-testing companies to anticipate, identify, and contest misuses of genetic studies and technologies. The task is difficult, since research into human origins is inherently political, often raising questions about groups' claimed attachments to land and wading into long-standing disputes about "who was here first." As we saw in chapter 2, it is made all the more tricky given that geneticists themselves disagree about the relevance of their science to political questions of identity and about what constitute "responsible" or even scientifically "correct" renderings of genetic ancestry.

As Catherine Nash has pointed out, there is an intrinsic weakness to the idea of staking antiracist struggles on claims of our genetic relatedness as a species—particularly when the evidence is presented in a way that demonstrates the abundant possibility of dividing the world up into relatively homogeneous and discrete genetic populations. According to Nash, "While studies of human genetic variation point to shared ancient ancestry and ancestral interconnectedness, the focus is on ascertaining and interpreting degrees of genetic relatedness. So if ancestral relatedness is celebrated as the basis of human unity, empathy, and harmony, it implies quite differently and unevenly distributed senses of care and solidarity."[15] Autosomal "ethnicity" analyses function by linking test-takers to a given number of contemporary genetic populations (albeit whose contents are highly "purified" by selective sampling methods), which stand in for "ancestral" groups dating to roughly the last 500 to 1,000 years. By the same token, these analyses categorically affirm the populations with which test-takers *do not* share ancestry. Hence, it is possible to be attributed "100 percent European" ancestry, for example—a claim feted by some White nationalists, but which obscures the deep histories of migration and mixture occurring among *Homo sapiens* (not to mention other archaic human species) for tens of thousands of years. As cultural anthropologists and queer theorists, among others, have long demonstrated, kinship ties are neither reducible to, nor contingent on, genetic-genealogical bonds: they are chosen and made in a multitude of ways—so why privilege these genetic links as a more "authentic" or "natural" source of human affinity?[16] It hardly needs saying that meaningful and durable interpersonal affiliations are constantly built up between individuals and communities—between friends, neighbors, people united by faith, or by political and humanitarian causes—without need for assumptions of common ancestry or kinship. And what of the potential for care and solidarity beyond Western conceptions of the human, extending to other-than-human species, ecosystems, and environments?[17]

The Momondo "DNA Journey" campaign invited viewers to write in explaining why they wanted to discover their genetic roots, and it offered selected participants the chance to travel to a country featured in their DNA report that they believed would "open their mind." Travel can be a way of cultivating cosmopolitan sensibilities, of learning to value other cultures and ways of life, of realizing that those who appear "foreign" are, in many ways, just like us. Yet opening one's mind is not an automatic process that comes with travel. Translation and interpretation are needed to make sense of things, to get beyond linguistic and cultural barriers. What's more, different types of travel may be viewed differently by receiving populations, depending on political and economic contexts. There is a certain irony, for instance, in 23andMe's decision to launch a similar initiative in partnership with Airbnb—a company accused of catalyzing patterns of gentrification in urban travel destinations in order to cater to the influx of tourists, in the process aggravating housing crises and fraying the fabric of local communities.[18] Meanwhile, it is not clear that the cosmopolitan sensibilities cultivated through travel will easily translate to political solidarity when those seeking care and affinity are not *there* but *here*: when they are migrants charged with "taking our jobs," or refugees accused of "invading our land" and "overwhelming our public services." Amidst the worsening climate and environmental crises, populations affected by flooding, drought, crop failures, and an associated rise in violent conflict will be forced to seek new homes elsewhere. So far, the responses of wealthy Western nations have largely been to tighten borders, cracking down on or banning migration from "undesirable" nations and creating "hostile environments" that make it increasingly difficult for foreign nationals to gain permanent residency. In the face of this global humanitarian crisis, fostering new modes of community living, based on values of equality, solidarity, and antiracism, is of the utmost importance. Once again, though, achieving these changes will require more than a shift in mindset: it will mean taking ambitious political, economic, and institutional action.

Healing the Wounds of the Past

Recent reports indicate that after three years of steep growth, global sales of DNA ancestry tests are now beginning to plateau.[19] For DNA ancestry companies, aside from finding new markets, the challenge is keeping existing customers interacting with their genomic profiles and uploading personal data to their websites. In part, the mission is financially motivated. Companies like 23andMe have based their business models on selling or loaning anonymized sets of genomic and medical data—contributed voluntarily by customers through online surveys—to biotech firms, pharmaceutical companies, and research laboratories.[20] Over the past decade, several DNA ancestry-testing services have integrated with online genealogy platforms, the idea being that autosomal admixture tests will act as a "hook" to get customers with little or no prior experience with family history research to begin working on their genealogies and pay for subscriptions to the companies' online databases. Businesses like AncestryDNA and MyHeritage have focused on developing their DNA relative-matching services, using algorithms that triangulate genomic and genealogical data to estimate the degree of genetic relatedness between customers and, where possible, suggest the identity of their most recent common ancestor—a concept known as "identity by descent" (IBD).[21] As more genetic profiles and genealogical data are uploaded, they become increasingly valuable tools for genealogists and adoptees, among others, who are seeking to locate genetic kin.

In recent years, genealogical models of kinship have suffered something of a fall from grace in anthropological thought.[22] Nonetheless, I argue that contemporary genealogical research, as a social practice, can have important political and therapeutic dimensions as a form of personal and collective truth-seeking about the past. The gradual rebranding of genealogy as "family history research" over the past three decades seems to reflect changing public attitudes toward this pursuit. Rather than being primarily concerned with the reconstruction of ancestral (usually paternal) bloodlines, genealogical investigations are increasingly regarded by practitioners as a way of encountering social histories through the lens of family experience and relationships.[23] During my fieldwork in the United States in 2014, I met several times with genealogists from an African American Special Interest Group (AASIG) that congregated each Monday at a Family History Center outside Washington, D.C. The majority of the group had taken one or more DNA ancestry tests, although it soon became clear that most were more interested in the tests' relative-matching features, and the clues they could offer for their research, than in their admixture or "ethnicity" reports per se. Each group member was working toward their particular research goals, and each had a story to tell about how they had become "hooked" on genealogy. For instance, Frank, a retired engineer from New Jersey, recalled that his first experience of genealogical research was as a young man, when he accompanied a cousin to a local archive to try and find out the whereabouts of the cousin's father. Years later, through a combination of research and speaking to older relatives, Frank learned that his uncle had been killed in a car accident in South Carolina back in the 1930s. He was astounded to learn that the driver—a member of a local White family who was known to Frank's relatives—reported to the authorities that "he just ran over something in the road . . . knowing that he had actually hit and killed him, or left him for dead." Such stories, Frank explained, were important to keep in families—not to scare or upset people, but to explain to the younger generations "why the family is the way it is, and why society is how it is today."

Bernice Bennett, a retired public health educator and the host of a BlogTalkRadio genealogy show, "Research at the National Archives and Beyond,"[24] traced her passion for genealogical research to the experience of restoring a photograph of her paternal grandmother, who had died when Bennett's father was young. Bennett recalled that her father always spoke of his mother with great affection, which made her curious to find out more about who she was and where she came from. Bennett's efforts to track down her grandmother's family origins led her on a remarkable and emotionally turbulent journey. Through her research, she learned for the first time that her grandmother had a brother, and that his descendants (Bennett's second cousins) were likewise trying to reconstruct their family history. Ultimately, their search to unravel their common roots led them back to a town in South Carolina where their ancestors had been enslaved in the mid-nineteenth century. For Bennett, one of the most astonishing aspects of this journey was that the crucial documents that allowed them to identify the names of their great-great-grandparents were provided by a descendant of the family who enslaved them. The two women have since maintained contact and continue to share information about their research into their common family history—something that Bennett believes that other descendants of slaveholders should also strive to do.[25]

DNA relative-matching services are already being used to great effect by African American genealogists who are seeking innovative ways to get around the historiographic challenges presented by the name changes, lack of surnames, and general scarcity of documents that normally hinder efforts to trace the family lineages of their enslaved ancestors. Testing for genetic matches between living relatives can help prove or disprove hypotheses about shared ancestral links, allowing genealogists to retrospectively reunite families who were separated by forced migrations or at the auction block and to solve mysteries of parentage that have long haunted their families. Many of the genealogists I interviewed portrayed their work as a labor of love, a way of fulfilling kinship obligations to their enslaved ancestors. In Bennett's words, "Our ancestors wanted us to know and find evidence of their existence. The voices of our ancestors called out to us and provided all of the clues we needed to make the connections. My great-great-grandparents created a legacy with the naming patterns of their children. They made certain that we would find evidence of their existence, even during the time of their enslavement."[26]

Another possible outcome of the expansion of online genetic-genealogical databases is that they may help bring to light "interracial" ancestral connections between White and Black Americans, dating to the time of slavery. Such revelations could help raise awareness among White Americans of their ancestors' connections to slavery, or allow descendants of known slaveholding families to confront histories that have become cloaked in silence and shame. In recent years, initiatives such as Coming to the Table (CTTT)—a nationwide network of groups that meet regularly "for truth-telling, building relationships, healing, and taking action to dismantle inequitable systems and structures based on 'race'"—have endorsed DNA ancestry testing as a technique that can foster recognition and reconciliation among those they refer to as the "linked descendants" of slavery, who are "related through ownership, kinship or violence."[27] CTTT was founded in 2005 with help from a small group of descendants of President Thomas Jefferson and Sally Hemings (an enslaved woman in the Jefferson household), who in turn met through the landmark 1998 DNA study that provided evidence Jefferson had likely fathered at least one of Hemings's children.[28] One key responsibility the group impresses on its members is telling the truth about slavery and the relationships it engendered, through the lens of each person's family history—a process designed to level the historic power differential between descendants of slaveholders and the enslaved and ensure all voices are heard equally.

Yet negotiating—and even accepting—these shared genetic bonds is far from easy. Genetic matches testify to histories of sex, and although common, sexual relationships between enslaved Black individuals and White slaveholders were always founded in steeply unequal, gendered power dynamics. Individuals who learn of such ancestral relationships in their own family trees may find it comforting to imagine these unions were born of mutual affection, even of love, "against the odds"—yet this is challenged by historical evidence of the fundamentally coercive and often violent nature of relationships between slaveholders and enslaved individuals.[29] As Hortense Spillers has remarked, it is likely that we will never truly be able to comprehend the nature of these relations because of the conditions of nonfreedom in which they took place.[30] For their part, slaveholder-descendant families have invested heavily in narratives that portray their patriarchs as all-American heroes and bearers of democracy and freedom; many are utterly unwilling to see their forebears' names defiled by allegations that they engaged in "sordid" relationships with enslaved women. Many of the descendants of Thomas and Martha Jefferson, for instance, continue to reject claims about the former's sexual relationship with Sally Hemings, despite the weight of supporting historical and genetic evidence.[31]

This example underscores a fact that I explored in chapter 5—namely, that while DNA tests can point to ancestral connections between living individuals, *reconstructing* kinship links involves active and reciprocal processes of recognition, including the exploration and negotiation of the histories and circumstances that gave rise to these ties. Whereas DNA relative-matching tools can generate connections between participating test-takers,[32] they cannot force individuals to follow up on these links—and indeed, many may prefer not to do so. While some of the African American genealogists I interviewed said they had managed to get in touch with slaveholder-descendants using these tools, others stated they found White Americans less prone to reply to their messages than other African Americans. One theory proposed to me was that these individuals may be reluctant to countenance evidence of "racial" mixture in their family histories, which could stain the "purity" of their White bloodlines.[33] Another possibility is that many White Americans are ignorant of the histories of "racial" mixture in which these connections are rooted. Genealogy blogger Melvin Collier notes that a common response received by African Americans who try to reach out to these genetic matches is: "I just don't see how we can be related because I am white."[34]

For their part, White members of CTTT have described the anxieties they felt on learning of their family connections to slavery; although many longed for the prospect of reconciliation with the descendants of those enslaved by their ancestors, they feared being asked to atone for their ancestors' crimes and wondered how they could possibly do so.[35] While some civil rights groups are currently pursuing financial reparations from U.S. federal and state governments, corporations, and wealthy families that profited from slavery on behalf of the descendants of enslaved Africans,[36] the genealogists I spoke with were generally interested in a different kind of reparation: the possibility of learning the truth about their ancestors' lives and identities, and having these truths heard and acknowledged by those whose ancestors benefited from the institution. In the words of one member of the African American genealogy group, the potential of DNA ancestry testing is the chance to "show actual proof of our connections to the descendants of other slave-owners. . . . Slavery existed, you know, you just can't wipe it out . . . and all kinds of relationships existed through slavery, so we are all related, and sometimes they don't necessarily want to accept that, but DNA will prove it." The existence of groups like CTTT indicates the need for mediation in these truth-finding processes, and for spaces in which to build trust and a shared vocabulary for exploring the inherited trauma and divisions created by slavery and its afterlives.

Permanent Markers?

Genealogical practices of the kind described above are not about condensing family histories into orderly bloodlines; on the contrary, they are about piecing together a range of human relationships and experiences in all their complexity, against a backdrop of extraordinarily complex and traumatic social histories. These encounters with the past can be profoundly painful, but also cathartic, moving, emancipatory. They provide insights into "why we are the way we are," not because of what they tell us about our genetic inheritance, but because of what they reveal about the experiences—the trials and the triumphs—that marked our ancestors, who in turn have marked us.

I am reminded here of an immersive performance called "The Flesh of History," by the French artist Fabienne Kanor, which I attended during a conference on slavery and authorship in New York in 2019. The performance took place in complete darkness, with the audience seated in a semicircle around a low stage on which Kanor danced and stomped, accompanied by a harmonica player, all the while reading a monologue from a piece of paper, lit by a handheld flashlight. Behind her, a screen showed a projected video of Kanor's body, dressed in a slip, weaving perpetually in a darkened room. The words of the monologue evoked the hold of the slave ship as well as other migrations, separations, and acts of racial violence. As Kanor later explained, the monologue was not prewritten but developed using fragments and ideas from the conference papers presented during the day. It was also inspired by her own memories of her parents' reluctance to talk about their past; as migrants who came to France from the Antilles as part of a controlled migration policy, they were obliged to "take up jobs that French people did not want to do." Kanor saw her intervention as a way of resisting the process of "calcification" or *blanchisation* (Whitening) of memory that threatened to let her family's stories disappear into colonial history. She described her performance as a reflection on the physicality of inheritance, which showed her "struggling against the paper, trying to force myself to tell a different story, or tell the story differently."[37]

The part of the performance that stands out most in my mind was a moment when Kanor began exploring the etymology of the word "trauma." She exclaimed, "Am I a historically modified organism? Am I a lesion?" Those words have stuck with me. The phrase "historically modified organism" evokes "genetically modified organisms" (GMO), a term usually associated with food cultivation, referring to organisms whose genetic material has been altered through bioengineering. Popular and political discourses about GMO crops often reflect fears about the "adulteration" of nature, resulting in hybrid "Frankenfoods" that, once created, take on a life of their own and cannot be returned to their "natural" state. What I found particularly incisive about Kanor's formulation is that it invokes the sense of horror, loss, and irreversibility that are intrinsic to concepts of genetic modification but links them instead to *historical* genealogies of enslavement, colonialism, imperialism, and racialization. Her question thus probes us to think of how the categories and hierarchies produced by these historical systems continue to scar and warp the fabric of our societies—not to mention our very bodies and minds—in a multitude of ways. These divisions continue to be reproduced in the form of racialized worldviews, identities, and kinship structures, and through the impacts of structural and institutional types of racism that condition access to education, wealth, health care; susceptibility to poverty, disease, criminalization, pollution, and violence. Are these marks permanent? Or can we find routes to healing and transformation by telling stories about the past differently, as Kanor suggests?

In Freudian psychoanalysis, trauma is conceived of as a wound whose truth has not been fully assimilated and which, even if suppressed, will continue to be reenacted unwittingly, thrusting itself into the present and haunting the psyche of those who bore witness to the original act of violence.[38] Ron Eyerman, whose work focuses on the United States, describes slavery as a "cultural trauma" that created the foundations of what it is to be African American through "a dramatic loss of identity and meaning, a tear in the social fabric, affecting a group of people that has achieved some degree of cohesion."[39] As Eyerman observes, African American intellectuals, artists, and activists have adopted diverse approaches to dealing with this trauma over time. Some have sought to leave slavery behind while others have tried to memorialize it; others have sought various ways to "return" to Africa in order to recover a "lost" identity. In Brazil, on the other hand—as in various other Latin American societies—the response of successive national governments was to induce citizens to forget slavery, an approach reinforced by acts of purposeful destruction such as the burning of archives. The descendants of enslaved Africans were offered the prospect of racial Whitening as a means to escape the stigma of Blackness; mixed-race

Brazilians were thus induced to suppress memories of slavery, cloaking them in shame and aligning themselves with the racial ideologies and cultural values of the colonizing class. Nonetheless, those who identify with the survivors of slavery have struggled against these processes of erasure, claiming the right to political recognition through their investment in maintaining cultural continuities with African and Afro-Brazilian pasts.

Ana Lucia Araujo has noted that the Akan symbol of the Sankofa (usually depicted as a heart or a bird with its head turned back over its body) is often featured on contemporary monuments, memorials, and heritage sites of the Atlantic slave trade. It is understood to refer to a West African proverb that states: "It is not a taboo to return and fetch it when you forget."[40] In this sense, searches for ancestry by members of the African diaspora can be understood as a way of reconstructing or even creating memory out of what has been forgotten about slavery. As I have shown throughout this book, DNA is increasingly being used as a tool for piecing together individual and collective histories. Yet it is not a form of evidence that can "speak" for itself; moreover, the insights it provides are always partial and fragmentary. DNA markers can be read in multiple ways, and often the narratives that lend themselves most readily to interpretation are the familiar national myths that have been instrumental in effacing or romanticizing histories of slavery. As Kanor indicates, it is always a struggle to depart from these narratives and find different perspectives on the past: a sense of context and multiple points of view are needed to read DNA against the grain of conventional histories.

Nor must memories of slavery be limited to the stories that can be read through markers in the genome, or on the surface of the body. In Brazil, the debate surrounding the administration of racially targeted university quotas has led some Black activist groups to pragmatically reorient their attempts at collective identity construction, making skin color the principle marker of Blackness.[41] This is one way to address the structural pigmentocracies installed by colonialism and slavery and cemented further by veiled forms of discrimination rooted in "color" prejudice. However, this body-centric approach must not come at the expense of more inclusive and expansive visions for engaging with the legacies of slavery in Brazil. Alexandre Emboaba da Costa, for example, has drawn attention to the concept of *ancestralidade* (ancestrality), put forward by some activist groups and cultural associations as a means of cultivating a historical identity, which is not limited to genetic notions of genealogy, nor to attempts to retrieve essentialized precolonial identities. Rather, "*ancestralidade* is both historically situated and emergent; it engages the past as formative of how individuals see themselves and their society in the present and how they envision possibilities for the future."[42] While these initiatives are partly focused toward the construction of Afro-Brazilian identities and subjectivities, they also encompass a concern with training White educators in antiracist pedagogies, to show how the legacies of slavery, colonialism, and racialization implicate all members of society.[43] This societal-level strategy is apt in that it extends the responsibility for addressing these histories of violence to all citizens and not merely those for whom the memories of trauma are most present. As Paul Gilroy has argued, at stake in breaking these cycles of violence is instilling a desire for justice in the majority of citizens who see themselves as affiliated neither with the victims nor the perpetrators of these systems. In Gilroy's terms, "this difficult stance challenges that unnamed group to witness sufferings that pass beyond the reach of words and, in so doing, to see how an understanding of one's own particularity or identity might be transformed as a result of a principled exposure to the claims of otherness."[44]

In 2020, at the time of writing, the current U.S. and Brazilian political administrations are openly hostile to attempts to redress the contemporary legacies of slavery and settler-colonialism. Relativism is weaponized as part of "post-truth" politics, so that attempts to expose episodes of racist violence are dismissed as "fake news" or countered with "alternative facts." In Brazil, the very institutions meant to uphold Afro-Brazilian interests are under assault. In late 2019, President Bolsonaro appointed Sérgio Camargo—a Black, right-wing journalist—as head of the Fundação Cultural Palmares, a governmental foundation dedicated to the promotion of Afro-Brazilian culture and history. Camargo is known for his apologist stance on slavery, which he claims has benefited the descendants of enslaved Africans, and for denying the severity of Brazilian racism, which he has dubbed "Nutella" in comparison to the "real racism" to be found in the United States.[45] Camargo opposed affirmative action policies and denies the structural character of racism, which he denounces as a fabrication of "victimist" Black activists. These attempts to portray slavery and racism as soft and benign—even perversely pleasurable—deny the violent effects of these phenomena. In contrast, those who seek to engage actively with memories of trauma know these claims to be false.

After her performance of "The Flesh of History," Kanor looked physically exhausted. When I asked her about it the next day, Kanor said that every time she performed the piece her body ended up feeling "so painful."

Despite the discomfort that confronting these histories can cause, there is nonetheless a truth to pain: it tells us that the past is not yet behind us and, in doing so, gives us the chance to understand how we came to be where we are, and to imagine how we might collectively transform our societies in the future.

Acknowledgments

My first and biggest "thank you" goes to each of the DNA test-takers and scientists who agreed to take part in my research and entrusted me with their stories. I hope I have done them justice.

During my fieldwork stints in Brazil and the United States, I encountered numerous instances of kindness and generosity. I would like to thank Maria Cátira Bortolini, Andrés Ruiz Linares, Ana Angélica Leal Barbosa, and the other members of the Consortium for the Analysis of Diversity and Evolution in Latin America (CANDELA) at the Universidade Federal do Rio Grande do Sul (UFRGS) and the Universidade Estadual do Sudoeste da Bahia (UESB) for their warm welcome and invaluable help with various aspects of my research. In particular, I am grateful for Virginia Ramallo's help in setting up interviews with volunteers. Thanks also to Cleidiana Ramos and Valdir Ferreira for their help locating articles in the documentation center of the newspaper *A Tarde*, and to Arthur Vinícius de Oliveira Moraes Cornélio for proofreading some of my Portuguese transcripts. I am extremely grateful to Fatimah Jackson, Ana Lucia Araujo, and Edna Medford for welcoming me to Howard University and providing countless pieces of advice to help get my fieldwork off the ground; to Jake Byrnes for sharing his expertise on the science of DNA ancestry testing; to Brian Donovan for his assistance during my fieldwork in Salt Lake City in 2017; to Bonnie Schrack and Shannon Christmas for their valuable insights into the world of genetic genealogy; and to Bernice Bennett for her generosity in sharing her genealogical expertise and experience and introducing me to members of the African American Special Interest Group. A warm thanks to Carlos da Silva Junior, Juliana Oliveira, Shaka Zulu, Caio Fernandes Barbosa, Jamille Oliveira, Camille Bolson, Ludmila Garcia, Kate McMahon-Ruddick, Tatiana Brofft, Evlondo Cooper, and Brian Duss for their friendship, generosity, and guidance during my time in Salvador, Jequié, Porto Alegre, and Washington D.C.

Over the past eight years I have been fortunate to benefit from the guidance and insights of several academic advisers and mentors. First and foremost, I am very grateful to my PhD supervisors Myriam Cottias, Véronique Boyer, and Odile Hoffmann for their careful readings, insightful comments, and warm encouragement of my work. I feel lucky to have conducted my PhD research as a member of the EUROTAST project, a Marie Skłodowska-Curie Initial Training Network, funded by the European Union under the Seventh Framework Programme (grant no. 290344), which provided regular opportunities for exchange and debate with international scholars and students from various disciplines. Thanks to Hannes Schroeder, Tom Gilbert, Temi Odumosu, and Colleen Morgan for their hard work in organizing dynamic and stimulating meetings and conferences between 2012 and 2015, and to the other network partners and EUROTAST fellows for countless thought-provoking discussions. My thanks also to Elisabeth Cunin, Antonio de Almeida Mendes, Jean Hébrard, Céline Flory, Ary Gordien, Sakiko Nakao, Giulia Bonazza, Nathalie Collain, and the other members of the Centre International de Recherches sur les Esclavages (CIRESC) for their feedback and encouragement over the course of my PhD research, and to Fatimah Jackson, Peter Fry, François Weil, and Hannes Schroeder for their comments on an earlier version of this manuscript.

The arguments developed in this book benefited greatly from my time working with Gísli Pálsson and the other members of the CitiGen project between 2016 and 2019, funded by Humanities in the European Research Area under the European Union's Horizon 2020 research and innovation program (grant no. 649307). Jean-Frédéric Schaub, Yasuko Takezawa, and the other members of the Zimbunken-TEPSIS collaborative were also influential in helping refine my critique of the antiracist potential of DNA ancestry technologies. During the final stage of writing and revision, I was supported financially by the British Academy's Postdoctoral Fellowship scheme (grant no. PF19/100026), and I am very grateful to my colleagues, friends, and students at the Centre of Latin American Studies of the University of Cambridge, who provided encouragement and inspiration for this last stretch. I would also like to express my sincere appreciation to the three anonymous reviewers of this book, and to Brandon Proia and the team at UNC Press, and Michelle Witkowski and Karen Brogno of Westchester Publishing Services, for their excellent editorial guidance and hard work preparing the final manuscript for publication.

I count myself lucky to have been accompanied on this journey by wonderful friends who have always been on hand with encouragement and moral support. Thanks in particular to Megan Ryburn, Lauren Harris, Tess Connell, Daphné Bédinadé, Marion Tremblay, Larissa Warnavin, Maria Thereza João, Gabriela Goldin Marcovich, Susannah Knights, Bastien Goursaud, Felipe Linden, and Elise Burton for numerous morale-restoring dinners, drinks, and *goûters* along the way. A special mention goes to Marcela Sandoval Velasco for her genetic fact-checking and numerous hours spent on Skype trying to cross disciplinary lines.

Lastly, I want to express my love and gratitude to my two families—British and Mexican—for encouraging me to go down this path, helping me through the hard times and making sure that I still kept sight of life outside the book manuscript. Mum and Dad, you always fed me with literature and encouraged me to travel with my imagination, and I think that was the real starting point of this project.

The biggest thank you goes to Rodrigo, for your love and companionship all along this journey, from nearby and afar.

Appendix

Interview Methodology

My methodology for chapter 4 is based primarily on qualitative interview data, collected from DNA ancestry test-takers in Brazil in 2013 and in the United States in 2014. In Brazil, I focused on a cohort of volunteers whose DNA was analyzed by the Consortium for the Analysis of Diversity and Evolution in Latin America (CANDELA). With kind permission and assistance from the CANDELA scientists, I conducted semistructured interviews with fifty volunteers who had recently received their DNA ancestry results (using an admixture test that calculated participants' "African," "European," and "Indigenous American" ancestry based on a panel of thirty ancestry informative markers, AIMs). Most interviewees were students, with a smaller number comprising teaching and administrative staff; thirty-seven were women and thirteen men. Eight interviewees were based at the Universidade Federal do Rio Grande do Sul (UFRGS) in Porto Alegre, a city in the south of Brazil, while the other forty-two were based at the Universidade Estadual do Sudoeste da Bahia (UESB) in Jequié, Bahia, a small city in Brazil's northeast. The interviewees were recruited on a semiopportunistic basis: an email advertising my study was sent out to all CANDELA volunteers in Porto Alegre and Jequié, and those who responded were invited to attend face-to-face interviews or fill in an email questionnaire. The CANDELA scientists also put me in touch with certain individuals who they remembered had a particularly enthusiastic reaction to their DNA results. While the recruitment email specified the study was about test-takers' perceptions of their African ancestry, the respondents represented a racial spectrum, identifying variously as *europeu/europeia, branco/a, pardo/a, mestiço/a, multiétnico/a, indígena, moreno/a, mulato/a,* and *negro/a.* All but two were attributed some proportion of African genomic ancestry. Each volunteer had filled out a pretesting questionnaire prepared by the CANDELA scientists, in which they expressed their expectations regarding their DNA ancestry results. I was therefore able to compare these with the posttesting responses gathered in my interviews. In addition, I analyzed 320 responses to a follow-up questionnaire sent round to all Brazilian participants of the CANDELA project (1,600 in total), which asked volunteers about their reactions to their DNA ancestry results. While I do not comment extensively on the follow-up questionnaire responses in chapter 4, I used them in my initial analysis to test the hypotheses formulated based on my core interview data.

During my fieldwork in the United States, I mainly recruited individuals who had taken commercial DNA ancestry tests, and I conducted a total of forty-one semistructured interviews (face-to-face or over Skype or email). The majority responded to interview requests through social networking platforms (primarily Instagram and

Facebook), where they had posted their DNA ancestry results; some were personal acquaintances; and a small percentage contacted me in response to blog-posts I published about DNA ancestry testing. I also interviewed members of an African American Special Interest Group who met regularly at a Family History Center (FHC) in Maryland, many of whom used DNA tests as part of their research. Overall, the test-takers were of varying ages and professional backgrounds, and they were spread out across the country (with a slight bias toward the Washington, D.C. area, where I was based); twenty-nine were women and twelve men. Like the Brazilian cohort, the people I interviewed in the United States were of varying racial backgrounds: just over half identified as African American or Black; around a quarter as White or Euro-descendant; and the rest as "mixed," "multiracial," or "diverse." The interviewees received their results from a range of different companies, and some had had their DNA analyzed by two or three services (one person had received six separate reports). In addition, I analyzed 620 posts to Instagram by DNA ancestry test-takers over the course of twenty-four weeks in 2014, which were tagged with the names of five prominent U.S. DNA testing companies (#23andMe, #AncestryDNA, #FamilyTreeDNA, #AfricanAncestry, and #Genographic). The posts included images of DNA testing kits (by people about to send off their genetic sample for analysis) and DNA ancestry reports (by people who had just received their results), with comments by test-takers and replies from other Instagram users. Again, while I do not comment extensively on these data in this book, collectively the posts provided additional insights into the public narratives given to results, as well as the significance of online social networking platforms as performative spaces in which test-takers "try out" their new genetic identities and receive feedback and validation from others.

Interview Scripts

How and when did you become interested in taking a DNA ancestry test?
[Brazilian respondents only] Had you heard of DNA ancestry testing before participating in the CANDELA project?
When did you first become interested in your ancestry?
In your family, do you often talk about family history, ancestors, and origins?
What was your aim in taking a DNA ancestry test?
Did you have any predictions or expectations about what the results would say?
[U.S. respondents only] Which companies and products did you look at when you were researching your DNA ancestry test? How did you choose between them?
What was your experience of waiting for the results from your DNA ancestry test?
What were the results of the test?
What was your reaction when you received the results?
Did you talk to your friends and family about the results? What were their reactions?
From what you knew beforehand about your family history, do you think the results give a decent reflection of your ancestry?

Which regions or populations highlighted in the results did you find most interesting, and why?

Has the experience of taking a DNA ancestry test made you think differently about your identity or other people's identity?

[U.S. respondents only] Have you become involved in any genealogy groups or related online communities since taking a DNA test?

Do you think the experience of taking a DNA ancestry test will have a lasting impact on your life? If so, in what way?

Do you think it is important for [Brazilians/Americans] to find out about their ancestry?

Do you think DNA ancestry testing could have any wider impact on society if more people took tests? If so, what?

Do you think DNA ancestry tests can tell us anything about "race," or is that something different?

How do you self-identify? In your opinion, what does it mean to self-identify in this way in Brazil/the United States today?

Notes

Introduction

1. Momondo, *Momondo—The DNA Journey*.
2. Sørensen, "Momondo—The DNA Journey"; D&AD, "The DNA Journey."
3. UNESCO, *Four Statements*.
4. "Reading the Book of Life," *New York Times*, June 27, 2000.
5. Bliss, *Race Decoded*.
6. The "umbilical cord" metaphor is used by Bryan Sykes, the founder of DNA testing company Oxford Ancestry, in his popular science book. Sykes, *The Seven Daughters of Eve*, 289.
7. Farr, "Consumer DNA Testing Has Hit a Lull."
8. Comments compiled from the Momondo Facebook page on June 5, 2016.
9. Reardon, *Race to the Finish*, 32–44.
10. In practice though, as Reardon points out, phenotypic and cultural differences have continued to be used as a guide for detecting potential genetic variation.
11. Gannett, "Making Populations."
12. Dobzhansky, "On Species and Races of Living and Fossil Man," 254.
13. Lewontin, "The Apportionment of Human Diversity," 397.
14. Provine, "Geneticists and the Biology of Race Crossing"; Barkan, *The Retreat of Scientific Racism*, 341–45.
15. Brattain, "Race, Racism, and Antiracism"; Selcer, "Beyond the Cephalic Index"; Segerstråle, *Defenders of the Truth*.
16. Fullwiley, "Race and Genetics"; Koenig, Lee, and Richardson, *Revisiting Race in a Genomic Age*; Wailoo, Nelson, and Lee, *Genetics and the Unsettled Past*; Wade et al., *Mestizo Genomics*; "Genetics for the Human Race"; Takezawa et al., "Human Genetic Research, Race, Ethnicity and the Labeling of Populations"; Chakravarti, *Human Variation*.
17. Rosenberg et al., "Genetic Structure of Human Populations"; Edwards, "Human Genetic Diversity."
18. Serre and Pääbo, "Evidence for Gradients of Human Genetic Diversity within and among Continents"; Kaplan and Winther, "Prisoners of Abstraction?"
19. Dunn, *Race and Biology*, 5.
20. Gannett, "Making Populations"; Royal and Dunston, "Changing the Paradigm from 'Race' to Human Genome Variation."
21. Bentley, Callier, and Rotimi, "Diversity and Inclusion in Genomic Research."
22. Jackson, "African-American Responses to the Human Genome Project."
23. Bliss, *Race Decoded*, 38.
24. Reich, "How Genetics Is Changing Our Understanding of 'Race.'"

25. The EUROTAST project was a Marie Skłodowska-Curie Initial Training Network (ITN) that ran from 2011 to 2015. See European Commission, "A European Initial Training Network on the History, Archaeology, and New Genetics of the Trans-Atlantic Slave Trade."

26. See, for example, Bastide, *Les Amériques noires*, 8–10.

27. Roberts, *Fatal Invention*; Nelson, *The Social Life of DNA*.

28. Wade, López Beltrán, and Santos, "Genomics, Race Mixture, and Nation in Latin America"; McLean, "Isolation by Distance and the Problem of the Twenty-First Century."

29. Pagden, *The Fall of Natural Man*.

30. Miramon and Van der Lugt, "Sang, hérédité et parenté au Moyen Âge"; Martínez, *Genealogical Fictions*.

31. Hall, *The Fateful Triangle*, 64.

32. M'charek, "Beyond Fact or Fiction," 423–24.

33. Bonilla-Silva, "Rethinking Racism."

34. Krieger, "The Science and Epidemiology of Racism and Health."

35. Hartigan, "Is Race Still Socially Constructed?"

36. Mukhopadhyay and Moses, "Reestablishing 'Race' in Anthropological Discourse," 526.

37. I borrow the concept of the "social management" of biology from Jean-Luc Bonniol's discussion of the production of the color line in colonial Antillean societies; see Bonniol, "Penser et gérer l'hérédité."

38. Benn Torres, Kittles, and Stone, "Mitochondrial and Y Chromosome Diversity in the English-Speaking Caribbean"; Gonçalves et al., "Sex-Biased Gene Flow in African Americans but Not in American Caucasians."

39. Bryc et al., "The Genetic Ancestry of African Americans, Latinos, and European Americans across the United States."

40. Hall, "Race—the Sliding Signifier," 45.

41. Zwart, "In the Beginning Was the Genome."

42. Wendy Roth describes racial schemas as "shared representations that are partly independent of individuals' beliefs," which are typically influenced by the institutionalization of racial categories by the state, schools, workplaces, families, social movements, and bureaucracies. Roth, *Race Migrations*, 13.

43. Seigel, "Beyond Compare."

44. Skidmore, *Black into White*; Stepan, *The Hour of Eugenics*.

45. UNESCO, *Four Statements*, 37.

46. Maio, "UNESCO and the Study of Race Relations in Brazil."

47. Telles and Project on Ethnicity and Race in Latin America, *Pigmentocracies*; Twine, *Racism in a Racial Democracy*.

48. Bourdieu and Wacquant, "On the Cunning of Imperialist Reason."

49. G. Reginald Daniel, for example, argues that the two countries are gradually converging on similar racial schemas and approaches to antiracism. Daniel, *Race and Multiraciality in Brazil and the United States*.

50. Wade, *Race and Ethnicity in Latin America*, 5.

51. Rotimi, "Genetic Ancestry Tracing and the African Identity."

52. Pereira, *O mundo negro*.

53. Twine, "A White Side of Black Britain."

54. The Consortium for the Analysis of Diversity and Evolution in Latin America, CANDELA, launched in 2011 and led by researchers at University College London (UCL), carried out simultaneous research projects in Brazil, Chile, Colombia, Mexico, and Peru and aimed to shed light on the contemporary consequences of the historic mixture between the region's three major ancestral populations: Europeans, Indigenous Americans, and Africans. See UCL Division of Biosciences, "Candela."

55. Gilroy, *Against Race*, 37.

56. Spillers, "Mama's Baby, Papa's Maybe," 67.

57. Zeuske, "The Second Slavery."

58. Keefer, "Marked by Fire."

59. Abel, Tyson, and Pálsson, "From Enslavement to Emancipation."

60. Gomez, *Exchanging Our Country Marks*; Edwards, *Hiding in Plain Sight*.

61. Gomez, *Exchanging Our Country Marks*, 117–20.

62. Cunha, *Negros, estrangeiros*; Schramm, *African Homecoming*, 40–45.

63. Cottias, *La question noire*, 42.

64. Véran, "Old Bones, New Powers," S247.

65. Boas, *Race, Language, and Culture*; Blackhawk and Wilner, *Indigenous Visions*; Du Bois, *The Souls of Black Folk*; Freyre, *Casa-grande e senzala*.

66. See, for example, Boas, *Race, Language, and Culture*, 60–75; Montagu, *Man's Most Dangerous Myth*.

67. Herskovits, *The Myth of the Negro Past*; Turner, *Africanisms in the Gullah Dialect*; Verger, *Flux et reflux de la traite des nègres*.

68. Maroons, or *quilombolas* in Portuguese, were individuals who escaped slavery, often banding together to form rural communities, *quilombos*. They survived by raiding surrounding plantations or sometimes setting up trade links with Indigenous groups and even communities of European settlers. On the 1988 Brazilian constitution and definitions of its beneficiaries, see French, "Dancing for Land"; Véran, *L'esclavage en héritage (Brésil)*.

69. The debate is summarized in Agier, "Frazier, Herskovits et la famille noire à Bahia."

70. French, "Dancing for Land"; Boyer, "Énoncer une 'identité' pour sortir de l'invisibilité."

71. La Roche and Blakey, "Seizing Intellectual Power"; Mack and Blakey, "The New York African Burial Ground Project."

72. Jackson et al., "Origins of the New York African Burial Ground Population," 88–89; see also Abel and Sandoval-Velasco, "Crossing Disciplinary Lines."

73. Roberts, *Fatal Invention*, 232; Nelson, *The Social Life of DNA*, 33.

74. Nelson, *The Social Life of DNA*, 95, 63–65.

75. Rabinow, *Essays on the Anthropology of Reason*, 102.

76. Sommer, "History in the Gene."

77. Canguilhem, "Le concept et la vie," 221.

78. M'charek, *The Human Genome Diversity Project*; Fullwiley, "The Biologistical Construction of Race"; Wailoo, Nelson, and Lee, *Genetics and the Unsettled Past*; Wade et al., *Mestizo Genomics*.

79. Twine, "Racial Ideologies and Racial Methodologies."

80. Jones, *Bad Blood*; Schwarcz, *O espetáculo das raças*; Skloot, *The Immortal Life of Henrietta Lacks*.

81. Roberts, *Fatal Invention*; Nelson, *The Social Life of DNA*.

82. Twine, "Racial Ideologies and Racial Methodologies," 2–3.

83. Fullwiley, "The 'Contemporary Synthesis'"; Walajahi, Wilson, and Hull, "Constructing Identities"; Abel and Tsosie, "Family History and the Global Politics of DNA."

84. Edwards, "Undoing Kinship," 46–47.

Chapter 1

1. Sweet, *African American Lives*, Episode 1, "Listening to Our Past."

2. Autosomal DNA refers to the autosomes, meaning all pairs of chromosomes (1–22) except the sex chromosomes (X and Y). Unlike the majority of mtDNA and Y-DNA, autosomal DNA is made up of a combination of genetic material from both biological parents (whose contributions constitute roughly 50 percent of their own autosomal DNA).

3. Judd, *African American Lives*, Episode 4, "Beyond the Middle Passage."

4. BBC Brasil, "Especial Raízes Afro-Brasileiras."

5. See, for instance, Leonard, "Black Like Me?"

6. Farrell and Forster, "'African American Lives.'"

7. BBC News Forums, "Você acha que o conceito de raça ainda faz sentido no Brasil?"

8. Azevedo, "A farsa neo-racista do Brasil em três momentos."

9. Ramos, "Frei entra na justiça contra pesquisador"; Ramos, "Pesquisa da BBC é apontada como estratégia contra cotas."

10. Simões, "Raízes e raças do Brasil."

11. Haraway, *Simians, Cyborgs, and Women*, 114.

12. Trouillot, *Silencing the Past*, xxiii.

13. Interview with author, May 2, 2014.

14. For example, Godwin, Appio, and Colton, *Wonders of the African World with Henry Louis Gates Jr.*

15. Haley, *Roots*; Chomsky et al., "Roots."

16. Taylor, "The Griot from Tennessee," 48; Moore, "Routes," 4.

17. Glazer and Moynihan, *Beyond the Melting Pot*; Moynihan, "The Negro Family."

18. Haley, *Roots*, 879.

19. Rushdy, *Remembering Generations*, 18.

20. Interview with author, May 2, 2014.

21. Gates, *In Search of Our Roots*, 5–6.

22. Weil, *Family Trees*.

23. McKay, "Genealogists and Records," 26; Forgie, "LDS Church Donates $2 Million to Create African-American Genealogy Museum"; MormonNewsroom.org,

"Church Presents Historic Freedmen's Bureau Database to African American Museum."

24. Blockson and Fry, *Black Genealogy*, 2.

25. Jacobson, *Roots Too*, 19–22.

26. Higham, *Strangers in the Land*, 242.

27. Novak, *The Rise of the Unmeltable Ethnics*, xvi.

28. Novak, xvii.

29. Novak.

30. African Ancestry, *Do You Know Where You're From?*

31. Interview with author, May 2, 2014.

32. Croasmun, "Jumping Chasms," 26.

33. Interview with author, May 2, 2014.

34. Wolfe, "Racial Integrity Laws (1924–1930)."

35. Du Bois, *The Souls of Black Folk*; Davis, *Who Is Black?* Jean-Luc Bonniol also provides an in-depth discussion of the logic of Whiteness, mixture, and the color line in the context of the French Antilles; see Bonniol, *La couleur comme maléfice*.

36. Nelson, *The Social Life of DNA*, 78.

37. Pinderhughes, "Black Genealogy Revisited."

38. Gates, "I'm White, but Tests Show I Have East African DNA. How?"; Gates, Pironti, and Siekman, "Did My White Ancestor Become Black?"; Gates, Pironti, and Siekman, "I'm White and Curious about My 'Free Colored' Ancestor"; Gates, "Who's Your (Irish) Daddy?"; Gates, "Exactly How 'Black' Is Black America?"; Gates, "High Cheekbones and Straight Black Hair?"

39. Glycerio, "'Brasil tem a cara do futuro,' diz professor." Gates later modified this statement. In 2011, he returned to Brazil to shoot an episode for his documentary series *Black in Latin America*. In the series, Gates noted that Brazil presents itself today as a racism-free country, but the reality is "much more complicated." Pollack, *Black in Latin America*, Episode 3, "Brazil: A Racial Paradise?"

40. Zack, "Mixed Black and White"; Hochschild, "Looking Ahead"; Warren and Sue, "Comparative Racisms," 34.

41. Schwarcz, "Usos e abusos da mestiçagem e da raça no Brasil."

42. Seigel, "Beyond Compare."

43. Freyre, *Casa-grande e senzala*, 70–71.

44. For a history of Brazil's Black movements, see Pereira, *O mundo negro*.

45. Nascimento, *O negro revoltado*, 67.

46. Skidmore, *O Brasil visto de fora*, 137; Daniel, *Race and Multiraciality in Brazil and the United States*, 183.

47. Fernandes, *O negro no mundo dos brancos*; Hasenbalg and Silva, *Estrutura social, mobilidade e raça*; Nascimento, "Aspects of Afro-Brazilian Experience"; Bucciferro, "Racial Inequality in Brazil from Independence to the Present"; Nascimento, *O genocídio do negro brasileiro*, 83–84.

48. Nascimento, *O genocídio do negro brasileiro*, 107.

49. Souza, *Multiculturalismo e racismo*, 16.

50. Fry, "Politics, Nationality, and the Meanings of 'Race' in Brazil," 100.

51. Martins, Medeiros, and Nascimento, "Paving Paradise," 800–803; Htun, "From 'Racial Democracy' to Affirmative Action," 68.

52. Moura and Barreto, *A Fundação Cultural Palmares na III Conferência Mundial*, 131.

53. Turra and Venturi, *Racismo cordial*, 13.

54. Lehmann, *The Prism of Race*, 34–37.

55. This same reasoning was used in 1978 by the U.S. Supreme Court to rule racial quotas illegal in the landmark *Regents of the University of California v. Bakke* case. Horn and Marín, *Realizing Bakke's Legacy*, 2.

56. Maggie, "Os novos bacharéis"; Maggie and Fry, "A reserva de vagas para negros nas universidades brasileiras."

57. Anthropologist Kabengele Munanga provides a discussion and critique of these and other objections to the quotas in Munanga, "Políticas de ação afirmativa em benefício da população negra no Brasil."

58. Fry, "A Viewpoint on the Dispute among Anthropologists over Racially Targeted Policies in Brazil."

59. Bourdieu and Wacquant, "On the Cunning of Imperialist Reason"; Fry et al., *Divisões perigosas*.

60. Azevedo, "Cota racial e estado," 215; Magnoli, *Uma gota de sangue*.

61. Carvalho and Segato, "Uma proposta de cotas," 18, 32. The theory about quotas promoting "interracial" mixing in universities was borne out in André Cicalo's ethnographic study among students in Rio de Janeiro. Cicalo, *Urban Encounters*.

62. Carvalho and Segato, "Uma proposta de cotas," 26–27; Kent and Wade, "Genetics against Race," 822.

63. Students who were rejected by the panel had the opportunity to appeal and could be invited to a formal interview in which they were asked to give further details about their racial identity. Maio and Santos, "Política de cotas raciais, os 'olhos da sociedade' e os usos da antropologia."

64. Pinho, "UnB rejeita um gêmeo e aceita outro nas cotas."

65. Interview with author, January 16, 2013.

66. Pena, "Brazilians and the Variable Mosaic Genome Paradigm," 102. The argument about the dissociation of "color" from DNA ancestry markers has since been contested; see Silva et al., "The Correlation between Ancestry and Color in Two Cities of Northeast Brazil."

67. Pena et al., "Retrato molecular do Brasil," 25.

68. Pena, *Igualmente diferentes*, 22; see also Pena, *À flor da pele*; Pena, *Humanidade sem raças?*

69. Pena and Bortolini, "Pode a genética definir quem deve se beneficiar das cotas universitárias e demais ações afirmativas?," 46, 43. The figure of 146 million was reached by extrapolating the findings of their population genetics studies in relation to recent census data on self-identified race. Based on this approach, the authors estimated that some 87 percent of all Brazilians had at least 10 percent African ancestry, meaning that "48% of Brazilian Afro-descendants self-identify as White."

70. See, for example, Edward, "Quem somos nós?"

71. Interview with author, August 22, 2013.

72. In *African American Lives*, the female guests received only mtDNA test results, whereas in *Raízes Afro-Brasileiras* the journalists gathered DNA from male relatives of the female celebrities to offer both sets of results to all participants. Two of the male guests on *African American Lives* received "African" Y-DNA results.

73. Glycerio, "Daiane dos Santos é 'protótipo da brasileira.'"

74. Glycerio and Salek, "Metade de negros em pesquisa tem ancestral europeu."

75. Santos and Maio, "Qual 'Retrato do Brasil'?," 86.

76. Fernandez, "The Color of Love"; Pinho, "White but Not Quite"; Moreno Figueroa, "Displaced Looks"; Hordge-Freeman, *The Color of Love*.

77. See, for example, Slenes, *Na senzala, uma flor*; Del Priore, "Brasil colonial"; Aidoo, *Slavery Unseen*; Smith, *Afro-Paradise*; Alves, *The Anti-Black City*.

78. Glycerio, "'Se fosse 100% negro, lutaria por indenização.'"

79. Mulot, "Le mythe du viol fondateur aux Antilles Françaises," 518.

80. Glycerio, "'Tenho orgulho de ser quase 100% africana.'"

81. See, for instance, Lafargue, "La ressemblance sert-elle à penser l'hérédité?"

82. Costa, "The (Un)Happy Objects of Affective Community," 35.

83. Glycerio, "Neguinho da Beija-Flor tem mais gene europeu."

84. Azevedo, "A farsa neo-racista do Brasil em três momentos."

85. Salek, "BBC Delves into Brazilians' Roots."

86. Kent and Wade, "Genetics against Race," 817.

87. Kent and Wade, 829.

88. The origins of EDUCAFRO are explored in Lehmann, *The Prism of Race*, 174–85.

89. Interview with author, August 15, 2013.

90. Ramos, "Frei entra na justiça contra pesquisador," 7.

91. Glycerio, "68% africano, ativista queria mais detalhes."

92. Glycerio.

93. Judd, *African American Lives*, Episode 4, "Beyond the Middle Passage."

94. Alberti and Pereira, "História do Movimento Negro no Brasil," 5–6.

95. Twine, *Racism in a Racial Democracy*; Silva and Paixão, "Mixed and Unequal."

96. Bailey, "Unmixing for Race Making in Brazil," 593; Silva and Paixão, "Mixed and Unequal," 192.

97. Alves, "From Necropolis to Blackpolis," 328; see also Smith, *Afro-Paradise*, 11.

98. Olopade, "Skip Gates Speaks."

99. Oprah.com, "The Importance of Ancestry."

100. Interview with author, May 2, 2014; D'Addario, "Henry Louis Gates."

101. Alves, *The Anti-Black City*, 123; Alves, "From Necropolis to Blackpolis," 326.

102. Alexander, *The New Jim Crow*.

103. Bonilla-Silva, "Rethinking Racism."

104. Silva and Paixão, "Mixed and Unequal."

105. Spivak, *In Other Worlds*, 205.

Chapter 2

1. Comaroff and Comaroff, *Ethnicity, Inc.*, 9.

2. The series of confrontations between the BritainsDNA executive and scientists and the UCL geneticists was chronicled extensively by the latter on their UCL home-page: see UCL Division of Biosciences, "The Moffat/BritainsDNA Saga." A summary of their account can also be found in Kennett et al., "The Rise and Fall of Britains-DNA." The issue of the libel claim was also discussed in "The Right to Speak Out," an editorial appearing in *Nature* later that year.

3. Thomas, "To Claim Someone Has 'Viking Ancestors' Is No Better than Astrology."

4. Gieryn, "Boundary-Work and the Demarcation of Science from Non-Science." In the BritainsDNA case, Thomas, Balding, and other geneticists kept up a steady criticism of the company and its claims to scientific authority, a discourse that was gradually taken up by BBC journalists, who in subsequent radio discussions took a more critical stance on BritainsDNA and other commercial ancestry-testing com-panies. As a result of the controversy, at the end of his three-year tenure as rector of the University of St. Andrews, Moffat was not offered an honorary degree by the senate—the award traditionally presented to holders of that title. See Bucks, "Mof-fat Not Nominated for Honorary Degree."

5. Nelson, *The Social Life of DNA*, 63–65.

6. A haplotype is a set of genetic variants inherited together from a single parent. In DNA ancestry testing, the term is often used to refer to sets of genes found in mtDNA and Y-DNA sequences, which are used to infer an individual's maternal or paternal biogeographical ancestry. For practical purposes, scientists have systematized known mtDNA and Y-DNA haplotypes, organizing related hap-lotypes into haplogroups, which are arranged into phylogenies (branching tree-like structures).

7. A summary of these arguments can be found in Rotimi, "Genetic Ancestry Tracing and the African Identity." They are also explored in more depth in Abel and Sandoval-Velasco, "Crossing Disciplinary Lines."

8. Baron, "Motherland: A Genetic Journey."

9. Jackson, "Concerns and Priorities in Genetic Studies"; Jackson, "African-American Responses to the Human Genome Project"; Jackson and Mulla, "In Con-versation with Fatimah Jackson."

10. Interview with author, May 26, 2014.

11. Nelson, *The Social Life of DNA*, 102.

12. Interview with author, May 26, 2014.

13. Nixon, "DNA Tests Find Branches but Few Roots."

14. Winstein, "Harvard's Gates Refines Genetic-Ancestry Searches for Blacks."

15. Kittles has also stated that this should be a role of DNA ancestry testing; see Shriver and Kittles, "Genetic Ancestry," 616.

16. For a further discussion of the scientific debates around DNA ancestry and African origins, see Abel and Sandoval-Velasco, "Crossing Disciplinary Lines."

17. Interview with author, May 19, 2014.

18. Also known as a phylogenetic trees, phylogenies are branching diagrams used by population geneticists to represent the evolutionary relationships of groups of organisms or populations within a species.

19. Ely et al., "African American Mitochondrial DNAs"; Ely, "Can a Database of MtDNA HVSI Sequences Properly Assign Africans to Their Country of Origin?"

20. Interview with author, May 7, 2014.

21. Ekeh, "Social Anthropology and Two Contrasting Uses of Tribalism in Africa"; Southall, "The Illusion of Tribe."

22. Heywood and Thornton, "Pinpointing DNA Ancestry in Africa."

23. AfricanDNA offered uniparental and continental admixture tests, which were processed by the company FamilyTreeDNA. Winstein, "Harvard's Gates Refines Genetic-Ancestry Searches for Blacks."

24. Interview with author, April 28, 2014.

25. Santos, Bortolini, and Maio, "No fio da navalha," 34.

26. UCL Division of Biosciences, "Candela."

27. Rio Grande do Sul is characterized by recent European immigration, in particular from Germany and Italy; Rondônia, in the heart of Amazonia, has a large Indigenous population; and Bahia is the area that received the greatest proportion of African migrations through the transatlantic trade.

28. A "SNP chip" is a technology designed to scan for specific genetic variants, known as single nucleotide polymorphisms, across the genome and indicate which allele is present in each case. Most SNP chips used for commercial ancestry-testing assay between 500,000 and 1 million genomic loci.

29. Personal email communication with Andrés Ruiz Linares, January 7, 2021. Details of the methods used to select the AIMs and reference populations for the CANDELA ancestry tests can be found in Ruiz-Linares et al., "Admixture in Latin America."

30. The HDGP-CEPH cell panel comprises 1,050 DNA samples from fifty-two "world populations," collected between the 1990s and 2000s by various laboratories participating in the Human Genome Diversity Project (HGDP) and the French Centre d'Étude du Polymorphisme Humain (CEPH). See CEPH Fondation Jean Dausset, "HGDP-CEPH Human Genome Diversity Cell Line Panel." The International HapMap Project was launched in 2002 as a tool to help researchers find genes and genetic variants that affect health and disease. The project produced a reference database that aimed for "global" coverage of human populations, and samples were identified by both ethnic and geographic tags (e.g., "Mexican Ancestry from Los Angeles USA," "Yoruba in Ibadan, Nigeria," "Japanese in Tokyo, Japan"). For a detailed account of how the HapMap Project chose and labeled these populations, see Reardon, "Race without Salvation."

31. Discussions of the principles and limitations of admixture testing can be found in Royal et al., "Inferring Genetic Ancestry," 667–69; Rajagopalan and Fujimura, "Making History via DNA, Making DNA from History"; Weiss and Lambert, "What Type of Person Are You?" On the underrepresentation of African groups in genomic datasets, see Bentley, Callier, and Rotimi, "Diversity and Inclusion in Genomic Research."

32. Interview with author, July 22, 2013.

33. M'charek, *The Human Genome Diversity Project*, 62–63.

34. Souza et al., "História da genética no Brasil"; Salzano and Freire-Maia, *Populações brasileiras*.

35. Novembre and Ramachandran, "Perspectives on Human Population Structure at the Cusp of the Sequencing Era," 246.

36. Pickrell and Reich, "Toward a New History and Geography of Human Genes Informed by Ancient DNA," 377.

37. The term first appeared in an 1864 pamphlet, published in New York under the title *Miscegenation: The Theory of the Blending of the Races, Applied to the American White Man and Negro*, which was later attributed to two Democrat (antiabolitionist) journalists, David Goodman Croly and George Wakeman. The pamphlet defined "miscegenation" as "the blending of the various races of men—the practical recognition of the brotherhood of all the children of the common father." Croly and Wakeman, *Miscegenation*; Lemire, *"Miscegenation": Making Race in America*.

38. Wade, "Race, Multiculturalism, and Genomics in Latin America," 214.

39. UNESCO, *Four Statements*, 44.

40. Interview with author, July 24, 2013.

41. UNESCO, *Four Statements*, 37.

42. Campbell and Tishkoff, "African Genetic Diversity."

43. Interview with author, July 22, 2013.

44. Interview with author, July 17, 2013.

45. Hu-DeHart and López, "Asian Diasporas in Latin America and the Caribbean"; Rustomji-Kerns, Srikanth, and Mendoza Strobel, *Encounters*.

46. Olarte Sierra and Díaz del Castillo H., "The Travels of Humans, Categories, and Other Genetic Products."

47. Pena, *À flor da pele*; Pena, *Humanidade sem raças?*; Pena, *Igualmente diferentes*.

48. Interview with author, July 30, 2013.

49. Pena and Bortolini, "Pode a genética definir quem deve se beneficiar das cotas universitárias e demais ações afirmativas?"

50. Gieryn, "Boundary-Work."

51. Gates, *In Search of Our Roots*, 10.

52. Interview with author, May 13, 2014. See also Keita and Stewart, "Ethics, Identity, Genetics, Patrimony and Power in the Harvesting of DNA from Africa."

53. Maio and Santos, "Política de cotas raciais, os 'olhos da sociedade' e os usos da antropologia."

54. See, for example, Barbosa et al., "Microsatellite Studies on an Isolated Population of African Descent in the Brazilian State of Bahia"; Santos and Barbosa, "O ciclo da vida em Queimadas"; Barbosa, *Comunidades quilombolas*.

55. Interview with author, September 5, 2013.

56. Bliss, *Race Decoded*.

57. Nelson, "Bio Science," 769.

58. Kent, Santos, and Wade, "Negotiating Imagined Genetic Communities"; Calvo-González and Rocha, "Está no sangue"; Calvo-González, "Usos políticos da leucopenia e diferença racial no Brasil contemporâneo."

59. Brodwin, "'Bioethics in Action' and Human Population Genetics Research."

Chapter 3

1. This was despite 23andMe being served a cease-and-desist order by the Food and Drug Agency (FDA) in late 2013 over the accuracy of its health estimates, forcing the company to temporarily refocus its commercial efforts on the genetic ancestry and relative-matching components of the test. Loftus, "Genetic Test Service 23andMe Ordered to Halt Marketing by FDA."

2. Comaroff and Comaroff, *Ethnicity, Inc.*, 40.

3. Comaroff and Comaroff.

4. Rutherford, *A Brief History of Everyone Who Ever Lived*, 364.

5. Rose and Novas, "Biological Citizenship," 447–48.

6. Foucault, "Technologies of the Self," 18; Pálsson, "Decode Me!"

7. See, for instance, Cannell, "English Ancestors"; Abel, "Linked Descendants."

8. Rose and Novas, "Biological Citizenship," 448.

9. Reardon, "The Human Genome Diversity Project"; Gannett, "Racism and Human Genome Diversity Research."

10. The International HapMap Project (2002), Genographic Project (2005), and 1000 Genomes Project (2008) are other examples of global projects aimed at mapping and cataloguing human genetic variation. Whereas the HapMap and 1000 Genomes projects were oriented toward medical research, the Genographic Project, a nonprofit run by National Geographic, was focused specifically on molecular anthropological research and ancestry testing.

11. Pálsson and Rabinow, "Iceland: The Case of a National Human Genome Project."

12. Interview with author, February 10, 2017; Anders, "For Utah Billionaire, Search for Roots Is Blooming Field."

13. As a private university, BYU is sponsored entirely by the LDS Church. According to Woodward, the decision to leave BYU and found the SMGF as an independent entity was to make it clear that the project was not associated with or endorsed by the LDS Church.

14. Hutchison, Myres, and Woodward, "Growing the Family Tree," 42.

15. See International Society of Genetic Genealogy Wiki, "GeneTree."

16. Interview with author, February 10, 2017. A similar debate took place among the HGDP scientists; see Reardon, *Race to the Finish*, 76–78.

17. Cavalli-Sforza, "Genes, Peoples, and Languages."

18. Bliss, *Race Decoded*, 62–63.

19. Interview with author, February 10, 2017.

20. Business Wire, "Sorenson Molecular Genealogy Foundation's Genetic Genealogy Database Crosses Historic Milestone with 100,000 DNA Samples."

21. Perego, Myres, and Woodward, "The Molecular Genealogy Research Project"; Solinas, *Ancestry*, 71.

22. Cannell, "The Christianity of Anthropology," 345.

23. Interview with author, February 10, 2017.

24. POPRES was an international project launched in 2005 by GlaxoSmithKline and intended to bring together a DNA sample set for extensive genotyping, to be

used primarily in pharmacogenetics research. See Nelson et al., "The Population Reference Sample, POPRES."

25. Novembre et al., "Genes Mirror Geography within Europe," 98.

26. Interview with author, May 20, 2014.

27. Ball et al., "Ethnicity Estimate White Paper." At the time of this writing, the AncestryDNA website states that its reference panel comprises over 16,000 DNA samples.

28. Interview with author, May 20, 2014.

29. A copy of AncestryDNA's West African PCA plot can be found in Granka, "AncestryDNA Makes Scientific Breakthrough in West African Ethnicity."

30. Interview with author, May 20, 2014.

31. Ball et al., "Ethnicity Estimate White Paper."

32. Interview with author, May 20, 2014.

33. Interview with author, May 20, 2014.

34. Interview with author, May 20, 2014.

35. M'charek, "Beyond Fact or Fiction," 434.

36. Wade, "Race, Ethnicity and Nation"; Nash, *Genetic Geographies*, 47–48.

37. Baloglu, "AncestryDNA Ethnicity Prediction."

38. See, for example, Dunham, "AncestryDNA and a Possible Faux Pa."

39. Bettinger, "Problems with AncestryDNA's Genetic Ethnicity Prediction?"

40. Estes, "Ancestry's Mythical Admixture Percentages."

41. Baloglu, "AncestryDNA Ethnicity Prediction."

42. Peter Wade has reported similar findings in his study of Latin American population genetics research. See Wade, *Degrees of Mixture, Degrees of Freedom*, 113.

43. Interview with author, May 20, 2014.

44. Interview with author, April 24, 2014.

45. Smith, *5 Truths about DNA Tests*.

46. For more on this topic, see Abel, "Linked Descendants."

47. Collier, "25 Do's and Don'ts of DNA."

48. Teil, "No Such Thing as Terroir?," 492.

49. Ibid., 491.

50. Nelson and Hwang, "Roots and Revelation."

51. See, for example, Ancestry Support, "Unexpected Ethnicity Results."

52. I am grateful to Fenella Cannell (personal communication) for suggesting this formulation.

53. The choice of SNP chip can affect results, based on the number and location of the genetic markers it assays. The chip used by many companies in 2014 (Illumina OmniExpress) was developed primarily using individuals of European descent, making it better at predicting European and African ancestry (since Europeans are genetically a subset of African populations) but less effective at predicting Asian or Native American ancestry. In 2016, AncestryDNA adopted a bespoke SNP chip that it claimed would provide greater insights into non-European populations.

54. A continental admixture test I took in 2014 from African Ancestry attributed me 73 percent (± 7 percent) genetic similarity to populations in Europe, and 27 percent (± 7 percent) similarity to populations in "India Subcontinent."

55. Latour, "Visualisation and Cognition," 14.

56. Comaroff and Comaroff, *Ethnicity, Inc.*, 40.

57. The comment can be heard in the recorded Q&A session following Byrnes's presentation at the conference. See Byrnes, "Synthesizing Genetic and Genealogical Data to Elucidate African American Ancestry."

58. Holger, "DNA Testing for Ancestry Is More Detailed for White People."

59. LivingDNA, "The Most Advanced DNA Test for People with African Ancestry."

60. Braun and Hammonds, "Race, Populations, and Genomics."

61. Some French Antillean groups, for instance, have strategically rejected the label "African-descendant" and have focused their efforts on recovering the identities of their enslaved ancestors in the Caribbean. See Abel, "Of African Descent?"

62. McLean, "Isolation by Distance and the Problem of the Twenty-First Century," 90.

63. Ball et al., "Genetic Communities White Paper."

64. Ancestry, "Ancestry Announces 94 New and Updated Communities for People of African American and Afro-Caribbean Descent."

65. Rose and Novas, "Biological Citizenship."

66. Harris, Wyatt, and Kelly, "The Gift of Spit."

67. Lumb, "23andMe Gives Pfizer Access to Its Genome Database."

68. Interview with author, February 10, 2017.

69. Mustian, "New Orleans Filmmaker Cleared in Cold-Case Murder."

70. TallBear, *Native American DNA*; Leroux, *Distorted Descent*.

71. Reardon and TallBear, "Your DNA Is Our History," S234.

72. The Israeli company MyHeritage announced an initiative aimed at gathering the genealogies of Indigenous tribes around the world, ostensibly with the aim of helping these communities preserve their own ancestral memories. See MyHeritage, "Tribal Quest Ecuador." Over the past few years, the company has been attempting to accrue vast datasets of genealogical data. MyHeritage's chief scientist, Yaniv Erlich, has stated an interest in constructing a genealogy that connects "everyone in the world"; see Zhang, "The 'Genome Hacker' Who Mapped a 13-Million-Person Family Tree."

73. Rose and Novas, "Biological Citizenship," 440.

74. Murphy, "Law and Policy Oversight of Familial Searches in Recreational Genealogy Databases"; Kennett, "Using Genetic Genealogy Databases in Missing Persons Cases and to Develop Suspect Leads in Violent Crimes"; Granja, "Long-Range Familial Searches in Recreational DNA Databases."

75. Westlake, "Family Tree DNA Opens Its Genealogy Database to FBI."

76. Abel, "What DNA Can't Tell." In a recent case study from Finland, Anna-Maria Tapaninen and Ilpo Helén have signaled, conversely, that "identity by descent" testing may be perceived as a useful resource in family migration cases where documentary proof of kinship is lacking. However, the risk remains that DNA test results may be used to contradict or overrule other forms of kinship evidence, providing a convenient mechanism for migration officials to refuse applications. Tapaninen and Helén, "Making up Families"; Weiss, "Strange DNA."

Chapter 4

1. Santos, Bortolini, and Maio, "No fio da navalha"; Palmié, "Genomics, Divination, 'Racecraft.'"

2. Nelson, "Bio Science"; Foeman, Lee Lawton, and Rieger, "Questioning Race"; Roth and Ivemark, "Genetic Options."

3. Waters, *Ethnic Options*; Haney López, "The Social Construction of Race"; Hickman, "The Devil and the One Drop Rule."

4. Abu El-Haj, *The Genealogical Science*, 162. Jennifer Wagner and Kenneth Weiss have observed that buying multiple tests is popular among White test-takers; see Wagner and Weiss, "Attitudes on DNA Ancestry Tests."

5. Grossi and Donovan, "Hate in the Blood"; Panofsky and Donovan, "Genetic Ancestry Testing among White Nationalists."

6. Genera, "A crescente demanda por testes de ancestralidade no Brasil."

7. Santos et al., "Color, Race, and Genomic Ancestry in Brazil."

8. Nogueira, "Preconceito racial de marca e preconceito racial de origem."

9. Calvo-González and Rocha, "Está no sangue."

10. Schwartz-Marín and Wade, "Explaining the Visible and the Invisible"; Nieves Delgado, García Deister, and Beltrán, "¿De qué me ves cara?"; Wade, *Degrees of Mixture, Degrees of Freedom*, 223–57.

11. Excerpts of this chapter were published in a different version in Abel, "Rethinking the 'Prejudice of Mark.'"

12. Telles, *Race in Another America*; Daniel, *Race and Multiraciality in Brazil and the United States*; Roth, *Race Migrations*.

13. Williams, "The Recursive Outcomes of the Multiracial Movement and the End of American Racial Categories." Kim Williams notes that Latinos, who might be the group most expected to use the "multiple race" option, are more likely to check "some other race," as if rejecting the official racial schema altogether.

14. Bonilla-Silva, "We Are All Americans!"; Hochschild, "Looking Ahead"; Omi and Winant, "Racial Formation Rules"; Telles and Project on Ethnicity and Race in Latin America, *Pigmentocracies*. Eduardo Bonilla-Silva argued in the early 2000s that the United States was heading for a "triracial" system of "Whites," "Honorary Whites," and "Collective Black," whose boundaries were not governed by conceptions of "blood" (ancestry) but by racial profiling based on appearance ("color").

15. *Branco* means "white"; the category *pardo* is often translated in English as "brown," or "mixed-race" but it also carries the meanings "dark," "dun," or "gray"; *preto* ("black") refers to the darkest skin tones, while *amarelo* ("yellow") typically refers to people of East Asian descent. *Indígena* (Indigenous) is not a "color" category per se, but refers (at least notionally) to individuals who maintain some elements of Indigenous culture and heritage.

16. Hasenbalg and Silva, *Estrutura social, mobilidade e raça*; Daniel, *Race and Multiraciality*, 245–57.

17. Sansone, *Blackness without Ethnicity*; Bailey and Telles, "Multiracial versus Collective Black Categories"; Silva and Paixão, "Mixed and Unequal."

18. Bailey, Fialho, and Loveman, "How States Make Race."

19. Sheriff, *Dreaming Equality*, 43–46.

20. Roth, *Race Migrations*, 13–14.

21. The metaphor of the "prism" is borrowed from David Lehmann's discussion of university quotas in Brazil; see Lehmann, *The Prism of Race*.

22. Nelson, *The Social Life of DNA*, 84–88.

23. I have used pseudonyms for all participants of the CANDELA project, in accordance with the project's ethical framework.

24. As I discuss later on, this ideal has been revised in the light of affirmative action debates, leading many activists to place greater emphasis on "color" as a principal marker of Blackness.

25. Paixão and Carvano, "Censo e demografia," 48–49.

26. Maggie, "Os novos bacharéis"; Gomes, *Sem perder a raiz*, 147–50.

27. Lehmann, *The Prism of Race*, 147.

28. Turra and Venturi, *Racismo cordial*; Silva and Paixão, "Mixed and Unequal," 207–14.

29. Silva and Paixão, "Mixed and Unequal."

30. Racusen, "Affirmative Action and Identity"; Kent and Wade, "Genetics against Race," 823.

31. Lempp, "With the Eyes of Society."

32. Lempp, "With the Eyes of Society." See also Dias and Tavares Junior, *Heteroidentificação e cotas raciais*.

33. Guimarães, "Recriando fronteiras raciais."

34. Hordge-Freeman, *The Color of Love*, 39, 50.

35. Santos et al., "Color, Race, and Genomic Ancestry in Brazil," 795.

36. Calvo-González and Rocha, "Está no sangue"; see also Calvo-González, "Usos políticos da leucopenia e diferença racial no Brasil contemporâneo."

37. Suarez-Kurtz et al., "Pharmacogenomic Diversity among Brazilians."

38. I borrow the term "made up" from Jeanette Edwards's study of concepts of inheritance in a northern English community. Edwards observed that personal identities were perceived to be made up of biological elements, as well as the influence of parental upbringing and personal experiences, each of which contributed in asymmetric and sometimes unpredictable ways to the expression of one's unique character. See Edwards, "Make-up."

39. Some of the names of the U.S. DNA test-takers interviewed in this chapter have been replaced by pseudonyms; in other cases, according to the interviewees' preferences, I have retained original names.

40. See, for example, Zack, "Mixed Black and White"; Hickman, "The Devil and the One Drop Rule."

41. Hickman, "The Devil and the One Drop Rule"; Williams, "The Recursive Outcomes of the Multiracial Movement and the End of American Racial Categories."

42. Roberts, *Fatal Invention*, 229.

43. Twine, "A White Side of Black Britain," 901.

44. Appiah, *Cosmopolitanism*; Comaroff and Comaroff, *Ethnicity, Inc.* Similar observations about African American DNA test-takers have been reported in Shim, Rab Alam, and Aouizerat, "Knowing Something versus Feeling Different."

45. Ernesto Schwartz-Marín and Peter Wade observed similar assumptions about the relation between genomic ancestry and regional origin among Colombian DNA test-takers. See Schwartz-Marín and Wade, "Explaining the Visible and the Invisible," 892–94.

46. Pinho, "White but Not Quite," 44.

47. See, for example, Bailey, Fialho, and Loveman, "How States Make Race."

48. Harris, "Whiteness as Property."

49. Roth and Ivemark, "Genetic Options," 175; see also Reardon and TallBear, "Your DNA Is Our History."

50. TallBear, *Native American DNA*; Golbeck and Roth, "Aboriginal Claims"; Walajahi, Wilson, and Hull, "Constructing Identities."

51. TallBear, *Native American DNA*, 46; Castro, "No Brasil, todo mundo é índio, exceto quem não é."

52. Golbeck and Roth, "Aboriginal Claims"; Roth and Ivemark, "Genetic Options."

53. See, for example, Kent and Santos, "'Os Charruas vivem' nos Gaúchos."

54. Bryc et al., "The Genetic Ancestry of African Americans, Latinos, and European Americans across the United States," 8.

55. See, for instance, Broyard, *One Drop*.

56. Abel, "Linked Descendants."

57. Kim, "Rachel Dolezal Breaks Her Silence."

58. Bouie, "Is Rachel Dolezal Black Just Because She Says She Is?"

59. An in-depth analysis of Dolezal's case and the commentary it received from across the political spectrum is provided in Brubaker, *Trans*.

60. I borrow this formulation from Kim TallBear, *Native American DNA*, 59.

61. Golbeck and Roth, "Aboriginal Claims," 417.

62. Harmon, "Seeking Ancestry in DNA Ties Uncovered by Tests."

63. Modarressy-Tehrani, "A DNA Test Revealed This Man Is 4% Black."

64. Ruiz-Linares et al., "Admixture in Latin America."

65. Pena, "Brazilians and the Variable Mosaic Genome Paradigm." See also Silva et al., "The Correlation between Ancestry and Color in Two Cities of Northeast Brazil."

66. Costa, *Reimagining Black Difference and Politics in Brazil*, 124.

67. Sovik, *Aqui ninguém é branco*.

68. Calvo-González and Rocha, "Está no sangue," 313.

69. Panofsky and Donovan, "Genetic Ancestry Testing among White Nationalists"; see also Grossi and Donovan, "Hate in the Blood."

70. Gates, "How Many 'White' People Are Passing?"

71. Genera, "A crescente demanda por testes de ancestralidade no Brasil"; Scherer, "Conheça o teste de ancestralidade desenvolvido por startup brasileira"; Brafrika, "Resultado do meu teste de DNA."

Chapter 5

1. Wade, *Race and Ethnicity in Latin America*, 5–24.

2. UNESCO, *Four Statements*, 31.

3. See, for example, Glick Schiller, "Blood and Belonging."

4. Rotimi, "Genetic Ancestry Tracing and the African Identity"; Abel and Sandoval-Velasco, "Crossing Disciplinary Lines"; Abel and Schroeder, "From Country Marks to DNA Markers."

5. Roberts, *Fatal Invention*, 253.

6. Nelson, *The Social Life of DNA*; Nelson, "Bio Science"; Nelson, "The Factness of Diaspora."

7. Nelson, *The Social Life of DNA*, 87.

8. Nelson, 93.

9. Comaroff and Comaroff, *Ethnicity, Inc.*, 1.

10. I borrow the notion of "socially activating" biological ties from Edwards, "Undoing Kinship," 46.

11. Weil, *Family Trees*, 62–66, 139, 186–89.

12. Nash, *Of Irish Descent*, 18.

13. Nash.

14. Cannell, "English Ancestors"; Cannell, "Ghosts and Ancestors," 208.

15. Blockson and Fry, *Black Genealogy*, 3–4.

16. See, for example, Blockson and Fry, *Black Genealogy*; Woodtor, *Finding a Place Called Home*; Burroughs, *Black Roots*.

17. AfriGeneas (www.afrigeneas.com), for example, offers a large collection of free genealogical resources, as well as message boards and a mailing list that are used to request and exchange information among researchers.

18. Doriott, "Genetic Codes Unraveled."

19. Oduah, "The DNA Debate."

20. Collier, "25 Do's and Don'ts of DNA."

21. Collier, *Mississippi to Africa*, 210–11. Studies of the personal names given to enslaved Africans suggest that naming may have been used as a way to mark kinship ties and ethnic affiliations among enslaved communities. See, for example, Cody, "There Was No 'Absalom' on the Ball Plantations"; Abel, Tyson, and Pálsson, "From Enslavement to Emancipation."

22. Collier, *Mississippi to Africa*, 199.

23. Chazkel, "History Out of the Ashes," 62–63.

24. Santos, "The Legacy of Slavery in Contemporary Brazil." A notable exception is the work of U.S. linguist Lorenzo D. Turner who, in a paper published in 1942, detailed the oral histories he collected among members of the last generation of Africans to be brought to Brazil under slavery; see Turner, "Some Contacts of Brazilian Ex-Slaves with Nigeria, West Africa."

25. Araujo, "Wounded Pasts."

26. Twine, *Racism in a Racial Democracy*, 122–32, 114.

27. Alberti and Pereira, "História do Movimento Negro no Brasil," 5–6.

28. Alberti and Pereira, 7.

29. Interview with author, August 15, 2013.

30. Goldani, "As famílias no Brasil contemporaneo e o mito da desestruturação."

31. Interview with author, August 15, 2013.

32. Interview with author, September 4, 2013.

33. Mattos, "'Remanescentes das comunidades dos quilombos.'" It should be noted that not all such communities have retained rich memories of their African pasts; as Véronique Boyer points out, communities wishing to claim legal status as *quilombos* must undergo processes to "excavate" these collective histories, often with the aid of professional historians and anthropologists. In Amazonas, the issue is further complicated by histories of mixture between Black and Indigenous groups. See Boyer, "Une forme d'africanisation au Brésil"; Boyer, "Énoncer une 'identité' pour sortir de l'invisibilité."

34. Capone Laffitte, *Searching for Africa in Brazil*, 11.

35. Guedj, *Panafricanisme, religion akan et dynamiques identitaires aux États-Unis*.

36. Abreu and Mattos, "Em torno das 'Diretrizes curriculares nacionais para a educação das relações étnico-raciais e para o ensino de história e cultura afro-brasileira e africana,'" 7–13.

37. Costa, *Reimagining Black Difference and Politics in Brazil*, 125–26.

38. Costa, 45–46.

39. Personal interview with member of *Brasil: DNA África* production team, July 31, 2015.

40. Interviews with author, June 24, 2015 and December 2, 2020.

41. Monteiro, Pires, and Alberto, *Brasil: DNA África*.

42. Cannell, "English Ancestors," 473.

43. The Fundação Cultural Palmares (Palmares Cultural Foundation) is linked to the Brazilian Ministry of Culture and is in charge of promoting the cultural, social, and economic value of the Black influence on Brazilian society.

44. Monteiro, Pires, and Alberto, *Brasil: DNA África*, Episode 1, "Bahia."

45. Fellet, "Na África, indaguei rei da minha etnia por que nos venderam como escravos."

46. Lafargue, "La ressemblance sert-elle à penser l'hérédité?"; Ohrt Fehler, "(Re)Constructing Roots."

47. Monteiro, Pires, and Alberto, *Brasil: DNA África*, Episode 1, "Bahia."

48. Edwards, "Make-up," 422.

49. Gilroy, *The Black Atlantic*, 74–79.

50. Ohrt Fehler, "(Re)Constructing Roots."

51. See The Aluna Method (www.alunamethod.com).

52. Boyle, "DNA Findings Point to Royal Roots in Africa."

53. Boyle, "Atlanta Family's Roots Get Tangled up in Africa."

54. Boyle.

55. Judd, "Beyond the Middle Passage"; Benn Torres et al., "Y Chromosome Lineages in Men of West African Descent."

56. Boyle, "Black History Saga Comes Full Circle."

57. Boyle, "Africans Visit Their American Cousins."

58. Boyle, "Genes Tell a Tale as Big as Africa."

59. Boyle.

60. Edwards, "A Feel for Genealogy."

61. Boyle, "African-American's Roots Revised."

62. Boyle.

63. Boyle.

64. Abel and Pálsson, "Detecting Ancestry."

65. Araujo, *Public Memory of Slavery*, 8; italics mine.

66. Benton and Shabazz, "Find Their Level," 499–500.

67. Hartman, *Lose Your Mother*, 5.

68. Hartman, 193; see also Ciarcia, *Le revers de l'oubli*, 71.

69. Boyle, "African-American Repatriates Tribal Treasures through eBay Diplomacy."

70. Boyle, "Genetic Quest Leads to African Apology for Role in Slave Trade."

71. Ciarcia, *Le revers de l'oubli*, 39.

72. Boyle, "African-American Repatriates Tribal Treasures through eBay Diplomacy."

73. Midlo Hall, *Slavery and African Ethnicities in the Americas*, 11.

74. Araujo, *Public Memory of Slavery*, 62–68.

75. See, for example, David and Jones, "Genetic Genealogical Methods."

76. DNA Tested African Descendants, "Our DNA Project."

77. Ohrt Fehler, "(Re)constructing Roots," 589.

78. Okona, "'Heritage Travel' Is Surging in the Era of DNA Testing."

79. Nelson, *The Social Life of DNA*, 106; BBC News, "American Rapper Ludacris Becomes Gabonese Citizen."

80. Schramm, "Diasporic Citizenship under Debate."

81. Reality Check Team, "African Diaspora."

82. Castro, "No Brasil, todo mundo é índio, exceto quem não é."

83. These arguments are elaborated further in Abel and Schroeder, "From Country Marks to DNA Markers."

84. Costa, *Reimagining Black Difference and Politics in Brazil*, 60–65.

85. Fellet, "Na África, indaguei rei da minha etnia por que nos venderam como escravos."

Epilogue

1. Regalado, "2017 Was the Year Consumer DNA Testing Blew Up." These figures are based on reported data from AncestryDNA, FamilyTreeDNA, 23andMe (all based in the United States), and the Israeli company MyHeritage; they do not take into account the multitude of smaller DNA ancestry-testing companies found elsewhere in Europe, the Americas, and Asia (for instance, the Chinese biotech company 23Mofang, which aimed to reach over 1 million customers by 2020).

2. Southern Poverty Law Center, "The Year in Hate."

3. Silva and Larkins, "The Bolsonaro Election, Antiblackness, and Changing Race Relations in Brazil," 898.

4. Twine, *Racism in a Racial Democracy*; Costa, "The (Un)Happy Objects of Affective Community."

5. Bonilla-Silva, "Rethinking Racism."

6. UNESCO, *Four Statements*, 51.

7. UNESCO, 22.

8. Mitchell-Walthour, "Racism in a Racialized Democracy," 226.

9. See also TallBear, *Native American DNA*.

10. Jacobson, *Roots Too*; Waters, *Ethnic Options*.

11. Roth and Ivemark, "Genetic Options."

12. Panofsky and Donovan, "Genetic Ancestry Testing among White Nationalists."

13. Kemp, *Four Flags*; Nash, *Genetic Geographies*, 115–16.

14. Leroux, *Distorted Descent*.

15. Nash, *Genetic Geographies*, 183.

16. Sahlins, *What Kinship Is—and Is Not*; Lorde, *Your Silence Will Not Protect You*.

17. Castro, *Cannibal Metaphysics for a Post-Structural Anthropology*; Kohn, *How Forests Think*.

18. 23andMe, "Travel as Unique as Your DNA with 23andMe and Airbnb"; Lee, "How Airbnb Short-Term Rentals Exacerbate Los Angeles's Affordable Housing Crisis."

19. Farr, "Consumer DNA Testing Has Hit a Lull."

20. Harris, Wyatt, and Kelly, "The Gift of Spit"; Hervé, Stoeklé, and Vogt, "'Un marché aux données génétiques' qui interroge."

21. Ancestry, "How Do We Find DNA Matches that Are Meaningful in Genealogy?"; MyHeritage, "What's Considered a Strong DNA Match?"

22. Ingold, *The Perception of the Environment*, 136.

23. De Groot, *Consuming History*, 73.

24. Bennett, "Research at the National Archives and Beyond."

25. Interviews with author, October 3, 2012 and May 12, 2014; Fox Carolina News, "Will Jones Reporter Interviews Bernice Bennett and Dr. Constance McNeill." Bennett's account of her search for her grandmother's origins has subsequently been published in a collected edition; see Bennett, "Finding My South Carolina Kin," 51–78. These experiences and those of other members of the AASIG are explored in depth in Abel, "Linked Descendants."

26. Bennett, "Finding My South Carolina Kin," 73.

27. Coming to the Table, "Linked Descendants Working Group."

28. Foster et al., "Jefferson Fathered Slave's Last Child"; Ford and Strauss, *Slavery's Descendants*.

29. Araujo, "The Problem of Using the Term 'Mistress' to Refer to Enslaved Women"; Aidoo, *Slavery Unseen*.

30. Spillers, "Mama's Baby, Papa's Maybe," 76.

31. Gordon-Reed, *The Hemingses of Monticello*. On the resistance of slaveholder-descendant families to recognize their links to descendants of the enslaved, see Ball, *Slaves in the Family*.

32. After a series of reports that commercial DNA ancestry-testing databases have been used by forensic and law-enforcement agencies in criminal and missing persons investigations and irregular migration cases, without the informed consent of customers, most companies now require clients to opt into these relative-matching services, rather than being included automatically. Murphy, "Law and Policy Oversight of Familial Searches in Recreational Genealogy Databases"; Abel, "What DNA Can't Tell"; Kennett, "Using Genetic Genealogy Databases in Missing Persons Cases

and to Develop Suspect Leads in Violent Crimes"; Granja, "Long-Range Familial Searches in Recreational DNA Databases."

33. According to African American genealogist and family therapist Elaine Pinderhughes, when she was researching her own family history in New Orleans, she found that several archivists erroneously claimed the files she was seeking had been destroyed or lost, in order to protect the reputations of local White lineages whose family histories of "racial" mixture had been kept diligently hidden for generations. Pinderhughes, "Black Genealogy Revisited," 118, 123.

34. Collier, "25 Do's and Don'ts of DNA."

35. Ford and Strauss, *Slavery's Descendants.*

36. Nelson, *The Social Life of DNA*, 121–40.

37. Kanor and Cottias, "Conversation between Fabienne Kanor and Myriam Cottias, on 'The Flesh of History.'"

38. Caruth, *Unclaimed Experience*, 1–5.

39. Eyerman, *Cultural Trauma*, 2.

40. Araujo, "Tourism and Heritage Sites of the Atlantic Slave Trade and Slavery," 285.

41. Guimarães, "Recriando fronteiras raciais"; Lempp, "With the Eyes of Society?"

42. Costa, "Afro-Brazilian Ancestralidade," 661.

43. Costa, *Reimagining Black Difference and Politics in Brazil.*

44. Gilroy, *Against Race*, 115.

45. Rodrigues, "Com futuro incerto, Sérgio Camargo volta à Fundação Palmares e quer equipe alinhada a seus ideais."

References

23andMe. "Travel as Unique as Your DNA with 23andMe and Airbnb." *23andMe* (blog), May 21, 2019. https://blog.23andme.com/ancestry-reports/travel -23andme-and-airbnb/.

Abel, Sarah. "Linked Descendants: Genetic-Genealogical Practices and the Refusal of Ignorance around Slavery." *Science, Technology & Human Values* (2021). https://doi.org/10.1177/01622439211021656.

———. "Of African Descent? Blackness and the Concept of Origins in Cultural Perspective." *Genealogy* 2, no. 1 (2018). https://doi.org/10.3390/genealogy 2010011.

———. "Rethinking the 'Prejudice of Mark': Concepts of Race, Ancestry, and Genetics among Brazilian DNA Test-Takers." *ODEERE* 5, no. 10 (2020): 186–221.

———. "What DNA Can't Tell: Problems with Using Genetic Tests to Determine the Nationality of Migrants." *Anthropology Today* 34, no. 6 (2018): 3–6.

Abel, Sarah, and Gísli Pálsson. "Detecting Ancestry: The Use of Genealogical Machines and Techniques in the Reconstruction of Family Histories." Translated by Zac Heyman. *Ethnologie française* 178, no. 2 (2020): 269–84.

Abel, Sarah, and Marcela Sandoval-Velasco. "Crossing Disciplinary Lines: Reconciling Social and Genomic Perspectives on the Histories and Legacies of the Transatlantic Trade in Enslaved Africans." *New Genetics and Society* 35, no. 2 (2016): 149–85.

Abel, Sarah, and Hannes Schroeder. "From Country Marks to DNA Markers: The Genomic Turn in the Reconstruction of African Identities." *Current Anthropology* 61, no. S22 (2020): S198–209.

Abel, Sarah, and Krystal Tsosie. "Family History and the Global Politics of DNA." *International Public History* 2, no. 2 (2019). https://doi.org/10.1515/iph-2019 -0015.

Abel, Sarah, George F. Tyson, and Gísli Pálsson. "From Enslavement to Emancipation: Naming Practices in the Danish West Indies." *Comparative Studies in Society and History* 61, no. 2 (2019): 332–65.

Abreu, Martha, and Hebe Maria Mattos. "Em torno das 'Diretrizes curriculares nacionais para a educação das relações étnico-raciais e para o ensino de história e cultura afro-brasileira e africana': Uma conversa com historiadores." *Estudos históricos* 21, no. 41 (2008): 5–20.

Abu El-Haj, Nadia. *The Genealogical Science: The Search for Jewish Origins and the Politics of Epistemology.* Chicago: University of Chicago Press, 2012.

African Ancestry. *Do You Know Where You're From?*, June 11, 2016. YouTube video, 1:30. https://www.youtube.com/watch?v=pZdorpGjEeo.

Agier, Michel. "Frazier, Herskovits et la famille noire à Bahia: Histoire d'une enquête ratée." *Cahiers du Brésil contemporain* 49/50 (2002): 39–48.

Aidoo, Lamonte. *Slavery Unseen: Sex, Power, and Violence in Brazilian History.* Durham, N.C.: Duke University Press, 2018.

Alberti, Verena, and Amilcar Araujo Pereira. "História do Movimento Negro no Brasil: Constituição de acervo de entrevistas de história oral." O Centro de Pesquisa e Documentação de História Contemporânea do Brasil (CPDOC), Rio de Janeiro, 2004. http://cpdoc.fgv.br/producao_intelectual/arq/1412.pdf.

Alexander, Michelle. *The New Jim Crow: Mass Incarceration in the Age of Colorblindness.* New York: New Press, 2010.

Alves, Jaime Amparo. *The Anti-Black City: Police Terror and Black Urban Life in Brazil.* Minneapolis: University of Minnesota Press, 2018.

———. "From Necropolis to Blackpolis: Necropolitical Governance and Black Spatial Praxis in São Paulo, Brazil." *Antipode* 46, no. 2 (2014): 323–39.

Ancestry. "Ancestry Announces 94 New and Updated Communities for People of African American and Afro-Caribbean Descent, Delivering More Historical Context than Ever Before." *Ancestry* (blog), February 19, 2019. https://blogs.ancestry.com/ancestry/2019/02/19/ancestry-announces-94-new-and-updated-communities-for-people-of-african-american-and-afro-caribbean-descent-delivering-more-historical-context-than-ever-before/.

———. "How Do We Find DNA Matches that Are Meaningful in Genealogy?" *Ancestry* (blog), 2021. https://www.ancestry.com/cs/dna-help/matches/meaningful-matches.

Ancestry Support. "Unexpected Ethnicity Results." *Ancestry Support*, 2021. https://support.ancestry.com/s/article/Unexpected-Ethnicity-Results.

Anders, George. "For Utah Billionaire, Search for Roots Is Blooming Field." *Wall Street Journal*, April 26, 2005. https://www.wsj.com/articles/SB111447552884616650.

Appiah, Kwame Anthony. *Cosmopolitanism: Ethics in a World of Strangers.* London: Penguin, 2006.

Araujo, Ana Lucia. "The Problem of Using the Term 'Mistress' to Refer to Enslaved Women." *A Historian's Views* (blog), March 1, 2017. http://www.historianviews.com/?p=249.

———. *Public Memory of Slavery: Victims and Perpetrators in the South Atlantic.* Amherst: Cambria Press, 2010.

———. "Tourism and Heritage Sites of the Atlantic Slave Trade and Slavery." In *A Companion to Public History*, edited by David Dean, 277–88. Hoboken, N.J.: Wiley, 2018.

———. "Wounded Pasts: Memory of Slavery and African Heritage in Brazil." In *African Heritage and Memories of Slavery in Brazil and the South Atlantic World*, edited by Ana Lucia Araujo. Amherst: Cambria Press, 2015.

Azevedo, Celia Maria Marinho de. "Cota racial e estado: Abolição do racismo ou direitos de raça?" *Cadernos de Pesquisa* 34, no. 121 (2004): 213–39.

Azevedo, Reinaldo. "A farsa neo-racista do Brasil em três momentos." *Veja*, May 30, 2007. http://veja.abril.com.br/blog/reinaldo/geral/farsa-neo-racista-brasil-em-tres-momentos/.

Bailey, Stanley R. "Unmixing for Race Making in Brazil." *American Journal of Sociology* 114, no. 3 (2008): 577–614.

Bailey, Stanley R., Fabrício M. Fialho, and Mara Loveman. "How States Make Race: New Evidence from Brazil." *Sociological Science* 5 (2018): 722–51.

Bailey, Stanley R., and Edward E. Telles. "Multiracial versus Collective Black Categories: Examining Census Classification Debates in Brazil." *Ethnicities* 6, no. 1 (2006): 74–101.

Ball, Catherine A., Mathew J. Barber, Jake K. Byrnes, Josh Callaway, Kenneth G. Chahine, Ross E. Curtis, Kenneth Freestone, et al. "Ethnicity Estimate White Paper." *AncestryDNA*, October 30, 2013. http://dna.ancestry.com/resource /whitePaper/AncestryDNA-Ethnicity-White-Paper.

Ball, Catherine A., Erin Battat, Jake K. Byrnes, Peter Carbonetto, Kenneth G. Chahine, Ross E. Curtis, Eyal Elyashiv, et al. "Genetic Communities White Paper: Predicting Fine-Scale Ancestral Origins from the Genetic Sharing Patterns among Millions of Individuals." *AncestryDNA*, 2018. https://www .ancestry.com/cs/dna-help/communities/whitepaper.

Ball, Edward. *Slaves in the Family.* New York: Farrar, Straus and Giroux, 1998.

Baloglu, Stephen. "AncestryDNA Ethnicity Prediction: Learning to Speak Genetics." *Ancestry Blog*, January 11, 2013. http://blogs.ancestry.com/ancestry /2013/01/11/ancestrydna-ethnicity-prediction-learning-to-speak-genetics/.

Barbosa, Ana Angélica Leal, ed. *Comunidades quilombolas: Outras formas de (re) existências.* Curitiba: Appris, 2020.

Barbosa, Ana Angélica Leal, Sandra Mara Bispo Sousa, Kiyoko Abé-Sandes, Carlos Alberto Alonso, Vicente Schneider, Denise C. C. Costa, Iglenir João Cavalli, and Eliane Elisa Souza Azevêdo. "Microsatellite Studies on an Isolated Population of African Descent in the Brazilian State of Bahia." *Genetics and Molecular Biology* 29 (2006): 23–30.

Barkan, Elazar. *The Retreat of Scientific Racism: Changing Concepts of Race in Britain and the United States between the World Wars.* Cambridge: Cambridge University Press, 1991.

Baron, Archie, dir. "Motherland: A Genetic Journey." Aired February 14, 2003, on BBC.

Bastide, Roger. *Les Amériques noires. Les civilisations africaines dans le Nouveau Monde.* 2nd ed. Paris: Payot, 1967.

BBC Brasil. "Especial Raízes Afro-Brasileiras." *BBC Brasil*, August 31, 2007. https://www.bbc.com/portuguese/noticias/cluster/2007/05/070427 _raizesafrobrasileiras.

BBC News. "American Rapper Ludacris Becomes Gabonese Citizen." *BBC News*, January 6, 2020. https://www.bbc.co.uk/news/world-africa-51008291.

BBC News Forums. "Você acha que o conceito de raça ainda faz sentido no Brasil?" *BBC News Forums*, May 28, 2007. http://newsforums.bbc.co.uk/ws /thread.jspa?sortBy=1&forumID=3129&start=435&tstart=0#paginator (site discontinued).

Benn Torres, J., R. A. Kittles, and A. C. Stone. "Mitochondrial and Y Chromosome Diversity in the English-Speaking Caribbean." *Annals of Human Genetics* 71 (2007): 782–90.

Benn Torres, Jada, Menahem B. Doura, Shomarka O. Y. Keita, and Rick A. Kittles. "Y Chromosome Lineages in Men of West African Descent." *PLoS One* 7, no. 1 (2012): e29687. https://doi.org/doi: 10.1371/journal.pone.0029687.

Bennett, Bernice Alexander. "Finding My South Carolina Kin." In *Our Ancestors, Our Stories*, by Harris Bailey Jr., Bernice Alexander Bennett, Ellen LeVonne Butler, Ethel Dailey, and Vincent Sheppard, 51–78. Suwanee: Write Image, 2014.

———. "Research at the National Archives and Beyond." *BlogTalkRadio*, 2021. https://www.blogtalkradio.com/bernicebennett.

Bentley, Amy R., Shawneequa Callier, and Charles N. Rotimi. "Diversity and Inclusion in Genomic Research: Why the Uneven Progress?" *Journal of Community Genetics* 8, no. 4 (2017): 255–66.

Benton, Adia, and Kwame Zulu Shabazz. "'Find Their Level': African American Roots Tourism in Sierra Leone and Ghana." *Cahiers d'Études africaines* 49, no. 1–2 (2009): 477–511.

Bettinger, Blaine. "Problems with AncestryDNA's Genetic Ethnicity Prediction?" *The Genetic Genealogist* (blog), June 19, 2012. http://thegeneticgenealogist.com /2012/06/19/problems-with-ancestrydnas-genetic-ethnicity-prediction/.

Blackhawk, Ned, and Isaiah Lorado Wilner, eds. *Indigenous Visions: Rediscovering the World of Franz Boas*. Yale University Press, 2018.

Bliss, Catherine. *Race Decoded: The Genomic Fight for Social Justice*. Kindle ed. Redwood City, Calif.: Stanford University Press, 2012.

Blockson, Charles L., and Ron Fry. *Black Genealogy*. Baltimore: Black Classic Press, 1991.

Boas, Franz. *Race, Language, and Culture*. New York: Free Press, Collier-Macmillan, 1940.

Bonilla-Silva, Eduardo. "Rethinking Racism: Toward a Structural Interpretation." *American Sociological Review* 62, no. 3 (1997): 465–80.

———. "We Are All Americans! The Latin Americanization of Racial Stratification in the USA." *Race & Society* 5 (2002): 3–16.

Bonniol, Jean-Luc. *La couleur comme maléfice: Une illustration créole de la généalogie des Blancs et des Noirs*. Paris: Albin Michel, 1992.

———. "Penser et gérer l'hérédité des caractères discriminants dans les sociétés esclavagistes et post-esclavagistes." *Rives nord-méditerranéennes* 24 (2006): 23–34.

Bouie, Jamelle. "Is Rachel Dolezal Black Just Because She Says She Is?" *Slate*, June 12, 2015. http://www.slate.com/articles/news_and_politics/politics/2015 /06/rachel_dolezal_claims_to_be_black_the_naacp_official_was_part_of_the _african.html.

Bourdieu, Pierre, and Loïc Wacquant. "On the Cunning of Imperialist Reason." *Theory, Culture & Society* 16, no. 1 (1999): 41–58.

Boyer, Véronique. "Énoncer une 'identité' pour sortir de l'invisibilité. La circulation des populations entre les catégories légales (Brésil)." *L'Homme* 214 (2015): 7–36.

———. "Une forme d'africanisation au Brésil: Les quilombolas entre recherche anthropologique et expertise politico-légale." *Cahiers d'Études africaines* 2, no. 198–199–200 (2010): 707–30.

Boyle, Alan. "African-American Repatriates Tribal Treasures through eBay Diplomacy." *NBC News Cosmic Log* (blog), January 19, 2013.

———. "African-American's Roots Revised." *NBC News Cosmic Log* (blog), May 14, 2012. https://www.nbcnews.com/science/cosmic-log/african-americans-roots -revised-flna771737.

———. "Africans Visit Their American Cousins." *NBC News Cosmic Log* (blog), July 4, 2011. https://www.nbcnews.com/science/cosmic-log/africans-visit-their -american-cousins-flna6c10403109.

———. "Atlanta Family's Roots Get Tangled up in Africa." *The Grio*, February 2, 2011. https://thegrio.com/2011/02/02/atlanta-familys-roots-get-tangled-up-in -africa/.

———. "Black History Saga Comes Full Circle." *NBC News Cosmic Log* (blog), March 1, 2011. https://www.nbcnews.com/science/cosmic-log/black-history -saga-comes-full-circle-flna6c10403293.

———. "DNA Findings Point to Royal Roots in Africa." *The Grio*, September 9, 2010. https://thegrio.com/2010/09/09/dna-findings-point-to-royal-roots-in -africa/.

———. "Genes Tell a Tale as Big as Africa." *NBC News Cosmic Log* (blog), November 5, 2011. https://www.nbcnews.com/science/cosmic-log/genes-tell -tale-big-africa-flna6c10402890.

———. "Genetic Quest Leads to African Apology for Role in Slave Trade." News website. *NBC News Cosmic Log* (blog), October 27, 2013. http://www.nbcnews .com/science/science-news/genetic-quest-leads-african-apology-role-slave -trade-f8C11467842.

Brafrika. "Resultado do meu teste de DNA." *Brafrika* (blog), February 13, 2021. https://brafrika.com.br/blogs/novidades/resultado-do-meu-teste-de-dna.

Brattain, Michelle. "Race, Racism, and Antiracism: UNESCO and the Politics of Presenting Science to the Postwar Public." *The American Historical Review* 112, no. 5 (2007): 1386–1413.

Braun, Lundy, and Evelynn Hammonds. "Race, Populations, and Genomics: Africa as Laboratory." *Social Science & Medicine* 67 (2008): 1580–88.

Brodwin, Paul. "'Bioethics in Action' and Human Population Genetics Research." *Culture, Medicine and Psychiatry* 29 (2005): 145–78.

Broyard, Bliss. *One Drop: My Father's Hidden Life—a Story of Race and Family Secrets.* New York: Back Bay Books, 2007.

Brubaker, Rogers. *Trans: Gender and Race in an Age of Unsettled Identities.* Kindle ed. Princeton, N.J.: Princeton University Press, 2016.

Bryc, Katarzyna, Eric Y. Durand, J. Michael Macpherson, David Reich, and Joanna L. Mountain. "The Genetic Ancestry of African Americans, Latinos, and European Americans across the United States." *American Journal of Human Genetics* 96 (2015): 37–53.

Bucciferro, Justin R. "Racial Inequality in Brazil from Independence to the Present." In *Has Latin American Inequality Changed Direction? Looking over the Long Run*, edited by Luis Bértola and Jeffrey Williamson, 171–94. Cham: Springer International, 2017.

Bucks, Jonathan. "Moffat Not Nominated for Honorary Degree." *The Saint*, November 27, 2014, 4.

Burroughs, Tony. *Black Roots: A Beginner's Guide to Tracing the African-American Family Tree*. New York: Fireside, 2001.

Business Wire. "Sorenson Molecular Genealogy Foundation's Genetic Genealogy Database Crosses Historic Milestone with 100,000 DNA Samples, Aided by Multi-Million Dollar Gift from Founder." *Business Wire*, April 28, 2010. https://www.businesswire.com/news/home/20100428005716/en/Sorenson -Molecular-Genealogy-Foundation%E2%80%99s-Genetic-Genealogy-Database (site discontinued).

Byrnes, Jake. "Synthesizing Genetic and Genealogical Data to Elucidate African American Ancestry." Paper presented at "The African Diaspora: Integrating Culture, Genomics and History," National Museum of Natural History, Smithsonian Institution, Washington, D.C., September 2013. YouTube video, 16:46. https://www.youtube.com/watch?v=Q2GKukY9jIU.

Calvo-González, Elena. "Usos políticos da leucopenia e diferença racial no Brasil contemporâneo." In *Identidades emergentes, genética e saúde: Perspectivas antropológicas*, edited by Ricardo Ventura Santos, Sahra Gibbon, and Jane Beltrão, 181–200. Rio de Janeiro: Fiocruz, Garamond, 2012.

Calvo-González, Elena, and Vera Rocha. "'Está no sangue': A articulação de ideias sobre 'raça', aparência e ancestralidade entre famílias de portadores de doença falciforme em Salvador, Bahia." *Revista de Antropologia* 53, no. 1 (2010): 277–320.

Campbell, Michael C., and Sarah A. Tishkoff. "African Genetic Diversity: Implications for Human Demographic History, Modern Human Origins, and Complex Disease Mapping." *Annual Review of Genomics and Human Genetics* 9 (2008): 403–33.

Canguilhem, Georges. "Le concept et la vie." *Revue philosophique de Louvain* 64, no. 82 (1966): 193–223.

Cannell, Fenella. "The Christianity of Anthropology." *Journal of the Royal Anthropological Institute* 11 (2005): 335–56.

———. "English Ancestors: The Moral Possibilities of Popular Genealogy." *Journal of the Royal Anthropological Institute* 17, no. 3 (2011): 462–80.

———. "Ghosts and Ancestors in the Modern West." In *A Companion to the Anthropology of Religion*, edited by Janice Boddy and Michael Lambek, 202–22. Chichester: Wiley-Blackwell, 2013.

Capone Laffitte, Stefania. *Searching for Africa in Brazil: Power and Tradition in Candomblé*. Translated by Lucy Lyall Grant. Durham, N.C.: Duke University Press, 2010.

Caruth, Cathy. *Unclaimed Experience: Trauma, Narrative, and History*. 20th anniversary ed. Baltimore: Johns Hopkins University Press, 2016.

Carvalho, José Jorge de, and Rita Laura Segato. *Uma proposta de cotas para estudantes negros na Universidade de Brasília*. Série antropologia 314. Brasília: Universidade de Brasília, 2002.

Castro, Eduardo Viveiros de. *Cannibal Metaphysics for a Post-Structural Anthropology*. Translated by Peter Skafish. Minneapolis: Univocal, 2014.

———. "No Brasil, todo mundo é índio, exceto quem não é." *Veja*, May 3, 2010, Brasil. http://veja.abril.com.br/brasil/no-brasil-todo-mundo-e-indio-exceto -quem-nao-e/.

Cavalli-Sforza, L. Luca. "Genes, Peoples, and Languages." *PNAS* 94 (1997): 7719–24.

CEPH Fondation Jean Dausset. "HGDP-CEPH Human Genome Diversity Cell Line Panel." *CEPH Fondation Jean Dausset*, 2020. http://www.cephb.fr/en/hgdp _panel.php#presentation.

Chakravarti, Aravinda, ed. *Human Variation: A Genetic Perspective on Diversity, Race, and Medicine*. Cold Spring Harbor, N.Y.: Cold Spring Harbor Laboratory Press, 2014.

Chazkel, Amy. "History out of the Ashes: Remembering Brazilian Slavery after Rui Barbosa's Burning of the Documents." In *From the Ashes of History: Loss and Recovery of Archives and Libraries in Modern Latin America*, edited by Carlos Aguirre and Javier Villa-Flores, 61–78. Raleigh, N.C.: A Contracorriente, 2015.

Chomsky, Marvin J., John Erman, David Greene, and Gilbert Moses, dirs. *Roots*. Aired 1977, on ABC.

Ciarcia, Gaetano. *Le revers de l'oubli: Mémoires et commémorations de l'esclavage au Bénin*. Paris: Karthala, 2016.

Cicalo, André. *Urban Encounters: Affirmative Action and Black Identities in Brazil*. New York: Palgrave Macmillan, 2012.

Cody, Cheryll Ann. "There Was No 'Absalom' on the Ball Plantations: Naming Practices in the South Carolina Low Country, 1720–1865." *American Historical Review* 92, no. 3 (1987): 563–96.

Collier, Melvin J. *Mississippi to Africa: A Journey of Discovery*. Self-published, Write Here, 2012.

———. "25 Do's and Don'ts of DNA." *Roots Revealed* (blog), November 7, 2018. https://rootsrevealed.com/2018/11/07/25-dos-and-donts-of-dna/.

Comaroff, John L., and Jean Comaroff. *Ethnicity, Inc.* Chicago: University of Chicago Press, 2009.

Coming to the Table. "Linked Descendants Working Group." *Coming to the Table*, 2019. https://comingtothetable.org/linked-descendants-working-group/.

Costa, Alexandre Emboaba da. "Afro-Brazilian Ancestralidade: Critical Perspectives on Knowledge and Development." *Third World Quarterly* 31, no. 4 (2010): 655–74.

———. *Reimagining Black Difference and Politics in Brazil: From Racial Democracy to Multiculturalism*. New York: Palgrave Macmillan, 2014.

———. "The (Un)Happy Objects of Affective Community." *Cultural Studies* 30, no. 1 (2016): 24–46.

Cottias, Myriam. *La question noire. Histoire d'une construction coloniale*. Paris: Bayard, 2007.

Croasmun, Jeanie. "Jumping Chasms." *Ancestry*, January/February 2006, 18–25.

Croly, David Goodman, and George Wakeman. *Miscegenation: The Theory of the Blending of the Races, Applied to the American White Man and Negro*. New York: H. Dexter, Hamilton, 1864.

Cunha, Manuela Carneiro da. *Negros, estrangeiros: Os escravos libertos e sua volta à África*. 2nd ed. São Paulo: Companhia das Letras, 2012.

D&AD. "The DNA Journey." *D&AD*, 2017. https://www.dandad.org/awards /professional/2017/pr/25835/the-dna-journey/.

D'Addario, Daniel. "Henry Louis Gates: 'Since Slavery Ended, All Political Movements Have Been about Race.'" *Salon*, October 20, 2013. http://www .salon.com/2013/10/20/henry_louis_gates_since_slavery_ended_all_political _movements_have_been_about_race/.

Daniel, G. Reginald. *Race and Multiraciality in Brazil and the United States: Converging Paths?* University Park: Pennsylvania State University Press, 2006.

David, LaKisha Tawanda, and Leia Jones. "Genetic Genealogical Methods Used to Identify African American Diaspora Relatives in the Study of Family Identity among Ghanaian Members of the Kassena Ethnic Group." *BioRxiv*, 2019, 833996. https://doi.org/10.1101/833996.

Davis, F. James. *Who Is Black? One Nation's Definition*. University Park: Pennsylvania State University Press, 1991.

De Groot, Jerome. *Consuming History: Historians and Heritage in Contemporary Popular Culture*. London: Routledge, 2009.

Del Priore, Mary Lucy Murray. "Brasil colonial: Um caso de famílias no femenino plural." *Cadernos de Pesquisa, São Paulo* 91 (1994): 69–75.

Dias, Gleidson Renato Martins, and Paulo Roberto Faber Tavares Junior, eds. *Heteroidentificação e cotas raciais: Dúvidas, metodologias e procedimentos*. Rio Grande do Sul, Brazil: IFRS Campus Canoas, 2018.

DNA Tested African Descendants. "Our DNA Project." *DNA Tested African Descendants*, 2020. https://www.dnatestedafricans.org/africanroyaledna.

Dobzhansky, Theodosius. "On Species and Races of Living and Fossil Man." *American Journal of Physical Anthropology* 2, no. 3 (1944): 251–65.

Doriott, Candace L. "Genetic Codes Unraveled: New Clues to Human History." *Ancestry*, January/February 2000, 15–21.

Du Bois, W. E. B. *The Souls of Black Folk*. Chicago: A. C. McClurg, 1903.

Dunham, Chris. "AncestryDNA and a Possible Faux Pa." *The Genealogue* (blog), June 13, 2012. http://www.genealogue.com/2012/06/ancestrydna-and-possible -faux-pa.html.

Dunn, Leslie Clarence. *Race and Biology*. Paris: UNESCO, 1951.

Edward, José. "Quem somos nós?" *Veja*, December 20, 2000, 102–9.

Edwards, A. W. F. "Human Genetic Diversity: Lewontin's Fallacy." *BioEssays* 25 (2003): 798–801.

Edwards, Erika Denise. *Hiding in Plain Sight. Black Women, the Law, and the Making of a White Argentine Republic.* Tuscaloosa: University of Alabama Press, 2020.

Edwards, Jeanette. "A Feel for Genealogy: 'Family Treeing' in the North of England." *Ethnos* 83, no. 4 (2018): 724–43.

———. "'Make-up': Personhood through the Lens of Biotechnology." *Ethnos* 70, no. 3 (2005): 413–31.

———. "Undoing Kinship." In *Relatedness in Assisted Reproduction: Families, Origins, and Identities,* edited by Tabitha Freeman, Susanna Graham, Fatemeh Ebtehaj, and Martin Richards, 44–60. Cambridge: Cambridge University Press, 2014.

Ekeh, Peter P. "Social Anthropology and Two Contrasting Uses of Tribalism in Africa." *Comparative Studies in Society and History* 32, no. 4 (1990): 660–700.

Ely, Bert. "Can a Database of MtDNA HVSI Sequences Properly Assign Africans to Their Country of Origin?," accessed January 14, 2021. http://research.cas.sc.edu/ely/African%20assignments.doc.

Ely, Bert, Jamie Lee Wilson, Fatimah Jackson, and Bruce A. Jackson. "African American Mitochondrial DNAs Often Match MtDNAs Found in Multiple African Ethnic Groups." *BMC Biology* 4, no. 1 (2006): 1–14.

Estes, Roberta. "Ancestry's Mythical Admixture Percentages." *DNAeXplained* (blog), October 24, 2012. http://dna-explained.com/2012/10/24/ancestrys-mythical-admixture-percentages/.

European Commission. "A European Initial Training Network on the History, Archaeology, and New Genetics of the Trans-Atlantic Slave Trade." *CORDIS EU Research Results,* October 31, 2016. https://cordis.europa.eu/project/id/290344.

Eyerman, Ron. *Cultural Trauma: Slavery and the Formation of African American Identity.* Cambridge: Cambridge University Press, 2001.

Farr, Christina. "Consumer DNA Testing Has Hit a Lull—Here's How It Could Capture the Next Wave of Users." *CNBC,* August 25, 2019. https://www.cnbc.com/2019/08/25/dna-tests-from-companies-like-23andme-ancestry-see-sales-slowdown.html.

Farrell, Leslie D., and Peter Forster. "'African American Lives.'" *Washington Post,* February 10, 2006. http://www.washingtonpost.com/wp-dyn/content/discussion/2006/02/09/DI2006020901668.html.

Fellet, João. "Na África, indaguei rei da minha etnia por que nos venderam como escravos." *BBC Brasil,* January 14, 2016. http://www.bbc.com/portuguese/noticias/2016/01/160113_dna_africano_zulu_jf_cc.

Fernandes, Florestan. *O negro no mundo dos brancos.* São Paulo: Difusão Européia do Livro, 1972.

Fernandez, Nadine T. "The Color of Love: Young Interracial Couples in Cuba." *Latin American Perspectives* 88, no. 23 (1996): 99–117.

Foeman, Anita, Bessie Lee Lawton, and Randall Rieger. "Questioning Race: Ancestry DNA and Dialog on Race." *Communication Monographs* (2014): 1–20.

Ford, Dionne, and Jill Strauss, eds. *Slavery's Descendants: Shared Legacies of Race and Reconciliation*. New Brunswick, N.J.: Rutgers University Press, 2019.

Forgie, Adam. "LDS Church Donates $2 Million to Create African-American Genealogy Museum." *KUTV*, February 28, 2019. https://kutv.com/news/local /lds-church-donates-2-million-to-create-african-american-genealogy-museum.

Foster, Eugene A., M. A. Jobling, P. G. Taylor, P. Donnelly, P. de Knijff, Rene Mieremet, T. Zerjal, and C. Tyler-Smith. "Jefferson Fathered Slave's Last Child." *Nature* 396 (1998): 27–28.

Foucault, Michel. "Technologies of the Self." In *Technologies of the Self: A Seminar with Michel Foucault*, edited by Luther H. Martin, Huck Gutman, and Patrick H. Hutton, 16–49. London: Tavistock, 1988.

Fox Carolina News. "Will Jones Reporter Interviews Bernice Bennett and Dr. Constance McNeill." *Fox Carolina News*, November 1, 2012. YouTube video, 5:54. https://www.youtube.com/watch?v=RCYXVL8Lv9k.

French, Jan Hoffman. "Dancing for Land: Law-Making and Cultural Performance in Northeastern Brazil." *Political and Legal Anthropology Review* 25, no. 1 (2002): 19–36.

Freyre, Gilberto. *Casa-grande e senzala: Formação da família brasileira sob o regime da economia patriarcal*. 48th ed. São Paulo: Global, 2003.

Fry, Peter. "Politics, Nationality, and the Meanings of 'Race' in Brazil." *Daedalus* 129, no. 2 (2000): 83–118.

———. "A Viewpoint on the Dispute among Anthropologists over Racially Targeted Policies in Brazil." *Lusotopie* 16, no. 2 (2009): 185–203.

Fry, Peter, Yvonne Maggie, Marcos Chor Maio, Simone Monteiro, and Ricardo Ventura Santos, eds. *Divisões perigosas: Políticas raciais no Brasil contemporâneo*. Rio de Janeiro: Civilização Brasileira, 2007.

Fullwiley, Duana. "The Biologistical Construction of Race: 'Admixture' Technology and the New Genetic Medicine." *Social Studies of Science* 38, no. 5 (2008): 695–735.

———. "The 'Contemporary Synthesis': When Politically Inclusive Genomic Science Relies on Biological Notions of Race." *Isis* 105, no. 4 (2014): 803–14.

———. "Race and Genetics: Attempts to Define the Relationship." *BioSocieties* 2 (2007): 221–37.

Gannett, Lisa. "Making Populations: Bounding Genes in Space and in Time." *Philosophy of Science* 70, no. 5 (2003): 989–1001.

———. "Racism and Human Genome Diversity Research: The Ethical Limits of 'Population Thinking.'" *Philosophy of Science* 68, no. 3 (2001): S479–92.

Gates, Henry Louis, Jr. "Exactly How 'Black' Is Black America?" *The Root*, February 11, 2013. https://www.theroot.com/exactly-how-black-is-black -america-1790895185.

———. "High Cheekbones and Straight Black Hair?" *The Root*, December 29, 2014. https://www.theroot.com/high-cheekbones-and-straight-black-hair -1790878167.

——. "How Many 'White' People Are Passing?" *The Root*, March 17, 2014. https://www.theroot.com/how-many-white-people-are-passing-1790874972.

——. "I'm White, but Tests Show I Have East African DNA. How?" *The Root*, January 23, 2015. https://www.theroot.com/i-m-white-but-tests-show-i-have -east-african-dna-how-1790858547.

——. *In Search of Our Roots: How 19 Extraordinary African Americans Reclaimed Their Past*. New York: Crown, 2009.

——. "Who's Your (Irish) Daddy?" *The Root*, March 17, 2010. http://www.theroot .com/whos-your-irish-daddy-1790878934.

Gates, Henry Louis, Jr., Eileen Pironti, and Meaghan Siekman. "Did My White Ancestor Become Black?" *The Root*, August 9, 2013. http://www.theroot.com /did-my-white-ancestor-become-black-1790897648.

——. "I'm White and Curious about My 'Free Colored' Ancestor." *The Root*, February 20, 2015. https://www.theroot.com/i-m-white-and-curious-about-my -free-colored-ancestor-1790858877.

Genera. "A crescente demanda por testes de ancestralidade no Brasil." *Genera* (blog), February 14, 2020. https://www.genera.com.br/blog/a-crescente -demanda-por-testes-de-ancestralidade-no-brasil.

"Genetics for the Human Race." Supplement, *Nature Genetics* 36, no. 11 (2004).

Gieryn, Thomas F. "Boundary-Work and the Demarcation of Science from Non-Science: Strains and Interests in Professional Ideologies of Scientists." *American Sociological Review* 48, no. 6 (1983): 781–95.

Gilroy, Paul. *Against Race: Imagining Political Culture beyond the Color Line*. Cambridge, Mass.: Harvard University Press, 2000.

——. *The Black Atlantic: Modernity and Double Consciousness*. Cambridge, Mass.: Harvard University Press, 1993.

Glazer, Nathan, and Daniel Patrick Moynihan. *Beyond the Melting Pot: The Negroes, Puerto Ricans, Jews, Italians, and Irish of New York City*. Cambridge, Mass.: MIT Press, 1963.

Glick Schiller, Nina. "Blood and Belonging: Long-Distance Nationalism and the World Beyond." In *Complexities: Beyond Nature & Nurture*, edited by Susan McKinnon and Sydel Silverman, 289–312. Chicago: University of Chicago Press, 2005.

Glycerio, Carolina. "'Brasil tem a cara do futuro', diz professor." *BBC Brasil*, May 28, 2007. https://www.bbc.com/portuguese/reporterbbc/story/2007/05 /printable/070528_dna_brasilfuturo_cg.shtml.

——. "Daiane dos Santos é 'protótipo da brasileira.'" *BBC Brasil*, May 28, 2007. http://www.bbc.co.uk/portuguese/reporterbbc/story/2007/05/070409_dna _daiane_cg.shtml.

——. "Neguinho da Beija-Flor tem mais gene europeu." *BBC Brasil*, May 29, 2007. http://www.bbc.co.uk/portuguese/reporterbbc/story/2007/05/070424_dna _neguinho_cg.shtml.

——. "'Se fosse 100% negro, lutaria por indenização.'" *BBC Brasil*, May 30, 2007. http://www.bbc.co.uk/portuguese/reporterbbc/story/2007/05/070409_dna _seujorge_cg.shtml.

———. "68% africano, ativista queria mais detalhes." *BBC Brasil*, May 31, 2007. http://www.bbc.co.uk/portuguese/reporterbbc/story/2007/05/070507_dna _freidavid_cg.shtml.

———. "'Tenho orgulho de ser quase 100% africana.'" *BBC Brasil*, May 31, 2007. http://www.bbc.co.uk/portuguese/reporterbbc/story/2007/05/070423_dna _sandradesa_cg.shtml.

Glycerio, Carolina, and Silvia Salek. "Metade de negros em pesquisa tem ancestral europeu." *BBC Brasil*, May 28, 2007. http://www.bbc.co.uk/portuguese /reporterbbc/story/2007/05/070326_dna_estudo_pena_cg.shtml.

Godwin, Nick, Helena Appio, and Nicola Colton. *Wonders of the African World with Henry Louis Gates Jr.* Documentary series. PBS, 1999.

Golbeck, Natasha, and Wendy D. Roth. "Aboriginal Claims: DNA Ancestry Testing and Changing Concepts of Indigeneity." In *Biomapping Indigenous Peoples: Towards an Understanding of the Issues*, edited by Susanne Berthier-Foglar, Sheila Collingwood-Whittick, and Sandrine Tolazzi, 415–32. Amsterdam: Rodopi, 2012.

Goldani, Ana Maria. "As famílias no Brasil contemporaneo e o mito da desestruturação." *Cadernos Pagu* 1 (1993): 67–110.

Gomes, Nilma Lino. *Sem perder a raiz: Corpo e cabelo como símbolos da identidade negra*. Belo Horizonte, Brazil: Autêntica, 2007.

Gomez, Michael A. *Exchanging Our Country Marks: The Transformation of African Identities in the Colonial and Antebellum South*. Chapel Hill: The University of North Carolina Press, 1998.

Gonçalves, V. F., F. Prosdocimi, L. S. Santos, J. M. Ortega, and Sérgio D. J. Pena. "Sex-Biased Gene Flow in African Americans but Not in American Caucasians." *Genetics and Molecular Research* 6, no. 2 (2007): 256–61.

Gordon-Reed, Annette. *The Hemingses of Monticello: An American Family*. New York: W. W. Norton, 2008.

Granja, Rafaela. "Long-Range Familial Searches in Recreational DNA Databases: Expansion of Affected Populations, the Participatory Turn, and the Co-Production of Biovalue." *New Genetics and Society* (2020): 1–22.

Granka, Julie. "AncestryDNA Makes Scientific Breakthrough in West African Ethnicity." *Ancestry Blog*, September 12, 2013. http://blogs.ancestry.com/techroots /ancestrydna-makes-scientific-breakthrough-in-west-african-ethnicity/.

Grossi, Élodie, and Joan Donovan. "Hate in the Blood: White Supremacists' Use of DNA Ancestry Tests." *Activist History Review*, October 20, 2017. https:// activisthistory.com/2017/10/20/hate-in-the-blood-white-supremacists-use-of -dna-ancestry-tests/.

Guedj, Pauline. *Panafricanisme, religion akan et dynamiques identitaires aux États-Unis: Le chemin du Sankofa*. Paris: L'Harmattan, 2011.

Guimarães, Antonio Sérgio Alfredo. "Recriando fronteiras raciais." *Sinais sociais* 11, no. 34 (2018): 21–43.

Haley, Alex. *Roots: The Enhanced Edition. The Saga of an American Family*. Kindle ed. New York: Vanguard, 2007.

Hall, Stuart. *The Fateful Triangle: Race, Ethnicity, Nation.* Cambridge, Mass.: Harvard University Press, 2017.

——. "Race—the Sliding Signifier." In *The Fateful Triangle: Race, Ethnicity, Nation,* 31–79. Cambridge, Mass.: Harvard University Press, 2017.

Haney López, Ian F. "The Social Construction of Race: Some Observations on Illusion, Fabrication, and Choice." *Harvard Civil Rights–Civil Liberties Law Review* 29, no. 1 (1994): 1–62.

Haraway, Donna. *Simians, Cyborgs, and Women: The Reinvention of Nature.* New York: Routledge, 1991.

Harmon, Amy. "Seeking Ancestry in DNA Ties Uncovered by Tests." *New York Times,* April 12, 2006, The DNA Age. https://www.nytimes.com/2006/04/12/us/seeking-ancestry-in-dna-ties-uncovered-by-tests.html.

Harris, Anna, Sally Wyatt, and Susan E. Kelly. "The Gift of Spit (and the Obligation to Return It): How Consumers of Online Genetic Testing Services Participate in Research." *Information, Communication & Society* 16, no. 2 (2013): 236–57.

Harris, Cheryl I. "Whiteness as Property." *Harvard Law Review* 106, no. 8 (1993): 1707–91.

Hartigan, John, Jr. "Is Race Still Socially Constructed? The Recent Controversy over Race and Medical Genetics." *Science as Culture* 17, no. 2 (2008): 163–93.

Hartman, Saidiya. *Lose Your Mother: A Journey along the Atlantic Slave Route.* New York: Farrar, Straus and Giroux, 2007.

Hasenbalg, Carlos, and Nelson do Valle Silva, eds. *Estrutura social, mobilidade e raça.* Rio de Janeiro: IUPERJ, Vértice, 1988.

Hernández, Candela L., Pedro Soares, Jean M. Dugoujon, Andrea Novelletto, Juan N. Rodríguez, Teresa Rito, Marisa Oliveira, et al. "Early Holocenic and Historic MtDNA African Signatures in the Iberian Peninsula: The Andalusian Region as a Paradigm." *PLOS ONE* 10, no. 10 (2015): e0139784. https://doi.org/10.1371/journal.pone.0139784.

Herskovits, Melville J. *The Myth of the Negro Past.* Boston: Beacon, 1941.

Hervé, Christian, Henri-Corto Stoeklé, and Guillaume Vogt. "'Un marché aux données génétiques' qui interroge." *Le Monde,* April 27, 2016, Idées. http://www.lemonde.fr/idees/article/2016/04/27/un-marche-aux-donnees-genetiques-qui-interroge_4909596_3232.html.

Heywood, Linda, and John Thornton. "Pinpointing DNA Ancestry in Africa." *The Root,* October 1, 2011. https://www.theroot.com/pinpointing-dna-ancestry-in-africa-1790866123.

Hickman, Christine B. "The Devil and the One Drop Rule: Racial Categories, African Americans, and the U.S. Census." *Michigan Law Review* 95, no. 5 (1997): 1161–1265.

Higham, John. *Strangers in the Land: Patterns of American Nativism 1860–1925.* 2nd ed. New York: Atheneum, 1975.

Hochschild, Jennifer L. "Looking Ahead: Racial Trends in the United States." *Daedalus* 134, no. 1 (2005): 70–81.

Holger, Dieter. "DNA Testing for Ancestry Is More Detailed for White People. Here's Why, and How It's Changing." *PCWorld*, December 4, 2018. https://www.pcworld.com/article/3323366/dna-testing-for-ancestry-white-people.html.

Hordge-Freeman, Elizabeth. *The Color of Love: Racial Features, Stigma, and Socialization in Black Brazilian Families.* Austin: University of Texas Press, 2015.

Horn, Catherine L., and Patricia Marín. *Realizing Bakke's Legacy: Affirmative Action, Equal Opportunity, and Access to Higher Education.* Sterling, VA: Stylus, 2008.

Htun, Mala. "From 'Racial Democracy' to Affirmative Action: Changing State Policy on Race in Brazil." *Latin American Research Review* 39, no. 1 (2004): 60–89.

Hu-DeHart, Evelyn, and Kathleen López. "Asian Diasporas in Latin America and the Caribbean: An Historical Overview." *Afro-Hispanic Review* 27, no. 1 (2008): 9–21.

Hutchison, Luke A. D., Natalie M. Myres, and Scott R. Woodward. "Growing the Family Tree: The Power of DNA in Reconstructing Family Relationships." In *Proceedings of the First Symposium on Bioinformatics and Biotechnology (BIOT-04)*, 42–49. Colorado Springs: University of Colorado, 2004.

Ingold, Tim. *The Perception of the Environment: Essays on Livelihood, Dwelling and Skill.* London: Routledge, 2000.

International Society of Genetic Genealogy Wiki. "GeneTree." *International Society of Genetic Genealogy Wiki*, February 1, 2013. https://isogg.org/wiki/GeneTree.

Jackson, F. L. C. "African-American Responses to the Human Genome Project." *Public Understanding of Science* 8, no. 3 (1999): 181–91.

———. "Concerns and Priorities in Genetic Studies: Insights from Recent African American Biohistory." *Seton Hall Law Review* 27, no. 3 (1997): 951–70.

Jackson, F. L. C., A. Mayes, M. E. Mack, A. Froment, S. O. Y. Keita, R. A. Kittles, M. George, K. J. Shujaa, M. L. Blakey, and L. M. Rankin-Hill. "Origins of the New York African Burial Ground Population: Biological Evidence of Geographical and Macroethnic Affiliations Using Craniometrics, Dental Morphology, and Preliminary Genetic Analyses." In *Skeletal Biology of the New York African Burial Ground Part I*, edited by Michael L. Blakey and Lesley M. Rankin-Hill, 69–94. Washington, D.C.: Howard University Press, 2009.

Jackson, Fatimah, and Sameena Mulla. "In Conversation with Fatimah Jackson: The Life and Career of an African American Muslim Biological Anthropologist." *Feminist Anthropology* 1, no. 2 (2020): 155–64.

Jacobson, Matthew Frye. *Roots Too: White Ethnic Revival in Post-Civil Rights America.* Cambridge, Mass.: Harvard University Press, 2006.

Jones, James H. *Bad Blood: The Tuskegee Syphilis Experiment.* New York: Free Press, 1993.

Judd, Graham, dir. *African American Lives.* Episode 4, "Beyond the Middle Passage." Aired February 8, 2006, on PBS.

Kanor, Fabienne, and Myriam Cottias. "Conversation between Fabienne Kanor and Myriam Cottias, on 'The Flesh of History.'" Presented at "Slavery,

Authorship and Literary Culture," Maison française, Columbia University, New York, January 2019.

Kaplan, Jonathan Michael, and Rasmus Grønfeldt Winther. "Prisoners of Abstraction? The Theory and Measure of Genetic Variation, and the Very Concept of 'Race.'" *Biological Theory*, 2012.

Keefer, Katrina H. B. "Marked by Fire: Brands, Slavery, and Identity." *Slavery & Abolition* (2019): 1–23.

Keita, Shomarka, and James Stewart. "Ethics, Identity, Genetics, Patrimony and Power in the Harvesting of DNA from Africa." *GeneWatch* 23, no. 3 (2010): 12–13.

Kemp, Arthur. *Four Flags: The Indigenous People of Great Britain: DNA, History and the Right to Existence of the Native Inhabitants of the British Isles.* 4th ed. Self-published, Ostara, 2012.

Kennett, Debbie. "Using Genetic Genealogy Databases in Missing Persons Cases and to Develop Suspect Leads in Violent Crimes." *Forensic Science International* 301 (2019): 107–17.

Kennett, Debbie, Adrian Timpson, David Balding, and Mark Thomas. "The Rise and Fall of BritainsDNA: A Tale of Misleading Claims, Media Manipulation and Threats to Academic Freedom." *Genealogy* 2, no. 4 (2018). https://doi.org/10.3390/genealogy2040047.

Kent, Michael, and Ricardo Ventura Santos. "'Os Charruas vivem' nos Gaúchos: A vida social de uma pesquisa de 'resgate' genético de uma etnia indígena extinta no Sul do Brasil." *Horizontes Antropológicos* 18, no. 37 (2012): 341–72.

Kent, Michael, Ricardo Ventura Santos, and Peter Wade. "Negotiating Imagined Genetic Communities: Unity and Diversity in Brazilian Science and Society." *American Anthropologist* 116, no. 4 (2014): 1–13.

Kent, Michael, and Peter Wade. "Genetics against Race: Science, Politics and Affirmative Action in Brazil." *Social Studies of Science* 45, no. 6 (2015): 816–38.

Kim, Eun Kyung. "Rachel Dolezal Breaks Her Silence on TODAY: 'I Identify as Black.'" *TODAY*, June 16, 2015. http://www.today.com/news/rachel-dolezal-speaks-today-show-matt-lauer-after-naacp-resignation-t26371.

Koenig, Barbara A., Sandra Soo-Jin Lee, and Sarah S. Richardson. *Revisiting Race in a Genomic Age.* New Brunswick, N.J.: Rutgers University Press, 2008.

Kohn, Eduardo. *How Forests Think: Toward an Anthropology beyond the Human.* Berkeley: University of California Press, 2013.

Krieger, Nancy. "The Science and Epidemiology of Racism and Health: Racial/Ethnic Categories, Biological Expressions of Racism, and the Embodiment of Inequality—an Ecosocial Perspective." In *What's the Use of Race? Modern Governance and the Biology of Difference*, edited by Ian Whitmarsh, 225–55. Cambridge, Mass.: MIT Press, 2010.

La Roche, Cheryl J., and Michael L. Blakey. "Seizing Intellectual Power: The Dialogue at the New York African Burial Ground." *Historical Archaeology* 31, no. 3 (1997): 84–106.

Lafargue, M.-M. Mady. "La ressemblance sert-elle à penser l'hérédité?" *Ethnologie française* 24, no. 1 (1994): 118–29.

Latour, Bruno. "Visualisation and Cognition: Drawing Things Together." In *Knowledge and Society: Studies in the Sociology of Cultural Past and Present*, edited by H. Kuklick, Vol. 6, 1–40. Greenwich, Conn.: Jai, 1986.

Lee, Dayne. "How Airbnb Short-Term Rentals Exacerbate Los Angeles's Affordable Housing Crisis: Analysis and Policy Recommendations." *Harvard Law and Policy Review* 10, no. 1 (2016): 229–54.

Lehmann, David. *The Prism of Race: The Politics and Ideology of Affirmative Action in Brazil.* Ann Arbor: University of Michigan Press, 2018.

Lemire, Elise. *"Miscegenation": Making Race in America.* Philadelphia: University of Pennsylvania Press, 2002.

Lempp, Sarah. "With the Eyes of Society? Doing Race in Affirmative Action Practices in Brazil." *Citizenship Studies* 23, no. 7 (2019): 703–19.

Leonard, John. "Black Like Me?" *New York Magazine*, January 26, 2006. http://nymag.com/arts/tv/reviews/15623/.

Leroux, Darryl. *Distorted Descent: White Claims to Indigenous Identity.* Winnipeg: University of Manitoba Press, 2019.

Lewontin, Richard. "The Apportionment of Human Diversity." *Evolutionary Biology* 6 (1972): 381–98.

LivingDNA. "The Most Advanced DNA Test for People with African Ancestry—Five Times the Detail of any other DNA Test." *LivingDNA* (blog), February 6, 2020. https://livingdna.com/blog/Over-70-new-African-genetic-ancestral-regions.

Loftus, Peter. "Genetic Test Service 23andMe Ordered to Halt Marketing by FDA." *Wall Street Journal*, November 25, 2013. http://www.wsj.com/articles/SB10001424052702304281004579219893863966448.

Lorde, Audre. *Your Silence Will Not Protect You.* London: Silver Press, 2017.

Lumb, David. "23andMe Gives Pfizer Access to Its Genome Database." *Fast Company*, January 13, 2015. https://www.fastcompany.com/3040864/23andme-gives-pfizer-access-to-its-genome-database.

Mack, Mark E., and Michael L. Blakey. "The New York African Burial Ground Project: Past Biases, Current Dilemmas, and Future Research Opportunities." *Society for Historical Archaeology* 38, no. 1 (2004): 10–17.

Maggie, Yvonne. "Os novos bacharéis: A experiência do pré-vestibular para negros e carentes." *Novos Estudos* 59 (2001): 193–202.

Maggie, Yvonne, and Peter Fry. "A reserva de vagas para negros nas universidades brasileiras." *Estudos Avançados* 18, no. 50 (2004): 67–80.

Magnoli, Demétrio. *Uma gota de sangue: História do pensamento racial.* São Paulo: Editora Contexto, 2009.

Maio, Marcos Chor. "UNESCO and the Study of Race Relations in Brazil: Regional or National Issue?" *Latin American Research Review* 36, no. 2 (2001): 118–36.

Maio, Marcos Chor, and Ricardo Ventura Santos. "Política de cotas raciais, os 'olhos da sociedade' e os usos da antropologia: O caso do vestibular da Universidade de Brasília (UnB)." *Horizontes Antropológicos* 11, no. 23 (2005): 181–214.

Martínez, María Elena. *Genealogical Fictions: Limpieza de Sangre, Religion, and Gender in Colonial Mexico*. Redwood City, Calif.: Stanford University Press, 2008.

Martins, Sérgio Da Silva, Carlos Alberto Medeiros, and Elisa Larkin Nascimento. "Paving Paradise: The Road from 'Racial Democracy' to Affirmative Action in Brazil." *Journal of Black Studies* 34, no. 6 (2004): 787–816.

Mattos, Hebe Maria. "'Remanescentes das comunidades dos quilombos': Memória do cativeiro e políticas de reparação no Brasil." *Revista USP* 68, no. dezembro/fevereiro (2005/2006): 104–11.

M'charek, Amade. "Beyond Fact or Fiction: On the Materiality of Race in Practice." *Cultural Anthropology* 28, no. 3 (2013): 420–42.

——. *The Human Genome Diversity Project: An Ethnography of Scientific Practice*. Cambridge: Cambridge University Press, 2005.

McKay, Aprille Cooke. "Genealogists and Records: Preservation, Advocacy, and Politics." *Archival Issues* 27, no. 1 (2002): 23–33.

McLean, Shay-Akil. "Isolation by Distance and the Problem of the Twenty-First Century." *Human Biology* 91, no. 2 (2019): 81–93.

Midlo Hall, Gwendolyn. *Slavery and African Ethnicities in the Americas: Restoring the Links*. Chapel Hill: The University of North Carolina Press, 2005.

Miramon, Charles de, and Maaike van der Lugt. "Sang, hérédité et parenté au Moyen Âge: Modèle biologique et modèle social. Albert le Grand et Balde." *Annales de démographie historique* 1 (2019): 21–48.

Mitchell-Walthour, Gladys. "Racism in a Racialized Democracy." In *Afro-Descendants, Identity, and the Struggle for Development in the Americas*, edited by Bernd Reiter and Kimberly Eison Simmons, 207–30. East Lansing: Michigan State University Press, 2012.

Modarressy-Tehrani, Caroline. "A DNA Test Revealed This Man Is 4% Black. Now He Wants to Abolish Affirmative Action." *Huffington Post*, September 19, 2019. https://www.huffingtonpost.co.uk/entry/dna-test-affirmative-action_n _5d824762e4b0957256afa986?.

Momondo. *Momondo—The DNA Journey*, June 1, 2016. YouTube video, 5:16. https://www.youtube.com/watch?v=tyaEQEmt5ls.

Montagu, M. F. Ashley. *Man's Most Dangerous Myth: The Fallacy of Race*. 3rd ed. New York: Harper and Brothers, 1952.

Monteiro, Mônica, Luciana Pires, and Carlos Alberto Jr., dirs. *Brasil: DNA África*. CineGroup, Globo Filmes, GloboNews. Screened June 2–16, 2016, Rio de Janeiro, São Paulo and Salvador da Bahia, Espaço Itaú Cinema.

——. *Brasil: DNA África*. Episode 1, "Bahia." CineGroup. Unpublished documentary, 2015, with permission.

Moore, David Chioni. "Routes: Alex Haley's 'Roots' and the Rhetoric of Genealogy." *Transition*, no. 64 (1994): 4–21.

Moreno Figueroa, Mónica G. "Displaced Looks: The Lived Experience of Beauty and Racism." *Feminist Theory* 14, no. 2 (2013): 137–51.

MormonNewsroom.org. "Church Presents Historic Freedmen's Bureau Database to African American Museum." *Church of Jesus Christ of Latter-day Saints*,

December 15, 2016. https://www.churchofjesuschrist.org/church/news
/church-presents-historic-freedmens-bureau-database-to-african-american
-museum.

Moura, C. A., and Jônatas Nunes Barreto. *A Fundação Cultural Palmares
na III Conferência Mundial de Combate ao Racismo, Discriminação Racial,
Xenofobia e Intolerância Correlata*. Brasília: Fundação Cultural Palmares,
2002.

Moynihan, Daniel Patrick. "The Negro Family: The Case for National Action."
Washington, D.C.: United States Department of Labor, 1965.

Mukhopadhyay, Carol C., and Yolanda T. Moses. "Reestablishing 'Race' in
Anthropological Discourse." *American Anthropologist* 99, no. 3 (1997):
517–33.

Mulot, Stéphanie. "Le mythe du viol fondateur aux Antilles Françaises." *Ethnologie
française* 37, no. 3 (2007): 517–24.

Munanga, Kabengele. "Políticas de ação afirmativa em benefício da população
negra no Brasil: Um ponto de vista em defesa de cotas." *Sociedade e Cultura* 4,
no. 2 (2001): 31–43.

Murphy, Erin. "Law and Policy Oversight of Familial Searches in Recreational
Genealogy Databases." *Forensic Science International* 292 (2018): e5–9.

Mustian, Jim. "New Orleans Filmmaker Cleared in Cold-Case Murder; False
Positive Highlights Limitations of Familial DNA Searching." *New Orleans
Advocate*, March 12, 2015. https://www.nola.com/news/article_d58a3d17-c89b
-543f-8365-a2619719f6f0.html.

MyHeritage. "What's Considered a Strong DNA Match?" *MyHeritage* (blog),
February 19, 2020. https://education.myheritage.com/article/whats
-considered-a-strong-dna-match/.

———. "Tribal Quest Ecuador: MyHeritage Documents the Family Histories of the
Achuar Tribe." *MyHeritage* (blog), December 15, 2019. https://blog.myheritage
.com/2019/12/tribal-quest-ecuador-myheritage-documents-the-family-histories
-of-the-achuar-tribe/.

Nascimento, Abdias do. *O genocídio do negro brasileiro. Processo de um racismo
mascarado*. Rio de Janeiro: Paz e Terra, 1978.

———. *O negro revoltado*. Rio de Janeiro: G.R.D., 1968.

Nascimento, Elisa Larkin. "Aspects of Afro-Brazilian Experience." *Journal of Black
Studies* 11, no. 2 (1980): 195–216.

Nash, Catherine. *Genetic Geographies: The Trouble with Ancestry*. Minneapolis:
University of Minnesota Press, 2015.

———. *Of Irish Descent: Origin Stories, Genealogy, and the Politics of Belonging*.
Syracuse, N.Y.: Syracuse University Press, 2008.

Nelson, Alondra. "Bio Science: Genetic Genealogy Testing and the Pursuit of
African Ancestry." *Social Studies of Science* 38, no. 5 (2008): 759–83.

———. "The Factness of Diaspora: The Social Sources of Genetic Genealogy." In
Revisiting Race in a Genomic Age, edited by Barbara A. Koenig, Sandra Soo-Jin
Lee, and Sarah S. Richardson, 253–68. New Brunswick, N.J.: Rutgers
University Press, 2008.

———. *The Social Life of DNA: Race, Reparations, and Reconciliation after the Genome.* Boston: Beacon Press, 2016.

Nelson, Alondra, and Jeong Won Hwang. "Roots and Revelation: Genetic Ancestry Testing and the YouTube Generation." In *Race after the Internet*, edited by Lisa Nakamura and Peter A. Chow-White, 271–90. New York: Routledge, 2012.

Nelson, Matthew R., Katarzyna Bryc, Karen S. King, Amit Indap, Adam R. Boyko, John Novembre, Linda P. Briley, et al. "The Population Reference Sample, POPRES: A Resource for Population, Disease, and Pharmacological Genetics Research." *American Journal of Human Genetics* 83, no. 3 (2008): 347–58.

New York Times. "Reading the Book of Life; White House Remarks on Decoding of Genome." *New York Times*, June 27, 2000. http://www.nytimes.com/2000/06/27/science/reading-the-book-of-life-white-house-remarks-on-decoding-of-genome.html.

Nieves Delgado, Abigail, Vivette García Deister, and Carlos López Beltrán. "¿De qué me ves cara?: Narrativas de herencia, genética e identidad inscritas en la apariencia." *Revista de Antropología Iberoamericana* 12, no. 3 (2017): 313–37.

Nixon, Ron. "DNA Tests Find Branches but Few Roots." *New York Times*, November 25, 2007. http://www.nytimes.com/2007/11/25/business/25dna.html?pagewanted=all&_r=0.

Nogueira, Oracy. "Preconceito racial de marca e preconceito racial de origem: Sugestão de um quadro de referência para a interpretação do material sobre relações raciais no Brasil." *Tempo Social* 19, no. 1 (2006): 287–308.

Novak, Michael. *The Rise of the Unmeltable Ethnics.* New York: Macmillan, 1973.

Novembre, John, Toby Johnson, Katarzyna Bryc, Zoltán Kutalik, Adam R. Boyko, Adam Auton, Amit Indap, et al. "Genes Mirror Geography within Europe." *Nature* 456 (2008): 98–103.

Novembre, John, and Sohini Ramachandran. "Perspectives on Human Population Structure at the Cusp of the Sequencing Era." *Annual Review of Genomics and Human Genetics* 12 (2011): 245–74.

Oduah, Chika S. "The DNA Debate: Can It Help Black Chicagoans Find African Relatives?" *Medill Reports Chicago*, December 1, 2009. http://newsarchive.medill.northwestern.edu/chicago/news.aspx?id=150565.

Ohrt Fehler, Benedicte. "(Re)Constructing Roots: Genetics and the 'Return' of African Americans to Ghana." *Mobilities* 6, no. 4 (2011): 585–600.

Okona, Nneka M. "'Heritage Travel' Is Surging in the Era of DNA Testing. It Has a Special Significance for Black Americans." *Vox*, September 25, 2019. https://www.vox.com/the-highlight/2019/9/18/20862468/heritage-african-american-ancestry-23-and-me-dna-testing.

Olarte Sierra, María Fernanda, and Adriana Díaz del Castillo H. "The Travels of Humans, Categories, and Other Genetic Products." In *Mestizo Genomics: Race Mixture, Nation, and Science in Latin America*, edited by Peter Wade, Carlos López Beltrán, Eduardo Restrepo, and Ricardo Ventura Santos, 135–60. Durham, N.C.: Duke University Press, 2014.

Olopade, Dayo. "Skip Gates Speaks." *The Root*, July 21, 2009, Culture. https://www.theroot.com/skip-gates-speaks-1790869826.

Omi, Michael, and Howard Winant. "Racial Formation Rules: Continuity, Instability, and Change." In *Racial Formation in the Twenty-First Century*, edited by Daniel Martinez HoSang, Oneka LaBennett, and Laura Pulido, 302–32. Berkeley: University of California Press, 2012.

Oprah.com. "The Importance of Ancestry." *Oprah.com*, September 3, 2010. http://www.oprah.com/oprahshow/Dr-Henry-Louis-Gates-Jr-Start-Your -Ancestry-Search.

Pagden, Anthony. *The Fall of Natural Man: The American Indian and the Origins of Comparative Ethnology*. Cambridge: Cambridge University Press, 1982.

Paixão, Marcelo, and Luiz M. Carvano. "Censo e demografia: A variável cor ou raça no interior dos sistemas censitários brasileiros." In *Raça: Novas perspectivas antropológicas*, edited by Osmundo Araújo Pinho and Livio Sansone, 2nd ed. Salvador: ABA, EDUFBA, 2008.

Palmié, Stephan. "Genomics, Divination, 'Racecraft.'" *American Ethnologist* 34, no. 2 (2007): 205–22.

Pálsson, Gísli. "Decode Me! Anthropology and Personal Genomics." *Current Anthropology* 53, no. 5 (2012): S185–95.

Pálsson, Gísli, and Paul Rabinow. "Iceland: The Case of a National Human Genome Project." *Anthropology Today* 15, no. 5 (1999): 14–18.

Panofsky, Aaron, and Joan Donovan. "Genetic Ancestry Testing among White Nationalists: From Identity Repair to Citizen Science." *Social Studies of Science* 49, no. 5 (2019): 653–81.

Pena, Sérgio D. J. *À flor da pele: Reflexões de um geneticista*. Rio de Janeiro: Vieira & Lent, 2007.

———. "Brazilians and the Variable Mosaic Genome Paradigm." In *Fifty Years of Human Genetics: A Festschrift and Liber Amicorum to Celebrate the Life and Work of George Robert Fraser*, edited by Oliver Mayo and Carolyn Leach, 98–104. Adelaide: Wakefield, 2007.

———. *Humanidade sem raças?* Ensaios, reportagens, entrevistas, série 21. São Paulo: PubliFolha, 2008.

———. *Igualmente diferentes*. Belo Horizonte: Editora UFMG, 2009.

Pena, Sérgio D. J., and Maria Cátira Bortolini. "Pode a genética definir quem deve se beneficiar das cotas universitárias e demais ações afirmativas?" *Estudos Avançados* 18, no. 50 (2004): 31–50.

Pena, Sérgio D. J., Denise R. Carvalho-Silva, Juliana Alves-Silva, Vânia Ferreira Prado, and Fabrício R Santos. "Retrato molecular do Brasil." *Ciência Hoje* 27, no. 159 (April 2000): 16–25.

Perego, Ugo A., Natalie M. Myres, and Scott R. Woodward. "The Molecular Genealogy Research Project," accessed January 14, 2021. http://vincentfamily .org/DNA/The_Molecular_Genealogy_Research_Project.pdf.

Pereira, Amilcar Araujo. *O mundo negro: Relações raciais e a constituição do Movimento Negro contemporâneo no Brasil*. Rio de Janeiro: Pallas, 2013.

Pickrell, Joseph K., and David Reich. "Toward a New History and Geography of Human Genes Informed by Ancient DNA." *Trends in Genetics* 30, no. 9 (2014): 377–89.

Pinderhughes, Elaine. "Black Genealogy Revisited: Restorying an African American Family." In *Re-Visioning Family Therapy*, edited by M. McGoldrick, 114–34. New York: Guilford, 1998.

Pinho, Angela. "UnB rejeita um gêmeo e aceita outro nas cotas." *Folha de S. Paulo.* June 8, 2007. http://www1.folha.uol.com.br/fsp/cotidian/ff0806200718.htm.

Pinho, Patricia de Santana. "White but Not Quite: Tones and Overtones of Whiteness in Brazil." *Small Axe* 29 (2009): 39–56.

Pollack, Ricardo, dir. *Black in Latin America.* Episode 3, "Brazil: A Racial Paradise?" Aired May 4, 2011, on PBS.

Provine, William B. "Geneticists and the Biology of Race Crossing." *Science* 182, no. 4114 (1973): 790–96.

Rabinow, Paul. *Essays on the Anthropology of Reason.* Princeton, N.J.: Princeton University Press, 1996.

Racusen, Seth. "Affirmative Action and Identity." In *Brazil's New Racial Politics*, edited by Bernd Reiter and Gladys L. Mitchell, 89–122. Boulder, Colo.: Lynne Rienner, 2010.

Rajagopalan, Ramya, and Joan H. Fujimura. "Making History via DNA, Making DNA from History: Deconstructing the Race-Disease Connection in Admixture Mapping." In *Genetics and the Unsettled Past: The Collision of DNA, Race, and History*, edited by Keith Wailoo, Alondra Nelson, and Catherine Lee, 143–63. New Brunswick, N.J.: Rutgers University Press, 2012.

Ramos, Cleidiana. "Frei entra na justiça contra pesquisador." *A Tarde*, June 24, 2007, Salvador & região metropolitana, 7.

———. "Pesquisa da BBC é apontada como estratégia contra cotas." *A Tarde*, June 24, 2007, Salvador e região metropolitana, 6.

Reality Check Team. "African Diaspora: Did Ghana's Year of Return Attract Foreign Visitors?" *BBC News*, January 30, 2020. https://www.bbc.co.uk/news/world-africa-51191409.

Reardon, Jenny. "The Human Genome Diversity Project: A Case Study in Coproduction." *Social Studies of Science* 31, no. 3 (2001): 357–88.

———. *Race to the Finish: Identity and Governance in an Age of Genomics.* Princeton, N.J.: Princeton University Press, 2005.

———. "Race without Salvation: Beyond the Science/Society Divide in Genomic Studies of Human Diversity." In *Revisiting Race in a Genomic Age*, edited by Barbara A. Koenig, Sandra Soo-Jin Lee, and Sarah S. Richardson, 304–19. New Brunswick, N.J.: Rutgers University Press, 2008.

Reardon, Jenny, and Kim TallBear. "Your DNA Is Our History: Genomics, Anthropology, and the Construction of Whiteness as Property." *Current Anthropology* 53, no. 5 (2012): S233–45.

Regalado, Antonio. "2017 Was the Year Consumer DNA Testing Blew Up." *MIT Technology Review*, February 12, 2018, Biotechnology. https://www.technologyreview.com/2018/02/12/145676/2017-was-the-year-consumer-dna-testing-blew-up/.

Reich, David. "How Genetics Is Changing Our Understanding of 'Race.'" *New York Times*, March 23, 2018, Opinion. https://www.nytimes.com/2018/03/23/opinion/sunday/genetics-race.html.

"The Right to Speak Out." *Nature* 496, no. 7444 (2013): 137.

Roberts, Dorothy. *Fatal Invention: How Science, Politics, and Big Business Re-Create Race in the Twenty-First Century*. New York: New Press, 2011.

Rodrigues, Maria Fernanda. "Com futuro incerto, Sérgio Camargo volta à Fundação Palmares e quer equipe alinhada a seus ideais." *Estadão*, February 27, 2020, Cultura. https://cultura.estadao.com.br/noticias/geral,com -futuro-incerto-sergio-camargo-volta-a-fundacao-palmares-e-quer-equipe -alinhada-a-seus-ideais,70003211896.

Rose, Nikolas, and Carlos Novas. "Biological Citizenship." In *Global Assemblages: Technology, Politics, and Ethics as Anthropological Problems*, edited by Aihwa Ong and Stephen J. Collier, 439–63. Oxford: Blackwell, 2005.

Rosenberg, Noah A., Jonathan K. Pritchard, James L. Weber, Howard M. Cann, Kenneth K. Kidd, Lev A. Zhivotovsky, and Marcus W. Feldman. "Genetic Structure of Human Populations." *Science* 298 (2002): 2381–85.

Roth, Wendy. *Race Migrations: Latinos and the Cultural Transformation of Race*. Redwood City, Calif.: Stanford University Press, 2012.

Roth, Wendy D., and Biorn Ivemark. "Genetic Options: The Impact of Genetic Ancestry Testing on Consumers' Racial and Ethnic Identities." *American Journal of Sociology* 124, no. 1 (2018): 150–84.

Rotimi, Charles N. "Genetic Ancestry Tracing and the African Identity: A Double-Edged Sword?" *American Journal of Human Genetics* 86 (2003): 661–73.

Royal, Charmaine D. M., and Georgia M. Dunston. "Changing the Paradigm from 'Race' to Human Genome Variation." *Nature Genetics Supplement* 36, no. 11 (2004): S5–7.

Royal, Charmaine D., John Novembre, Stephanie M. Fullerton, David B. Goldstein, Jeffrey C. Long, Michael J. Bamshad, and Andrew G. Clark. "Inferring Genetic Ancestry: Opportunities, Challenges, and Implications." *American Journal of Human Genetics* 86 (2010): 661–73.

Ruiz-Linares, Andrés, Kaustubh Adhikari, Victor Acuña-Alonzo, Mirsha Quinto-Sanchez, Claudia Jaramillo, William Arias, Macarena Fuentes, et al. "Admixture in Latin America: Geographic Structure, Phenotypic Diversity and Self-Perception of Ancestry Based on 7,342 Individuals." *PLOS Genetics* 10, no. 9 (2014). https://doi.org/10.1371/journal.pgen.1004572.

Rushdy, Ashraf H. A. *Remembering Generations: Race and Family in Contemporary African American Fiction*. Chapel Hill: The University of North Carolina Press, 2001.

Rustomji-Kerns, Roshni, Rajini Srikanth, and Leny Mendoza Strobel, eds. *Encounters: People of Asian Descent in the Americas*. Lanham, Md.: Rowman and Littlefield, 1999.

Rutherford, Adam. *A Brief History of Everyone Who Ever Lived: The Stories in Our Genes*. E-book ed. London: Weidenfeld and Nicolson, 2016.

Sahlins, Marshall. *What Kinship Is—and Is Not*. Chicago: University of Chicago Press, 2013.

Salek, Silvia. "BBC Delves into Brazilians' Roots." *BBC News*, July 10, 2007. http://news.bbc.co.uk/2/hi/6284806.stm.

Salzano, Francisco M., and Newton Freire-Maia. *Populações brasileiras: Aspectos demográficos, genéticos e antropológicos.* São Paulo: Editora Nacional, Editora da Universidade, 1967.

Sansone, Livio. *Blackness without Ethnicity: Constructing Race in Brazil.* New York: Palgrave Macmillan, 2003.

Santos, Jamille Pereira Pimentel dos, and Ana Angélica Leal Barbosa. "O ciclo da vida em Queimadas: As etnicidades geracionais presentes no nascer, viver e morrer." *ODEERE* 5, no. 9 (2020): 205–33.

Santos, Myrian Sepúlveda dos. "The Legacy of Slavery in Contemporary Brazil." In *African Heritage and Memories of Slavery in Brazil and the South Atlantic World*, edited by Ana Lucia Araujo. Amherst, N.Y.: Cambria Press, 2015.

Santos, Ricardo Ventura, Maria Cátira Bortolini, and Marcos Chor Maio. "No fio da navalha: Raça, genética e identidades." *Revista USP* 68 (2006): 22–35.

Santos, Ricardo Ventura, Peter H. Fry, Simone Monteiro, Marcos Chor Maio, José Carlos Rodrigues, Luciana Bastos-Rodrigues, and Sérgio D. J. Pena. "Color, Race, and Genomic Ancestry in Brazil: Dialogues between Anthropology and Genetics." *Current Anthropology* 50, no. 6 (2009): 787–819.

Santos, Ricardo Ventura, and Marcos Chor Maio. "Qual 'Retrato do Brasil'?: Raça, biologia, identidades e política na era da genômica." *MANA* 10, no. 1 (2004): 61–95.

Scherer, Felipe. "Conheça o teste de ancestralidade desenvolvido por startup brasileira." *Exame* (blog), June 10, 2020. https://exame.com/blog/inovacao-na -pratica/conheca-o-teste-de-ancestralidade-desenvolvido-por-startup -brasileira/.

Schramm, Katharina. *African Homecoming: Pan-African Ideology and Contested Heritage.* London: Routledge, 2010.

———. "Diasporic Citizenship under Debate." *Current Anthropology* 61, no. S22 (2020): S210–19.

Schwarcz, Lilia K. Moritz. *O espetáculo das raças: Cientistas, instituições e questão racial no Brasil 1870–1930.* São Paulo: Companhia das Letras, 1993.

———. "Usos e abusos da mestiçagem e da raça no Brasil: Uma história das teorias raciais em finais do século XIX." *Afro-Ásia* 18 (1996): 77–101.

Schwartz-Marín, Ernesto, and Peter Wade. "Explaining the Visible and the Invisible: Public Knowledge of Genetics, Ancestry, Physical Appearance and Race in Colombia." *Social Studies of Science* 45, no. 6 (2015): 886–906.

Segerstråle, Ullica. *Defenders of the Truth: The Battle for Science in the Sociobiology Debate and Beyond.* Oxford: Oxford University Press, 2000.

Seigel, Micol. "Beyond Compare: Comparative Method after the Transnational Turn." *Radical History Review* 91 (Winter 2005): 62–90.

Selcer, Perrin. "Beyond the Cephalic Index: Negotiating Politics to Produce UNESCO's Scientific Statements on Race." *Current Anthropology* 53, no. 5 (2012): S173–84.

Serre, David, and Svante Pääbo. "Evidence for Gradients of Human Genetic Diversity within and among Continents." *Genome Research* 14 (2004): 1679–85.

Sheriff, Robin E. *Dreaming Equality: Color, Race, and Racism in Urban Brazil.* New Brunswick, N.J.: Rutgers University Press, 2001.

Shim, Janet K., Sonia Rab Alam, and Bradley E. Aouizerat. "Knowing Something versus Feeling Different: The Effects and Non-Effects of Genetic Ancestry on Racial Identity." *New Genetics and Society* 37, no. 1 (2018): 44–66.

Shriver, Mark D., and Rick A. Kittles. "Genetic Ancestry and the Search for Personalized Genetic Histories." *Nature Reviews* 5 (2004): 611–18.

Silva, Antonio José Bacelar da, and Erika Robb Larkins. "The Bolsonaro Election, Antiblackness, and Changing Race Relations in Brazil." *Journal of Latin American and Caribbean Anthropology* 24, no. 4 (2019): 893–913.

Silva, Graziella Moraes da, and Marcelo Paixão. "Mixed and Unequal: New Perspectives on Brazilian Ethnoracial Relations." In *Pigmentocracies: Ethnicity, Race, and Color in Latin America*, edited by Edward E. Telles and Project on Ethnicity and Race in Latin America, 172–217. Chapel Hill: The University of North Carolina Press, 2014.

Silva, Thiago Magalhães da, M. R. Sandhya Rani, Gustavo Nunes de Oliveira Costa, Maria A. Figueiredo, Paulo S. Melo, João F. Nascimento, Neil D. Molyneaux, et al. "The Correlation between Ancestry and Color in Two Cities of Northeast Brazil with Contrasting Ethnic Compositions." *European Journal of Human Genetics* 23, no. 7 (2015): 984–89.

Simões, Rogério. "Raízes e raças do Brasil." *BBC Brasil: Blog do Editor*, June 4, 2007. http://www.bbc.co.uk/blogs/portuguese/2007/06/raizes_e_racas_do_brasil.shtml.

Skidmore, Thomas E. *Black into White: Race and Nationality in Brazilian Thought*. Durham, N.C.: Duke University Press, 1993.

———. *O Brasil visto de fora*. Rio de Janeiro: Paz e Terra, 1994.

Skloot, Rebecca. *The Immortal Life of Henrietta Lacks*. United Kingdom: Pan MacMillan, 2011.

Slenes, Robert W. *Na senzala, uma flor. Esperanças e recordações na formação da família escrava: Brasil Sudeste, século XIX*. Rio de Janeiro: Nova Fronteira, 1999.

Smith, Christen A. *Afro-Paradise: Blackness, Violence, and Performance in Brazil*. Urbana: University of Illinois Press, 2015.

Smith, Nicka. *5 Truths about DNA Tests (23andMe, Ancestry DNA, Family Tree DNA, MyHeritage DNA, LivingDNA)*. September 21, 2016. YouTube video. 4:49. https://www.youtube.com/watch?v=UhQoYYHcHRE.

Solinas, Pier Giorgio. *Ancestry: Parentele elettroniche e lignaggi genetici*. Florence: editpress, 2015.

Sommer, Marianne. "History in the Gene: Negotiations between Molecular and Organismal Anthropology." *Journal of the History of Biology* 41, no. 3 (2008): 473–528.

Sørensen, Stine Gjevnøe. "Momondo—The DNA Journey: How It Was Made." *Momondo*, June 10, 2016. https://www.momondo.com/discover/momondo-the-dna-journey-how-it-was-made.

Southall, Aidan W. "The Illusion of Tribe." In *Perspectives on Africa: A Reader in Culture, History, and Representation*, edited by Roy Richard Grinker, Stephen C. Lubkemann, and Christopher B. Steiner, 2nd ed., 83–94. Chichester, U.K.: Wiley-Blackwell, 2010.

Southern Poverty Law Center. "The Year in Hate: Trump Buoyed White Supremacists in 2017, Sparking Backlash among Black Nationalist Groups." *Southern Poverty Law Center* (blog), February 21, 2018. https://www.splcenter .org/news/2018/02/21/year-hate-trump-buoyed-white-supremacists-2017 -sparking-backlash-among-black-nationalist.

Souza, Jessé, ed. *Multiculturalismo e racismo: Uma comparação Brasil—Estados Unidos.* Brasília: Paralelo 15, 1997.

Souza, Vanderlei Sebastião de, Rodrigo Ciconet Dornelles, Carlos E. A. Coimbra Júnior, and Ricardo Ventura Santos. "História da genética no Brasil: Um olhar a partir do Museu da Genética da Universidade Federal do Rio Grande do Sul." *História, Ciências, Saúde—Manguinhos* 20, no. 2 (2013): 675–94.

Sovik, Liv. *Aqui ninguém é branco.* Rio de Janeiro: Aeroplano, 2009.

Spillers, Hortense J. "Mama's Baby, Papa's Maybe: An American Grammar Book." *Diacritics* 17, no. 2 (1987): 64–81.

Spivak, Gayatri. *In Other Worlds: Essays in Cultural Politics.* New York: Routledge, 1988.

Stepan, Nancy Leys. *The Hour of Eugenics: Race, Gender, and Nation in Latin America.* Ithaca, N.Y.: Cornell University Press, 1991.

Suarez-Kurtz, Guilherme, Sergio Danilo Juno Pena, Claudio José Struchiner, and Mara Helena Hutz. "Pharmacogenomic Diversity among Brazilians: Influence of Ancestry, Self-Reported Color, and Geographical Origin." *Frontiers in Pharmacology* 3 (2012): 1–7.

Sweet, Jesse, dir. *African American Lives.* Episode 1, "Listening to Our Past." Aired February 1, 2006, on PBS.

Sykes, Bryan. *The Seven Daughters of Eve: The Science That Reveals Our Genetic Ancestry.* Kindle ed. New York: Norton, 2001.

Takezawa, Yasuko, Kazuto Kato, Hiroki Oota, Timothy Caulfield, Akihiro Fujimoto, Naoyuki Kamatani, Shoji Kawamura, et al. "Human Genetic Research, Race, Ethnicity and the Labeling of Populations: Recommendations Based on an Interdisciplinary Workshop in Japan." *BMC Medical Ethics* 15, no. 33 (2014). https://doi.org/doi: 10.1186/1472-6939-15-33.

TallBear, Kim. *Native American DNA: Tribal Belonging and the False Promise of Genetic Science.* Minneapolis: University of Minnesota Press, 2013.

Tapaninen, Anna-Maria, and Ilpo Helén. "Making up Families: How DNA Analysis Does/Does Not Verify Relatedness in Family Reunification in Finland." *BioSocieties* 15 (2020): 376–93.

Taylor, Helen. "'The Griot from Tennessee': The Saga of Alex Haley's Roots." *Critical Quarterly* 37, no. 2 (1995): 46–62.

Teil, Geneviève. "No Such Thing as Terroir?: Objectivities and the Regimes of Existence of Objects." *Science, Technology & Human Values* 37, no. 5 (2011): 478–505.

Telles, Edward E. *Race in Another America: The Significance of Skin Color in Brazil.* Princeton, N.J.: Princeton University Press, 2004.

Telles, Edward E., and Project on Ethnicity and Race in Latin America. *Pigmentocracies: Ethnicity, Race, and Color in Latin America.* Chapel Hill: The University of North Carolina Press, 2014.

Thomas, Mark. "To Claim Someone Has 'Viking Ancestors' Is No Better than Astrology." *The Guardian*, February 25, 2013, Science. http://www.theguardian.com/science/blog/2013/feb/25/viking-ancestors-astrology.

Trouillot, Michel-Rolph. *Silencing the Past: Power and the Production of History.* Boston: Beacon, 1995.

Turner, Lorenzo D. *Africanisms in the Gullah Dialect.* Chicago: University of Chicago Press, 1949.

——. "Some Contacts of Brazilian Ex-Slaves with Nigeria, West Africa." *Journal of Negro History* 27, no. 1 (1942): 55–67.

Turra, Cleusa, and Gustavo Venturi. *Racismo cordial.* São Paulo: Ática, 1995.

Twine, France Winddance. "Racial Ideologies and Racial Methodologies." In *Racing Research, Researching Race: Methodological Dilemmas in Critical Race Studies*, edited by France Winddance Twine and Jonathan W. Warren, 1–34. New York: NYU Press, 2000.

——. *Racism in a Racial Democracy: The Maintenance of White Supremacy in Brazil.* New Brunswick, N.J.: Rutgers University Press, 1998.

——. "A White Side of Black Britain: The Concept of Racial Literacy." *Ethnic and Racial Studies* 27, no. 6 (2004): 878–907.

UCL Division of Biosciences. "Candela." *UCL Division of Biosciences*, 2021. https://www.ucl.ac.uk/biosciences/departments/genetics-evolution-and-environment/candela/.

——. "The Moffat/BritainsDNA Saga." *UCL Division of Biosciences*, 2021. https://www.ucl.ac.uk/biosciences/departments/genetics-evolution-and-environment/research/molecular-and-cultural-evolution-lab/debunking-genetic-astrology/britainsdna-saga/moffatbritainsdna-saga.

UNESCO. *Four Statements on the Race Question.* Paris: UNESCO, 1969.

Véran, Jean-François. *L'esclavage en héritage (Brésil): Le droit à la terre des descendants de marrons.* Paris: Karthala, 2003.

——. "Old Bones, New Powers." *Current Anthropology* 53, no. 5 (2012): S246–55.

Verger, Pierre. *Flux et reflux de la traite des nègres entre le Golfe de Bénin et Bahia de Todos os Santos du XVIIe au XIXe siècle.* Paris: Mouton, École Pratique des Hautes Études, 1968.

Wade, Peter. *Degrees of Mixture, Degrees of Freedom: Genomics, Multiculturalism, and Race in Latin America.* Durham, N.C.: Duke University Press, 2017.

——. *Race and Ethnicity in Latin America.* London: Pluto Press, 1997.

——. "Race, Ethnicity and Nation: Perspectives from Kinship and Genetics." In *Race, Ethnicity and Nation: Perspectives from Kinship and Genetics*, edited by Peter Wade, 1–31. New York: Berghahn, 2009.

——. "Race, Multiculturalism, and Genomics in Latin America." In *Mestizo Genomics: Race Mixture, Nation, and Science in Latin America*, edited by Peter Wade, Carlos López Beltrán, Eduardo Restrepo, and Ricardo Ventura Santos, 211–39. Durham, N.C.: Duke University Press, 2014.

Wade, Peter, Carlos López Beltrán, Eduardo Restrepo, and Ricardo Ventura Santos, eds. *Mestizo Genomics: Race Mixture, Nation, and Science in Latin America.* Durham, N.C.: Duke University Press, 2014.

Wade, Peter, Carlos López Beltrán, and Ricardo Ventura Santos. "Genomics, Race Mixture, and Nation in Latin America." In *Mestizo Genomics: Race Mixture, Nation, and Science in Latin America*, 1–32. Durham, N.C.: Duke University Press, 2014.

Wagner, Jennifer K., and Kenneth M. Weiss. "Attitudes on DNA Ancestry Tests." *Human Genetics* 131, no. 1 (2012): 41–56.

Wailoo, Keith, Alondra Nelson, and Catherine Lee, eds. *Genetics and the Unsettled Past: The Collision of DNA, Race, and History.* New Brunswick, N.J.: Rutgers University Press, 2012.

Walajahi, Hina, David R. Wilson, and Sara Chandros Hull. "Constructing Identities: The Implications of DTC Ancestry Testing for Tribal Communities." *Genetics in Medicine* 21 (2019): 1744–50.

Warren, Jonathan, and Christina A. Sue. "Comparative Racisms: What Anti-Racists Can Learn from Latin America." *Ethnicities* 11, no. 1 (2011): 32–58.

Waters, Mary C. *Ethnic Options: Choosing Identities in America.* Berkeley: University of California Press, 1990.

Weil, François. *Family Trees: A History of Genealogy in America.* Cambridge, Mass.: Harvard University Press, 2013.

Weiss, Kenneth M., and Brian W. Lambert. "What Type of Person Are You? Old-Fashioned Thinking Even in Modern Science." In *Human Variation: A Genetic Perspective on Diversity, Race, and Medicine,* edited by Aravinda Chakravarti, 15–28. Cold Spring Harbor, N.Y.: Cold Spring Harbor Laboratory Press, 2014.

Weiss, Martin G. "Strange DNA: The Rise of DNA Analysis for Family Reunification and Its Ethical Implications." *Genomics, Society and Policy* 7 (2011): 1–19.

Westlake, Adam. "Family Tree DNA Opens Its Genealogy Database to FBI." *Slash Gear,* February 2, 2019. https://www.slashgear.com/family-tree-dna-opens-its-genealogy-database-to-fbi-02564465/.

Williams, Kim M. "The Recursive Outcomes of the Multiracial Movement and the End of American Racial Categories." *Studies in American Political Development* 31, no. 1 (2017): 88–107.

Winstein, Keith J. "Harvard's Gates Refines Genetic-Ancestry Searches for Blacks." *Wall Street Journal,* November 15, 2007. http://www.wsj.com/articles/SB119509026198193566.

Wolfe, Brendan. "Racial Integrity Laws (1924–1930)." In *Encyclopedia Virginia,* February 25, 2021. https://www.encyclopediavirginia.org/Racial_Integrity_Laws_of_the_1920s.

Woodtor, Dee Parmer. *Finding a Place Called Home: A Guide to African-American Genealogy and Historical Identity.* New York: Random House, 1999.

Zack, Naomi. "Mixed Black and White Race and Public Policy." *Hypatia* 10, no. 1 (1995): 120–32.

Zeuske, Michael. "The Second Slavery: Modernity, Mobility, and Identity of Captives in Nineteenth-Century Cuba and the Atlantic World." In *The Second Slavery: Mass Slaveries and Modernity in the Americas and in the Atlantic Basin,* edited by Javier Laviña and Michael Zeuske, 113–42. Berlin: LIT Verlag, 2014.

Zhang, Sarah. "The 'Genome Hacker' Who Mapped a 13-Million-Person Family Tree." *The Atlantic*, March 1, 2018. https://www.theatlantic.com/science/archive/2018/03/yaniv-erlich-genomes-pedigrees-myheritage/554441/.

Zwart, Hub A.E. "In the Beginning Was the Genome: Genomics and the Bi-Textuality of Human Existence." *The New Bioethics* 24, no. 1 (2018): 26–43.

Index

AfricanDNA, 70, 205n23
African Royale DNA Project, 172
AfriGeneas, 213n17
Afro-descendant populations, Brazilian:
ambiguous meaning of term, 24,
123–24; and census categories, 116;
genetic definitions of, 48, 202n69;
genetic studies of, 84
afrodescendente. See African-
descendant: definitions of; Afro-
descendant populations, Brazilian
AIMs (ancestry informative markers),
72–75, 78, 104, 193, 205n29
Airbnb, 107, 181
Alves, Jaime, 54, 55
Amerindian. *See* Indigenous American:
ancestry, genetic
ancestralidade, 156, 188
ancestry: African American approaches
to, 23, 32–35, 70, 109, 149–51;
biogeographical, 9, 61, 76, 204n6;
Brazilian approaches to, 24, 152–56;
as situated knowledge, 31; social
versus genetic concepts of, 5, 27,
68–69, 71–72, 78, 82, 89, 119–28,
142–43, 161–62. *See also* activists,
Afro-Brazilian: ancestry, interest in;
admixture; *ancestralidade*; anthropology: and African ancestry, reconstruction of; "color": and ancestry,
genetic; DNA ancestry testing; family
history; Indigenous American; Native
American; race: and ancestry; United
States: ancestry, laws of; United
States: ancestry, uneven access to
Ancestry.com, 58, 87, 89, 93. *See also*
AncestryDNA
AncestryDNA, 1, 27, 87, 89, 103, 106,
176, 194; commercial partnerships, 1,
106, 176; critiques of, 97, 99–102,
108–9; database size, 94, 109, 176,
208n27; Ethnicity Reference Panel,
95–97; "ethnicity" test, genetic, 89,
94–98, 100–102, 112; Eurocentric
bias, 98, 109, 208n53; European

admixture, 96, 99–100, 101, 104–5;
Genetic Communities feature, 110–11;
relative-matching feature, genetic,
103, 182; results, author's, 105–6;
results, test-takers', 99–100, 102, 129,
132; U.S.-centric bias, 109; West
African admixture, 95–96, 101–2,
108. *See also* Byrnes, Jake; Chahine,
Ken
anthropology: and African ancestry,
reconstruction of, 9, 19–21, 32;
authenticating identity, used for, 20,
46, 174; and genealogical models of
kinship, 182; genetic, 11, 22, 62; and
race, concepts of, 2–3, 6, 8, 10–11, 42;
and race science, 18–19; reconstructive, 19; salvage, 113
anthropometry, 18, 19, 72, 88
antiracialism, 47, 74
antiracism, 24, 27, 45, 133, 158, 181,
189; and DNA testing, 27; genetic
approaches to, 8, 180. *See also* Brazil:
antiracism, approaches to; Indigenous American: antiracism; United
States: antiracism, approaches to
Araujo, Ana Lucia, 152, 170, 188
Araújo, Zulu, 159–60, 163, 175
Asian-descendant populations, 75, 78
autosomal: definition of, 28, 200n2;
DNA analyses, 53, 109, 115, 130, 162,
180, 181; testing products, 87, 94, 108,
114, 144, 150; DNA test providers, 101,
103, 109, 172. *See also* admixture
Azevedo, Reinaldo, 52

Balding, David, 59–60, 61, 204n4
Banton, Michael, 178
Barbosa, Ana Angélica Leal, 84
BBC Brasil, 29, 31, 41, 46, 53, 152; forum
on race in Brazil, online, 30, 51.
See also *Raízes Afro-Brasileiras*;
Salek, Silvia; Simões, Rogério
Beija-Flor, Neguinho da, 29, 30, 52, 85
Bennett, Bernice, 183
Bettinger, Blaine, 99

165; market logic, 14, 98; and pharmaceutical sector, 88, 89, 112, 181; privacy issues, 113; prohibited in France, 4; and racism, 4, 5, 15, 27, 52, 55, 81, 114, 143, 177–79, 180; reliability of results, 25, 27, 60–62, 67–69, 73, 89, 99, 101–3, 120, 162, 207n1; unexpected results, 53, 70, 99, 104, 119–20, 122–6, 142, 161–62. *See also* admixture; autosomal; CANDELA; mitochondrial DNA; relative-matching; uniparental; Y-chromosome DNA; *and individual testing companies*

"The DNA Journey," 1, 27, 176, 180

DNAme, 59

DNA Tested African Descendants, 172

DNA test-takers: communities of, 23, 98–99, 118, 182–83; heterogeneity among, 15–16, 23–26; reasons for taking a test, 68–69, 81, 103, 109, 119, 128, 136, 163. *See also* CANDELA: results, test-takers'; DNA ancestry testing: unexpected results; ethnicity: DNA test-takers' conceptions of; *and under individual testing companies*

Dobzhansky, Theodosius, 6

Dolezal, Rachel, 138, 146

Donovan, Joan, 143

Du Bois, W.E.B., 19

Dunn, Leslie, 77

Durban: Third World Conference on Racism, 44

EDUCAFRO, 53, 153

Edwards, Jeanette, 164, 211n38

Ellis Island: Immigration Museum, 28; genealogy database, 34

Ely, Bert, 66–67

Erlich, Yaniv, 209n72

Estes, Roberta, 99

ethnicity; African, genetic reconstruction of, 8, 15, 17, 19–21, 36–37, 60, 61–70, 95–96, 109; anthropological conceptions of, 2, 14, 25, 68–69, 87,

106, 147–48; and authenticity, 27, 56, 69, 147, 151, 156, 165, 173–74, 180; and choice, 88, 114, 117, 120, 130, 133–34, 148, 159–61, 163, 178; DNA test-takers' conceptions of, 48–51, 117–18, 123, 128–29, 134, 135, 144, 148, 158–65, 173–74, 178–79; genetic bases of, 6, 64–67, 97, 110; genetic "ethnicity," construction of, 15, 25, 27, 87, 89, 93–106, 108–10, 112; geneticization of, 3, 9, 12, 21, 147; and "purity," notions of, 68, 117. *See also under* Brazil; identity; United States

ethnocentrism, 68, 83

eugenics, 2, 9, 13, 88. *See also* Whitening

Eurocentrism, 7, 10, 14, 19, 27, 62, 109, 208n53

EUROTAST project, 8, 198n25

Eyerman, Ron, 187

Facebook, 2, 4, 118, 194

family history: genetic approaches to, 16, 36–37, 81–82, 129, 146, 150, 182–84; genetic approaches to, critiques of, 70, 102–3, 151; and identity, 135, 145, 148, 179, 185; as kinship work, 89, 149, 182–83, 186; knowledge, social value of, 24–25, 35, 37, 149, 167; market, 58; research, popularization of, 33–34, 149, 182; resources, 34, 91, 98–99, 149; school assignments, 34–35; shows, 30, 37; and slavery, 26, 32–33, 37–38, 70, 83, 101, 110, 149–50, 183. *See also* Brazil: family history, approaches to; United States: ancestry, uneven access to; United States: genealogical practices in

FamilyTreeDNA, 58, 87, 109, 194; results, author's, 105, 108; results, test-takers', 161

"The Flesh of History," 186, 189

Florentino, Manolo, 49, 50

Fodio, Usman dan, 163

Food and Drug Agency, 207n1

HGDP-CEPH Cell Line Panel, 94,
  205n30
historically modified organism, 187
Holland, William, 166–70, 171, 172
Howard University, 20, 62, 68, 138
Human Genome Diversity Project
  (HGDP), 90, 207n16
Human Genome Project (HGP), 3, 63, 90
Hünemeier, Tábita, 77–78, 82
hypodescent, 130. *See also* race: and
  "one-drop rule"

identity: and authenticity, 20, 26, 69,
  138, 148, 156, 163, 174; biocultural, 15;
  biosocial, 21; Brazilian, 41, 48, 51, 56,
  116, 145, 157; and choice, 26, 88, 106,
  114, 117, 120, 148, 159, 163–64, 175,
  178; claims, 20, 26, 35, 83, 107,
  112–13, 120, 139, 174, 189; collective,
  15, 17, 35, 39, 52, 68, 82, 97, 125,
  174–75, 188; commercialization of,
  59, 87; by descent, 103, 182; discourses, 5, 16, 27, 48, 51, 86; and DNA
  ancestry testing, 3–5, 16, 27–31,
  67–72, 80–84, 114–46, 147–48,
  157–75, 180, 195; DNA as key to, 1, 4,
  21–22, 25, 54–57, 92, 177; ethnic, 1, 17,
  23, 35–37, 56, 85, 147–49, 158–75,
  178; effacement of, 9, 17, 28, 170, 175,
  187; fluidity of, 20, 69, 120, 123, 130,
  132, 144–45; formation, 15, 50, 80, 82,
  89, 118, 174, 177, 188–89; genetic, 21,
  26, 117–19, 148, 157, 194; and genetics,
  relationship to, 4, 9, 14–15, 26, 39,
  60, 84, 97, 101, 177; hyphenated, 36,
  157; myths of, 27, 42, 56, 115, 143;
  national, 1, 4, 24, 25, 31, 71, 107, 113,
  114–16; and official forms, 115–16,
  123–24, 130; oppositional, 5, 24;
  "preslavery," 63, 147; projects, 56–57,
  82; and race, 12, 14, 16, 29–30, 71, 79,
  114–46, 152–57, 179; reconstruction
  of, 5, 17, 19–22, 29, 63, 81, 110, 149,
  155–57, 174, 188; transracial, 138;
  "unmarked," 18, 135; U.S., 36, 55, 157.

See also biraciality: as racial identity;
  Blackness; body: and identity;
  ethnicity; family history: and
  identity; positionality: author's; race;
  racism: and identity, effects on;
  slavery: and identity, impacts on;
  Whiteness
Illumina OmniExpress, 208n53
indígena: racial category, 116, 193,
  210n15. *See also* Indigenous American: ancestors
Indigenous American: ancestors, 126;
  ancestry, genetic, 29, 47, 48, 49,
  73–75, 76; antiracism, 19, 113;
  critiques of DNA testing, 112–13;
  populations, 10, 53, 71, 73, 74, 76, 78,
  199n54. *See also* Native American
índio/a, 49, 122, 135, 136
inheritance, 179, 186; of abilities and
  talents, 50–51; cultural, 27, 51, 147;
  genetic, 2, 4, 126, 186; genomic, 21,
  37, 96, 104, 117, 127, 147; and memory,
  51; of personal characteristics, 16,
  211n38; of physical traits, 16, 126, 127;
  systems of, 19
Instagram, 23, 118, 128, 132, 179,
  193–94
interdisciplinarity: between social
  sciences and genetics, 8, 177

Jackson, Bruce, 66–68
Jackson, Fatimah, 62–63, 64, 66, 68, 83
Jacobson, Matthew Frye, 35
Jefferson, Thomas, 184
Jones, Quincy, 37, 51

Kanor, Fabienne, 186–87, 188, 189
Keita, Shomarka, 68–69, 83
kinship, 55: and DNA testing, 21, 25–26,
  27, 92, 114, 148, 173, 175, 185; and
  ethnicity, 37, 66, 97–98, 175; and
  genealogy, 89, 148, 149, 157, 180,
  182–84; geneticization of, 3; and
  racism, 10, 187; and slavery, 9,
  19–20, 26, 32, 149, 154, 175, 182–84

Kittles, Rick, 62, 83, 85; and African Ancestry, 21, 37, 66, 167; and New York African Burial Ground Project, 61

Laboratório GENE, 47, 48
Latour, Bruno, 105
Latter-day Saints, Church of Jesus Christ of, 34, 58, 92, 149, 207n13; and genealogy, theological significance of, 90, 92–93
Lawrence-Lightfoot, Sara, 39
Lehmann, David, 124, 211n21
Lewontin, Richard, 6
LivingDNA: African "ethnicity" estimates, 109; results, author's, 105
Luna, Juliana, 157–59, 160, 163, 165, 170

Maio, Marcos Chor, 70, 74
markers: DNA, scientific approaches to, 22, 47, 72–75, 78, 91, 96, 147, 161, 164; DNA, social interpretations of, 17, 26–27, 51, 56, 75, 126–27, 147, 169, 174, 188; of inequality, 16; "racial," 16, 27, 47, 115, 117–18, 125–27, 143, 146, 188. See also AIMs; mitochondrial DNA: as marker of ancestry; permanent markers, concept of; skin color: as "racial" marker; uniparental: markers; Y-chromosome DNA: as marker of ancestry
maroon communities. See quilombos
Mattos, Hebe, 155
M'charek, Amade, 10, 75, 97
McLean, Shay-Akil, 110
mestiçagem, 42, 49, 76, 78, 126, 145; definition of, 42, 76; genetic dynamics of, 16, 60, 71; as racial schema, 42–43, 71, 78, 115
mestiço/a: national identity, 42, 116, 155; racial category, 193
mestizaje, 16, 78
methodology, author's, 23–26, 118, 143–144, 193–94
Middle Passage, 17, 29, 39, 83, 146, 171, 172

Midlo Hall, Gwendolyn, 172
miscegenation, 12, 13, 30, 50, 77; origins of term, 76, 206n37
miscigenação, 12, 42, 84, 140; origins of term, 76. See also miscegenation
mitochondrial DNA (mtDNA): analyses, in commercial testing, 36, 48, 61, 114, 157; analyses, in population studies, 11, 21, 47–48, 66–67; inheritance, mode of, 11, 29, 36; as marker of ancestry, 37, 59, 61–62, 69, 92; and relative-matching, 150; results, test-takers', 29, 37, 48–50, 53, 63, 66, 130–31, 137, 158, 161–62
"mitochondrial Eve," 92
mixture, "racial": and African identities, erasure of, 18, 24, 131; in Brazil, 12, 41–44, 47–56, 71–79, 84, 119–28, 135, 140–42, 157, 214n33; ideologies of, 13, 24, 43, 49–50, 78, 117, 145; and elimination of race, 13, 41–42, 47, 51, 54, 56; in United States, 12, 40–41, 55, 68, 128, 132, 137, 185, 217n33. See also admixture; Brazil: mixture, hegemonic discourses of; Brazil: mixture, public discourses of; CANDELA: mixture, conceptions of; mestiçagem; mestizaje; miscigenação; United States: mixture, hegemonic discourses of; United States: mixture, public conceptions of; Whiteness: and "racial" mixture
Moffat, Alistair, 59, 60, 204n4
Momondo, 1, 3, 27, 107, 176, 180
Mormons, 89–91, 129. See also Latter-day Saints, Church of Jesus Christ of
Moses, Yolanda T., 11
Motherland: A Genetic Journey, 62, 83
Mukhopadhyay, Carol C., 11
Mulot, Stéphanie, 50
multiculturalism, 36, 43, 55, 85, 155; critiques of, 20
multiraciality, 52, 133; and census, U.S., 117; as racial category, 130–31, 133,

145, 194; as racial schema, 43, 54, 55, 128, 130–31, 145. *See also* activists, multiracial

Munanga, Kabengele, 202n57

MyHeritage, 89, 109, 144, 182, 209n72

naming practices: and genealogy, 32, 33, 34, 103, 151, 183; renaming ceremonies, African, 158–59, 160, 167, 170; and slavery, 17, 149–50

Nascimento, Abdias do, 42, 43

Nash, Catherine, 149, 180

nationalism, 2; ethnic, 179; White, 114, 143, 176, 179, 180

Native American: ancestors, 63, 129, 162; ancestry, appropriation of, 112, 136, 139, 146, 179; ancestry, genetic, 4, 11, 29, 137, 162, 208n53; critiques of DNA testing, 112–13; populations, 35, 68, 75. *See also* Indigenous American

nature/culture debates, 2, 6

Nazism, 2, 45

negro/a, 43, 45, 46, 49, 152–54; as census category, 116, 152; as racial identification, test-takers', 117, 122, 124, 135, 140, 193

Nelson, Alondra, 39, 41, 61, 63, 119, 147–48

New York African Burial Ground Project (NYABGP), 20–21, 61–62, 68

Novak, Michael, 36

Novas, Carlos, 89, 111

Novembre, John, 93, 97

Obama, Barack, 132

objectivity, 86, 120; of DNA ancestry estimates, 21, 26, 27, 47, 56, 89, 103–4, 121, 144; in genetics, 6, 60, 66

Ohrt Fehler, Benedicte, 172–73

Okundaye, Nike, 158, 165

Paige, Gina, 21

Pálsson, Gísli, 88

Panofsky, Aaron, 143

pardo/a, 43, 45; as census category, 116, 210n15; as racial identification, test-takers', 117, 121–22, 140, 145, 193

passing: as African, 164; as Black, 146; as White, 11, 136

Pena, Sérgio Danilo, 74, 79, 141; DNA ancestry testing, views on, 48, 56; Frei David, dispute with, 53; on race, 47–48, 54; and *Raízes Afro-Brasileiras*, 47–49

Perego, Ugo, 91

permanent markers, concept of, 16, 186–190

personal genomics industry, 3

phenotype: and genetics, 47, 53, 71; and race, 52, 116, 124, 125, 127, 130, 144, 145. *See also* "color"; physical appearance

phylogenies, 66, 67; definition of, 204n6, 205n18

physical appearance: and ancestry, genetic, 30, 46; and ethnicity, 164; and race, 39, 45, 50, 52, 117, 124, 135, 138, 144. *See also* "color"; phenotype

Pinderhughes, Elaine, 217n33

population genetics, 6–8, 11, 63, 76, 82, 85, 90, 94, 179; admixture, definitions of, 76; nonhegemonic approaches to, 78–79; and race, definitions of, 6–7, 77, 202n69; sampling strategies in, 7, 90–92

Population Reference Sample project (POPRES), 93

positionality: author's, 9, 23–26

postraciality, 13. *See also* mixture, "racial": and elimination of race

quilombos, 20, 43, 84, 155, 157, 199n68, 214n33

quotas, university, 22, 30–31, 44, 54, 71, 144; BBC Brasil statement on, 31; constitutionality of, 52, 202n55; criticisms of, 44–46, 52, 202n57; defense of, 45, 202n57; DNA test-takers' views on, 115, 122, 123, 124, 144;

quotas (cont.)
eligibility criteria for, 44–45; and fraud, 45, 124, 146; geneticists' views on, 47–48, 74, 80, 83; law, 52, 80; objectives of, 124; and racial identification, impacts on, 116, 117, 145, 188; verification commissions, 45, 125, 202n63. *See also* affirmative action; Universidade de Brasília

Rabinow, Paul, 21
race: and ancestry, 5, 10, 38–39, 116, 126, 130; in anthropological thought, 2–3, 6, 8, 10–11, 18–19, 42; biocultural approaches to, 9–11, 97–98; biological bases of, beliefs in, 4, 10–11, 124; biological determinist conceptions of, 2, 18–19; biological-essentialist conceptions of, 8, 71, 114; and class, 43, 54, 124, 133, 142, 152, 177; deconstruction of, 5, 10, 14–15, 19, 39, 47, 55, 71, 74; definitions of, 7, 9–11, 44, 116, 123; discourses of, 5, 12, 14, 16, 60, 80, 117, 121, 177; embodied experiences of, 5, 11, 13, 138; and ethnicity, similarities between, 147; genetic bases of, discussions on, 3, 6–9, 47–48, 76–77, 123–27, 144–45; geneticization of, 3, 8–9, 26, 114, 144; history of concept, 10, 16–19; human, 3; and ideology, 6–7, 10–11, 14–15, 24, 55, 117, 120, 133, 143, 153–55, 188; national narratives of, 16, 31, 41–43, 49, 56, 71, 115–17, 178; and "one-drop rule," 38–39, 41, 115, 117, 126, 130, 132; public understandings of, 4, 16, 22, 30–31, 46, 60, 114–46, 195; and "purity," 1–2, 11, 29, 38–42, 48–49, 71, 114, 137–38, 142–43, 177–79, 185; relations, 13, 43; "science," 60, 84; as social construct, 2, 4, 9, 14, 39, 114, 136, 145; as structural phenomenon, 5, 10–11, 13, 85–86, 116, 127, 133, 177–78, 184, 187–88; transnational construction of, 13–15. *See also*

admixture: and race; affirmative action: and racial identification, impacts on; Blackness; body: and race; Brazil: race, hegemonic discourses of; Brazil: race, public conceptions of; "color"; genetic diversity: and race; genetic variation: and race; genomic data: and race; identity: and race; markers: "racial"; mixture, "racial"; phenotype: and race; physical appearance: and race; population genetics: and race, definitions of; quotas, university: and racial identification, impacts on; racism; skin color: as "racial" marker; UNESCO: Statements on Race; United States: race, hegemonic discourses of; United States: race, public conceptions of; Whiteness; Whitening
racialization: experiences of, 117, 130, 145, 146; of physical traits, 16, 116, 119, 125; of populations, 74, 112, 127, 177, 178; processes of, 19, 113, 187, 189
racial profiling, 54–55
racial schemas, 10, 12, 14, 17, 116, 117, 130, 144; definition of, 198n42
racism: and African-descendant populations, impacts on, 9, 15, 24, 44, 54, 134, 160; biological, 9; and colonialism, 15, 17–19, 50, 90, 179, 187; combating, 5, 14, 22, 46, 61, 176; and DNA ancestry testing, 4, 5, 15, 27, 52, 55, 81, 114, 143, 177–179, 180; embodied experiences of, 5, 10–11, 13, 17, 24–25, 107, 117; everyday, 116; genetic approaches to, 8, 46–47, 60–61, 63, 70, 80; as ideology, 3, 11, 45, 139, 145, 176–79, 189; and identity, effects on, 5, 17, 187; institutional, 11, 54, 55, 127, 178, 187; and love, 49–51; and narratives of "racial" mixture, 41–44, 142, 145; and police violence, 55, 177; and prejudice, 4, 8, 13, 43, 50, 60, 135, 139, 189; and race, relationship to, 10–11;

www.ingramcontent.com/pod-product-compliance
Lightning Source LLC
Chambersburg PA
CBHW030355270326
41926CB00009B/1114